Contents

List of figures

Wheat, Europe and the GATT

Wheat, Europe and the GATT

A political economy analysis

Peter W. B. Phillips

Pinter Publishers, London

© Peter W.B. Phillips

First published in Great Britain in 1990 by
Pinter Publishers Limited
25 Floral Street, London WC2E 9DS

British Library Cataloguing in Publication Data

A CIP catalogue record for this book is available from the British Library

ISBN 0 86187 125 1

Typeset by The Castlefield Press Ltd, Wellingborough, Northants in Ehrhardt 10/12 point.
Printed and bound in Great Britain by Biddles Ltd.

List of tables

Abbreviations

AGPB	Association Générale des Producteurs de Blé (French wheat producers association)
ASC	*Agricultural Situation in the Community*, published annually by the Commission
B	billion (1 B = 1,000 M)
BEUC	Bureau Européen des Unions des Consommateurs (EC consumer lobby)
CAP	Common Agricultural Policy
CDU	German Christian Democratic Union
Ch	change
CIAA	Confédération des Industries Agro-Alimentaires de la CEE (EC food and drink federation)
COFACE	Compagnie Français d'Assurances pour le Commerce Extérieur (French Export Credit Agency)
COM	communication from the Commission
COPA	Committee of Professional Agricultural Associations
CPE	centrally planned economy
CSU	German Christian Social Union
DBV	Deutsche Bauernverband, German farmers union
DG–VI	Commission Directorate General responsible for agriculture
DM	Deutschmark
EAGGF	European Agricultural Guidance and Guarantee Fund, also known as FEOGA after French acronym
EC	European Community(ies)
ECGD	Export Credit Guarantee Department (UK)
ECSC	European Coal and Steel Community
ECU	European currency unit
EEB	European Environmental Bureau
EEC	European Economic Community, now called EC
EMS	European Monetary System
EP	European Parliament, also known as the Assembly
ESC	Economic and Social Committee
FAO	Food and Agriculture Organization

FDP	German Free Democratic Party (Liberal)
FNSEA	Fédération Nationale des Syndicats d'Exploitants Agricoles (French farm lobby)
GATT	General Agreement on Tariffs and Trade
GDP	Gross Domestic Product
ha	hectare
H-GCA	Home-Grown Cereals Authority (UK)
ICA	international commodity agreement
IMF	International Monetary Fund
IPE	international political economy
IWA	International Wheat Agreement
IWC	International Wheat Council
M	million
MAFF	UK Ministry of Agriculture, Fisheries and Food
MCA	Monetary Compensatory Amount
MEP	Member of the European Parliament
Mo	month
nc	no change
NC	national currency
NFU	National Farmers Union of England and Wales
OECD	Organization for Economic Co-operation and Development
OJ	*Official Journal* of the EC
ONIC	Office National Interprofessionnel pour les Céréales
SAFER	Société d'Aménagement Foncier et d'Etablissement Rural
SCA	Special Committee for Agriculture
SPD	German Social–Democratic Party
t	tonne (metric)
UA	Unit of Account
UK	United Kingdom
UNICE	Union of Industries in Europe
US	United States of America
USSR	Union of Soviet Socialist Republics
VAT	value-added tax

Foreword and acknowledgements

The bulk of this study was completed as part of a doctoral dissertation at the London School of Economics and Political Science. I would like to thank especially Professor Susan Strange and Mr Michael Donelan for their support and advice during my studies and Dr Rosemary Fennell for her useful and detailed critique of my work.

I acknowledge the time and effort expended on my behalf by many individuals within the European farm policy community. Their comments were extremely useful.

My parents, Bob and Tanyss Phillips, as usual provided the most incisive comments and useful suggestions. I owe them a great debt for the time they gave to reading my work.

I must also acknowledge the following agencies for financial support: George B. Sanderson Trust, Saskatchewan Wheat Pool, William Lyon MacKenzie King Trust, Social Science and Humanities Research Council of Canada, and Committee of Vice-Chancellors and Principals of the Universities of the UK.

Finally, I could not have started, let alone completed, this work without Wanda's support and encouragement.

Chapter 1

Alternative approaches to policy analysis

The trinity of grain, flour, bread is to be found everywhere in the history of Europe. It was the major preoccupation of towns, states, merchants and ordinary people for whom life meant 'eating one's daily bread'.[1]

Economic historian Fernand Braudel's observation refers to the period between the fifteenth and eighteenth centuries but is equally apt today. The trinity, frequently expressed in public policy debates as simply 'wheat', continues to generate great interest in business, government and the press. Since 1958 the European Community (EC) wheat policy has been at the forefront of debate in the European system and, in 1982, was elevated to the top of the world trade agenda. The current round of multilateral trade negotiations (MTN) in the General Agreement of Tariffs and Trade (GATT), more than any in the past, will be judged a success only if there is agreement on wheat trade.

Trade policy, however, 'is the stuff of domestic politics'[2] so any examination of the GATT must necessarily begin with a review of the domestic policy system. This study therefore examines the political and economic changes in the domestic and international organization and operation of the EC Common Agricultural Policy (CAP) for wheat during the 1973–88 period to demonstrate the opportunities and constraints in the current GATT round. An international political economy approach is adopted in order to highlight the key power structures – security, production, finance and knowledge – and to demonstrate how they transformed the interlocking and overlapping set of bargains that determines policy.

Throughout the 1970s, the CAP wheat price and trading system focused on achieving social objectives. Prices after 1972 were generally based on the 'objective method criterion' to provide smaller and less competitive farmers with an income comparable to non-farm workers (for a more detailed discussion see Chapter 4). Market concerns were largely ignored. This domestic orientation neither required nor allowed much of an external policy for agriculture. Trade policy was used almost entirely to secure domestic supplies of wheat for European consumers; export was regarded as a cheap means of disposing of surpluses.

This study shows that the four power structures surrounding the wheat system shifted fundamentally during the post-war period, causing in the 1980s a breakdown of some of the underlying bargains that determine policy outcomes and the formation or strengthening of others. World-wide political and military tension lessened and production of all goods became internationally inter-dependent, so total food self-sufficiency became neither necessary nor feasible. New production techniques and seed varieties, meanwhile, expanded output but made farms more vulnerable to the increasingly uncertain market, inflation, exchange and financial risks. Technological change drove producers, consumers and policy-makers to adapt quickly to the new opportunities. Domestically, these changes reshaped the policy community, so that the farm lobby no longer dominated. Bale and Koester note that beginning in 1980 there was 'a fundamental change in the source of criticism':[3] agitation for change moved from outside the system (i.e. consumers, the press, manufacturers and academics) to within the Commission, Council, European Parliament (EP), Economic and Social Committee (ESC) and even into some of the farm organizations.

By 1989 the price system was fundamentally different from the one prevailing in the 1970s. Debate over prices in the late 1980s was largely motivated by market concerns while the Community structures policy addressed social concerns. Farmers in 1989 received well below the 'guarantee' implied by the intervention price:[4] two cereals co-responsibility levies and a fundamentally different intervention system (that operates as a market of last resort and not an alternative market) ensure that market prices at least partially reflect market conditions. In the future price changes will be largely dictated by the super levy system which triggers automatic price cuts whenever the maximum guaranteed quantity is exceeded and by the 1988 budget agreement which limits growth in EC agricultural outlays to less than overall budgetary growth (see overview in Chapter 3).

This new system provides a firm basis for the Community to develop a lasting export presence. Encouraged by the incomes-based price policy of the 1970s, wheat yields surged. By the mid-1980s EC wheat production was highly competitive, which created inexorable pressure for the Community to move into world wheat markets as a commercial exporter. Beginning in the 1980s, the Community developed a greater variety of trade instruments. By 1989 the full scope of the complete EC wheat trade policy was clear: it would include targeted marketing with selected refund offers, flexible commercial and concessionary credit, credit guarantees, multi-annual supply agreements and an active storage system.

During the Tokyo Round of the GATT in 1973–79 the Community adopted a highly defensive posture in line with its domestic orientation. But the new international focus of the CAP now makes the EC a formidable participant in the GATT. The EC, as an outward-looking, export-competitive participant, is positioned to take an active role in developing the rules and procedures for world wheat trade. If other parties at the GATT recognize and accept this transformation, the changes in EC policy should enhance the potential for a political resolution to the subsidy dispute which has dominated the world wheat trade during the 1980s. Unfortunately the agricultural trade negotiations between 1984 and 1990 demonstrate that the other participants have not yet recognized these transformations. Unless negotiators acknowledge and accommodate the new EC wheat policy, the Uruguay Round could fail and the GATT could be seriously impaired.

Traditional approaches to study of farm policy

The analytical approach chosen to study farm policy frequently forces the researcher to focus either on the microeconomic issues (e.g. farmers, consumers) or on the macroeconomic concerns (e.g. national security, economic growth) and to ignore the political context. Consequently, these analyses miss the critical linkages among the microeconomic, macroeconomic and political concerns. Most agriculture research, for example, examines ECU prices and production averages for the Community, thereby ignoring that farmers, who are after all the basic unit in the system, work and live in a national context: farmers are concerned with national currency prices and often divergent national market pressures and have their most direct access to policy-makers through national organizations and national political systems. Nevertheless, the policy system and many of the key economic pressures facing farmers and policy-makers are set in an international setting. Analyses that ignore the national and international dimensions are incomplete. An examination of international agricultural affairs requires analytic tools to examine national industries, domestic politics, international markets and high politics.

The US approach

US farm trade policy is firmly based on classical economic analysis which concludes that the CAP wheat policy is inefficient and wasteful. UK farm economist Brian Hill says it best: 'The basic problem of the CAP is that it attempts to defy the underlying forces of economic development.' He, like many economists, concludes that: 'If the CAP continues as it is at present the costs of surplus disposal will bankrupt the Community.'[5] The US Export Enhancement Program, introduced in 1985, is an effort to increase the budgetary cost of the CAP wheat policy and thereby precipitate EC farm policy reform.[6] In summary, economic logic says that the policy must be reformed.

Available evidence, however, does not support that conclusion. The Australian government has estimated that the annual economic cost of defying the 'underlying forces of economic development' averaged only 27 ECUs per capita (or 0.3 per cent of Community GDP) in Europe during the 1975–83 period.[7] This suggests that economists have overestimated the importance of market efficiency.

A plethora of macroeconomic studies concur that protectionist policies in the EC cause deadweight losses for the Community. These argue that producer prices supported above the world market-clearing price encourage farmers to over-produce and the higher consumer prices depress domestic demand for food, reducing consumer surplus.[8] The partial equilibrium studies in Table 1.1 estimate that the losses ranged from 0.13 per cent to 1.3 per cent of Community gross domestic product (GDP) between 1976 and 1985.

General equilibrium models show larger losses because higher food prices reduce household resources available to save or to spend on manufactured goods and services, while higher farm production attracts resources (including entrepreneurs) from other sectors, which reduces non-farm growth. EC farm support is estimated to depress GDP between 0.9 per cent (Spencer for 1980) and 2.7 per

Table 1.1 Cost of agricultural support in the EC: partial equilibrium (intersectoral and multisectoral) studies

Ref. year	Study	Commodities & policies (EC9 unless stated)	Base prices	Deadweight (DW) loss	DW loss as % GDP
1976	Bale & Lutz (1981)	CAP & state policies in France, Germany & UK; cereals, sugar, beef	C	1.2 BECU	0.13%
1978	Morris: IFS (1980)	Cereals, dairy, sugar, beef, pigs, poultry, eggs & olive oil	C	6.2 BECU	0.53%
			82	9.3 BECU	—
1978	BAE (1985)	All policies (CAP & national) for all CAP commodities	82	11.2 BECU	0.48%
1980	Buckwell et al. (1982)	All CAP commodities & policies			
		(a) diff. from self-sufficiency	C	3.2 BECU	0.13%
		(b) diff. from free trade	C	11.1 BECU	0.55%
		(b) diff. from free trade	82	13.5 BECU	—
1980	BAE (1985)	As above	82	8.1 BECU	—
1980	Tyers (1985)	Cereals, meats, dairy, sugar	80	22.3 BECU	1.10%
1980–82	Tyers & Anderson (1987)	Cereals, meat, dairy, sugar; EC10	80	4.9 BECU	0.27%
1983	BAE (1985)	As above	82	8.0 BECU	0.32%
			C	8.6 BECU	0.25%
1983	Devereau & Morris (1985)	All CAP commodities & policies	C	14.0 BECU	0.40%
1984	Harvey & Thomson (1985)	All CAP commodities & policies	C	13.8 BECU	0.37%
1985	Tyers & Anderson (1986)	All policies (CAP & national) for all major commodities	80	24.1 BUS$	1.30%

Notes: C means current year; otherwise date is year to which prices are deflated
Sources: Walters (1987); BAE (1985); Buckwell et al. (1982); and IMF (1988)

cent (Burniaux and Waelbroeck for 1985) (Table 1.2). Stoeckel (1985) estimated EC farm support in 1980 increased exports from the agriculture, food, beverage and tobacco industries by an average 37 per cent and caused related imports to fall by more than 20 per cent. This increase in the trade balance boosted the average European exchange rate by 4.4 per cent which caused a 4 per cent drop in manufacturing exports and a loss of approximately one million jobs (1 per cent). More than 400,000 of the jobs lost would have been in manufacturing.[9] It is important to remember that these studies assume total factor mobility between sectors, which is not necessarily true for either labour or capital in the farm sector, so loss estimates could be too high, especially in the short run.

Table 1.2 Cost of agricultural support in the EC: general equilibrium studies

Ref. year	Study	Commodities & policies (EC9 unless stated)	Deadweight (DW) loss	DW loss as % GDP
1980	Spencer (1985)	All CAP commodities & policies	na	approx 0.9%
1980	Stoeckel (1985)	All policies (CAP & national) for all CAP commodities	approx 1 million jobs	na
1985	Burniaux & Waelbroeck (1985)	All policies (CAP & national) for all CAP commodities	na	2.7%

Sources: See Table 1.1

Agricultural policies are not unique in creating deadweight losses. Although national defence imposes a loss, few argue that the economic calculus in that case is the full story. The numbers really only provide an estimate of the cost of providing public policies. Both agriculture and national defence policies have non-quantifiable benefits, such as protection from coercion from other countries and greater social harmony through greater equality of incomes.

The economic paradigm of supply and demand curves is a powerful tool for analysing questions of efficiency and wealth creation, but operates only by imposing severe limits on the variables that are considered: non-quantifiable costs and benefits are assumed to be insignificant or constant and therefore are not considered. Economic analysis is perhaps most severely hindered by the explicit separation of political and economic processes. Economics implicitly assumes that a 'black box' political system simultaneously resolves all conflicting demands, achieving a new equilibrium.[10] This obviously does not happen in real life. Policy compromises are achieved recursively, as power and interlocking bargains shift. US farm economist Timothy Josling believes that 'preoccupation with efficiency of resource allocation and disregard for analysis of income transfers has been a major cause for the frustration of many economists who see agricultural policy as a jumble of politically motivated and expensive follies.'[11]

The Cairns Group[12] approach

Australia, as leader of the Cairns Group, in line with Josling's advice adopted a welfare economics approach to explain the CAP and to examine alternative strategies. That approach improves on classical economics because it identifies the transfers that flow among consumers, producers and taxpayers and thereby provides estimates of which groups in society bear the economic costs and acquire the benefits of the policy (Table 1.3). The Australian research concludes that 'the best prospects for agricultural policy reform lie in groups outside agriculture realising their common interests in substantially changing the political will of governments to reform bad policies.'[13] The solution therefore is to educate European consumers, the unemployed and industrialists to the costs of the CAP.

The welfare approach, however, does not necessarily identify the potential for change. There are two problems. First, the theory incorrectly assumes that the bargaining position of each actor in the system is based solely on its assessment of relative benefits and costs. When opinion surveys are compared with the benefits or costs of the CAP, some of the results refute close economic links between economic self-interest and bargaining positions. German farmers, for example, get an average 33 per cent more support per capita than other Community farmers,[14] yet are the least satisfied that the CAP is 'on balance . . . worthwhile.'[15] More importantly, however, this approach, like economics, still assumes that politics takes place in a black box. The distribution of winners and losers is usually presented as yielding an obvious outcome. But the political system does not work that way. Economic calculus of income transfers ignores often more important social, political and cultural concerns that determine policy.

Trade diplomats and journalists

Those who have worked in the area of or studied European affairs or agricultural trade frequently believe that the economic aspects of the CAP wheat policy are secondary to its key role in sustaining the political bargain between Germany and France, which is the foundation of the EC (and, in turn, bolsters the Western European alliance against Soviet expansionism). This approach (supported by many academics in international relations (IR)) fails largely because it focuses almost exclusively on state–state relations and on international security issues. The CAP cannot be understood completely without examining the great variety of both state and non-state actors and the increasing commercial orientation of its international dealings.

As shown in Chapter 2, the CAP was designed to contribute to post-war economic and political reconstruction in Europe. The CAP provided the means for the original six Community members to strengthen their farm structures and to increase European agricultural production and ultimately to contribute to a stronger and more integrated European economy. As such, it contributed to the western security alliance.

This approach does not fully explain the policy processes and developments in the CAP in recent years. By underemphasizing all but security motives, it has

Table 1.3 Inter-sectoral transfers caused by the EC Common Agricultural Policy (ECU)

Ref. year	Study	Policies and commodities (EC9 unless stated)	Base prices	Consumer loss	Producer gain	Taxpayer loss
1976	Bale & Lutz (1981)	CAP & state policy; Fr., FRG, & UK; cereals, sugar, & beef	C	3.9 B	4.7 B	0.2 B
1978	Morris: IFS (1980)	Cereals, dairy, sugar, beef, pigs, eggs, poultry & oils	78	23.3 B	21.5 B	5.1 B
1980	Buckwell et al. (1982)	All CAP products & policies	C	24.8 B	22.0 B	8.3 B
1979–81	OECD (1987)	All policies for EC10 (total consumer & taxpayer losses)	C	56.5 B	—	inc.
1983	BAE (1985)	All policies (CAP & state) for all CAP commodities	82	30.6 B	47.5 B	24.9 B
1984	Harvey & Thomson (1985)	All CAP products & policies	C	42.5 B	46.5 B	17.8 B
1985	Tyers & Anderson (1986)	All policies (CAP & state) for major products for EC10	80	$49.0 B	$27.2 B	$2.2 B

Sources: See Table 1.1

reduced ability to contribute to the discussion of largely economic and trade-related issues. Henry Kissinger, US Secretary of State during the Nixon and Ford administrations, said in 1975 that 'a new and unprecedented kind of issue has emerged.' He explained that: 'The problems of energy, resources, environment, population, the uses of space and the seas now rank with questions of military security, ideology and territorial rivalry which have traditionally made up the diplomatic agenda.'[16] IR does not provide a means to analyse such issues.

Runge and Witzke argue that 'the economist's penchant for treating the institutional framework as "given" has left little to say about the CAP other than to cite its negative economic benefits.'[17] International relations, by ignoring both the economics of the CAP and the connections between domestic and international politics, has similarly reduced its ability to assist analysis.

An alternative approach: international political economy

This study uses the theory of international political economy and Susan Strange's structures–bargains model presented in *States and Markets* to examine the EC wheat policy. She has presented a schematic approach to social science studies that illuminates and reconciles the relationship among the separate approaches outlined above. She argues that society balances four conflicting goals: individual, group, or national security; wealth creation or maintenance; economic, social or legal justice for individuals or groups; and freedom of choice or action for either individuals or groups. No society can elevate all these goals to equal status because they are often contradictory. The relative power of government and private actors determines the balance among the various goals, which thereby determines the organization of markets and states.

Each of the approaches examined in the previous section concentrates on a single segment of this balancing act. By examining the key focus of each discipline, it is easy to determine the linkage among the 'bureaucratic creations' of the social sciences. Economics examines wealth creation, welfare economics concentrates on distribution issues (also sometimes on the trade-off between wealth creation and distribution) and international relations focuses on questions of security.

In contrast, international political economy attempts to examine the balance among these conflicting goals. By accepting the inseparability of politics and economics at both the domestic and international levels, IPE provides the means to deal with the second-best[18] world of agriculture. IPE analyses begin with the basic question of 'cui bono'[19] or who benefits, but go beyond the economic calculus to look at social, political and philosophical issues and conflicts.

IPE, therefore, is a focus of inquiry which 'denotes an area of investigation, a particular range of questions and a series of assumptions about the nature of the international "system".'[20] Strange's model provides a means of putting into practice this rather general pronouncement.[21] She argues that 'power' decides the mix and change in balance of state and market control.[22] The best approach is to examine changes in the four key 'power' structures in the system (i.e. security, production, finance and knowledge, which relate to the four goals in society) and to determine how they cause the essential bargains in the system to change. These usually overlapping and interlocking bargains among consumers, producers, governments and non-state actors provide the true background and explanation of system changes.

The theory of bargains

Strange asserts 'drawing bargaining maps will . . . reveal the domestic roots of international agreements, and tell us about what is likely to be permanent and what will probably prove ephemeral about them.'[23] All theoretical disciplines need a focus for analysis. Bargains can provide the same power and depth to IPE as the invisible hand of the market and the balance of military power provide for economics and international relations.[24]

The concept of bargains has been largely undefined and unexplained. The dictionary defines bargain as: 'n. agreement on terms of a transaction; beyond the strike terms, moreover; make or strike a . . .; come to terms.'[25] This definition is constrained by its contractual focus (e.g. union-management bargains or international treaties). If bargains are always formal agreements or transactions and have explicit strike terms, important tacit understandings that often fundamentally influence policy would be excluded. The concept of bargains must also include understandings ('n. agreement, harmony, convention, thing agreed upon') and conventions ('n. agreement between parties; agreement between states, less formal than a treaty; general (often implicit) consent').[26] Therefore, bargains in IPE include all explicit or implicit agreements, understandings and conventions that underlie the operation of a modern economy.

Bargains in political economy provide a means for people to acquire power. The quest for power and the forging of bargains are therefore closely intertwined. Almost everyone would welcome an opportunity to bargain to increase their power. To a great extent, however, 'he who has, gets.' Bargains only convert potential sources of power into actual power, or exchange power over one area for power in another. The four power structures (i.e. security, production, finance and knowledge) and the existing rules systems (treaties, laws, etc.) apportion power among the various actors in the system. Therefore, shifts in the power structures cause power to ebb and flow between actors. Bargains are weakened or new bargains are struck to accommodate the changes.

By implication, there are limits to bargains. They cannot create power where it does not exist; they just make that power effective. Some bargains that provide structural power may create power that no other group had been able to use. Nevertheless, that power was always available. Bargains by their very nature also limit independent action by creating greater certainty. Individuals, groups, corporations and governments make either explicit or implicit bargains that let all parties know how each will react to specific developments. The converse is that each party to a binding bargain gives up freedom to react in exchange for this greater certainty.

The variety of bargains is almost as great as the number of actors in the system. Issues often overlap and interlock, so that adversaries on some issues may be allies on others. It is not possible, therefore, to identify an archetypical bargain that encompasses all possibilities. 'The bargain struck is apt to consist of a highly variable mix of political and economic benefits conferred and opportunities opened up. Bargains will reflect both the positive goals the parties severally wish to achieve and the negative risks and threats from which they want to find some security.'[27]

Leadership is the key imponderable variable in analysis of bargains. Public policy is created by persons who act for both rational and irrational reasons. Consequently, the ebb and flow of bargains is not necessarily continuous. By sheer force of personality, strong leaders can forge new bargains before the relevant structures have fully developed or can sustain failing bargains beyond their natural lifespan. Alternatively, weak leaders can precipitate the destruction of some bargains that would otherwise survive for a time or fail to create new bargains despite supportive structures.

Relationship between bargains and power structures

Bargains and the underlying power structures are often interrelated and simultaneous. When parties to a bargain acquire structural power – to decide how things will be done – they also acquire the ability to build or alter their own environment. This creates a complex problem of how to begin to analyse a simultaneous system, where bargains create the structures which in turn either support or change the bargains.

This is not a problem unique to international political economy. All social scientists must approach and disentangle interrelated motives, markets and power relationships to understand the world. In economics, for example, macroeconomists build large, simultaneous econometric models to approximate the linkages between sectors. They start by setting the exogenous variables and then allow their model to iterate towards a stable and unique solution.

The IPE framework provides the means to do likewise. Chapter 2 shows that many power structures are influenced or determined by events well beyond the scope of any of the related bargains. Especially for this sectoral analysis of the European wheat market, most of the security and knowledge structures are determined by bargains outside the agricultural policy community. Consequently, those power structures can be examined in isolation from the related bargains. For the rest, where bargains bestow structural power on actors in the system, an iterative approach is necessary, starting with the baseline set of power structures and bargains and then examining how, over time, existing bargains are influenced by and influence the power structures. This study of European wheat policy confronts this problem directly by sequentially examining the power structures and bargains and then returning to re-examine the power structures.

The structures–bargains approach differs fundamentally from the approaches reviewed in the previous section in that non-economic factors are elevated to an equal status with economic ones. This is in stark contrast particularly to economics, which frequently ignores or assumes constant all non-economic factors because they are often non-quantifiable. The focus on quantification and comparative statics diverts most theoretical and applied economists' attention away from the important institutional and political constraints on economic policy. IPE uses the bargain approach to reveal the implicit value attached to these non-economic variables and to restore them to their rightful position.

IPE and European wheat policy

Strange and Tooze posit that 'sectoral analysis (by which we mean any study of the political economy of a specific industry in its world context, or of specific markets for goods and services) will illuminate the key bargains, whether these are inter-governmental, company-government, inter-company or intra-company, or between the company and its labour force or its financial backers.'[28]

The European wheat market has been transformed since the mid-1970s. The use of Strange's model reveals that change. Comparison of snapshots of the priorities of the system in the early years and again in the late 1980s shows that the system has shifted significantly away from security–distribution concerns towards wealth creation. The priorities, in descending order of importance in the early 1970s were security, justice, wealth and freedom. By the late 1980s these had been reversed, so that wealth and freedom preceded justice and security. The relative ranking of some of the goals is subjective but even a cursory examination of Community action shows that security and food self-sufficiency no longer drive the CAP policy. Commission reports now pay much more attention than they once did to the role and position of agriculture in the entire economy and its contribution towards economic growth and development. This substitution of goals has required a concomitant shift towards market control and away from administrative direction.

Most studies of the CAP attempt to encompass all of the agricultural producers and products in the Community, which usually results in a vague analysis that does not truly capture the subtleties of the situation. It is necessary to go beyond the general to the specific. In contrast, this study focuses on common wheat[29] and on the relations between consumers, producers and governments in France, West Germany, the United Kingdom and at the European level. Wheat was chosen because it plays a critical role in the domestic food industry; cereals were the first set of commodities for which the Community was able to negotiate a common market regime and still remain the focus of much attention.

Wheat producers are also the most influential non-government actors in the agricultural system in Europe. In France, the power of the wheat growers' organization often makes them 'the spokesmen' for all agricultural interests, especially in the European domain, even though they represent only a small part of French agriculture. In Germany and the UK cereal producers also dominate the national farm lobbies and represent their farmers in the various Community professional groups and consultative bodies.[30]

Wheat, as well as dominating CAP diplomacy, is a key export commodity that has attracted international attention. The issue was raised at the G7 Summit in Tokyo in 1986 and discussions continued at the Vancouver and San Francisco meetings of agricultural and trade ministers from the big five exporters during the following 12 months. Wheat trade issues also were prominent in the opening meeting of the Uruguay Round of the GATT and then paralysed the mid-term review meeting in Montreal in December 1988.

Finally, within the Community, the three predominant nations in the fields of wheat production and agriculture policy formulation are France, Germany and the UK. By 1984–6 the three countries accounted for more than 84 per cent of the EC common wheat output compared with only 72.5 per cent in 1969–71. The other six members of the EC9 are either net importers or insignificant exporters of wheat. Italy, although a major producer of durum and the only remaining large importer of wheat, 'had only an intermittent and on the whole marginal influence on the creation and early development of the CAP,'[31] and continues to have little impact on wheat policy. Greece, Spain and Portugal all joined the Community in the 1980s, adding significantly to the potential wheat production base, but their impact on the policy has been minimal and they are excluded from this study. Observers of the Community assert that the key pressures on farm policy will continue to come from the 'big, not the small, countries – and from the north not the south' which means in effect France, Germany or the UK.[32] As the pace of political reform in Eastern Europe accelerated in early 1990, the dominance of the large countries has increased (see Chapter 2).

The body of this study consists of an examination of the fundamental changes in the four key power structures and explanation of how these have affected the vital interlocking and overlapping bargains that sustain and support the European wheat system. Chapter 2 examines the critical structural changes that have influenced the IPE of wheat in Europe since the mid-1970s. Chapters 3–7 examine domestic reforms centred on the price-fixing during 1972–89, with a focus on how the shifting structures caused the pattern of interlocking bargains to change. Chapters 8 and 9 show when, how and why the CAP has developed a comprehensive commercial policy for wheat. Finally, Chapter 10 draws some general lessons for the major world wheat exporting countries.

Notes

1. Braudel (1981), p. 143.
2. Spero (1985), p. 91.
3. Bale and Koester (1983), pp. 387–8.
4. 'Guaranteed price' refers to the effective support provided for farm-gate prices by the institutional (intervention and threshold) prices.
5. Hill (1984), pp. 158–9, concluded that bankruptcy would occur in 1984.
6. *Financial Times*, 6–9–84, reported that the USDA estimated that US outlays for wheat support would rise US$10 for every US$1 increase inflicted on the EC. Other sources estimated the range was from 5–1 to 19–1. Thus, the EEP was an imperfect means of achieving this goal.
7. Bureau of Agricultural Economics (1985), p. 108.
8. Deadweight losses do not include income transfers, whether from or to consumers, producers or governments.
9. Stoeckel (1985), pp. 40–1.
10. Black box theory attempts to link input to output in a political system without describing the mechanisms involved.
11. Josling quoted in Haen, Johnson and Tangermann (1985), p. 32.

12. This group of 14 self-styled 'fair traders', which acts as a unit in the GATT farm trade negotiations, includes three large wheat exporters: Australia, Canada and Argentina.
13. Centre for International Economics (1988), p. 6.
14. Buckwell, et al. (1982), p. 141, table 9.1. Producer benefits in Germany were estimated at 4207 EUA/head compared with the EC9 estimate of 2793 EUA/head.
15. *Eurobarometre*, 27 (June 1987), p. A118. Only 37 per cent of German farmers agreed that: 'Although there is a lot to criticize and to put right in the EC CAP, on balance it is worthwhile.' About 44 per cent disagreed. The nearest percentage of national farmers which disagreed was 31 per cent in France.
16. Keohane and Nye (1977), p. 26.
17. Runge and Witzke (1987), p. 213.
18. The general theory of the second-best optimum states that 'if there is introduced into a general equilibrium system a constraint which prevents the attainment of one of the Paretian conditions, the other Paretian conditions, although still attainable, are, in general, no longer desirable.' *The New Palgrave, V.4* (1987), p. 280.
19. Strange (1985), p. 23.
20. R. Tooze, 'Perspectives and theory: a consumer's guide,' in Strange (1984), p. 2.
21. Gilpin (1987), pp. 9 and 25, proposes that the solution is 'an eclectic mixture of analytic methods and theoretical perspectives.' Eclecticism may be fine for well-read analysts but is an inadequate base upon which to build a discipline.
22. Strange (1988), p. 23.
23. Strange (1983), p. 353.
24. Regime theory (Krasner, ed. (1983), p. 275) appears to answer the same questions as bargains but poses a number of problems. Because it is directed primarily at how states conduct their affairs in a non-hegemonic power system, it ignores non-state actors that are increasingly important in the development and determination of policy. Regime theory is also static: each regime has a variety of norms that determine how states act and if even one norm changes a new regime develops. Consequently, regime analysis, because it compares relative fixed situations, is similar to comparative statics in economics. Bargains, in contrast, highlight the dynamic nature of systems and are therefore comparable to general dynamics theory in economics. See Phillips (1989), pp. 24–6.
25. *The Concise Oxford Dictionary of Current English*, 6th ed. (Oxford, 1976).
26. *Ibid.*
27. Strange (1983), p. 353.
28. Strange and Tooze (1981), p. 12.
29. European farm policy distinguishes between hard wheats and soft wheats (frequently called common wheat). Within the common wheat class, the policy also differentiates between wheat of bread-making quality and feed-grade wheat.
30. Averyt (1977), p. 44.
31. Neville-Rolfe (1984), p. 149.
32. Duchêne, Szczepanik and Legg (1985), p. 181.

Chapter 2

Changing power structures

The CAP wheat policy has been influenced by a myriad of events which on the surface appear completely unrelated to wheat production, consumption or trade. New power structures in the post-war period provided the basis for the creation of the CAP. Since then changes in the interconnected security, production, finance and knowledge structures have accelerated, forcing reform of the CAP wheat policy.

Increased complexity stands out as the most striking difference between the environment in the 1980s and conditions in the 1950s. In the first two post-war decades the security structure was often characterized as 'black and white': nations were either friendly or hostile. National security was to be assured by military might and food self-sufficiency. Production patterns and methods were largely unchanged from times of the agricultural revolution; small, atomistic farm units accounted for most of the acreage and production. World-wide, production and trade was predominantly in and among the developed countries. Farmers and national governments also relied on a relatively stable set of financial structures (interest, exchange and inflation rates) and the knowledge base was comfortably constant, with few developments that required farmers, governments, consumers or traders to adjust.

The pace of change accelerated in the 1970s and 1980s and made life more uncertain and complex for farmers, consumers and governments. Each shift in a power structure precipitated changes in the other structures, so that the stability of the earlier period was replaced with perpetual adjustment.

The simple security structure of the immediate post-war period was replaced by an interdependent world where superpower (nuclear) war now seems unthinkable and strict national security is almost impossible because of the interdependence of production of both food and strategic goods.

The agricultural investment boom of the 1970s and 1980s generated two different types of farms. About three-quarters of Community wheat now is produced on high-volume and low-margin commercial farms which depend on a stable supply of imported inputs, access to financial capital and a properly functioning distribution and trading system. These farmers often produce only a few products and have little opportunity to shift production. The rest of the farms in the EC are low-volume and high-margin and remain small, undercapitalized and largely removed from commercial and financial pressures. This division within the farm sector complicated policy development at both farm organization and government levels.

Meanwhile, the expansion of farm credit opened the sector to the uncertainties of impersonal financial markets: interest rates change frequently, exchange rates vary greatly and inflation occasionally causes havoc.

When the Community became a major exporter in the 1980s it found that competition increased as developed country markets were replaced by new opportunities in lesser developed countries (LDCs) and centrally planned economies (CPEs).

Finally, the knowledge explosion in the 1970s and 1980s radically changed the opportunities and pressures on the CAP. Better communications and data processing systems allowed farmers to use the latest production and market information to adapt their enterprises. These rapid shifts, however, forced governments to re-examine their goals and instruments because quick action by farmers increasingly thwarted government attempts to manage the market.

Security structures

The world security system has changed radically since the 1950s. Following the Second World War, the system was dominated by two large, expanding power blocs, led respectively by the United States of America (US) and the Union of Soviet Socialist Republics (USSR). Cold war prevailed for more than two decades, interspersed with periods of fierce but isolated fighting. It was generally viewed as a bad time to be outside one of the alliances. Rhetoric and anxiety both reached a high level. The threat of war seemed real.

After the Second World War food self-sufficiency remained a key security interest of most nations. The war had shown that food was a strategic resource: Japan had annexed Manchuria in 1936 partly to gain rice fields; Germany had sought control of the wheat lands of the Western steppes when it invaded the USSR in 1941; and ships were diverted from military use to transport food from North America to the food deficient UK.[1] In the immediate post-war period, Western European governments set food security as a top priority for national reconstruction.

Since then, a series of economic and military failures have caused the two power blocs to reassess their positions and seek less confrontation. Meanwhile, the economic structure of the world economy became increasingly inter-dependent, so that food self-sufficiency now is both less essential and less attainable than in earlier times. The CAP, built in response to the cold war climate of the 1950s and 1960s, is incompatible with the interdependence of the 1980s. National economies require guaranteed access to world markets for output and to ensure supplies of inputs. In the opinion of many, the CAP, by dampening overall industrial output in Europe[2] and providing a visible target for trade disputes, threatens to destabilize the very features that underlie the security structure of the western world in the 1980s.

Security in the Cold War

The battered, weakened and divided Western European states concentrated on economic and social reconstruction in the post-war period. The US provided all of the national security in those countries immediately after the war but was determined to strengthen Western Europe in order to provide a bulwark against Soviet expansion. Thus, the US encouraged Western Europeans to join the NATO alliance and accept military and economic support. The Organization for European Economic Co-operation (OEEC), set up in 1948 to administer the Marshall Plan, is generally credited with successfully rebuilding European industry.

The Marshall Plan, however, did not assist farmers directly. Immediately after the war, continental governments wished to assure the survival of farm jobs (more than 30 per cent of the German work force and almost 40 per cent of French employment) in the hope that grateful farmers would support the new democratic governments. The West German farm economy was in particularly poor shape because it had lost the large efficient farms in Prussia and was left with mostly small and inefficient farms.[3] Immediately following the war, food was scarce; in the winter of 1947 food was rationed and thousands died of starvation. Although the Allies provided food aid, the German government did not want to depend on imports. In response, Germany raised both subsidies and import duties to encourage production. This policy both assisted many refugees from the East to resettle into farming and allowed the nation to use its scarce foreign exchange reserves to rebuild its industrial infrastructure. The other continental governments also concentrated on reconstruction. Although these policies allowed food production in the EC6 to match pre-war levels by 1951,[4] the six remained large net importers of all major foods.

When the European Coal and Steel Community (ECSC), founded in 1950 by the 'Six' to manage the continental resources of coal and steel, demonstrated the economic and political benefits of European co-operation, continental farmers began to agitate for a similar agricultural arrangement. Although unification proposals failed in 1954 because of the collapse of the European Defence Community initiative, the European movement continued. Negotiations to create the EEC finally began in 1956 and, in 1958, the French and German governments reached agreement. German industry got access to the French market in exchange for French farmers' access to German consumer markets.

In the absence of UK participation, the CAP was created in line with continental concerns. Pearce argues that the main decision of the 1958–62 negotiations was 'that the policy's chief objective would be to maintain farm income and that its principal instrument would be price support.'[5] The common set of prices, therefore, became the most important feature of the CAP wheat regime (Figure 2.1). Until 1976, the Council annually set the target (ceiling) price to support farmers in the consuming regions (i.e. Duisburg in Germany) while the intervention (floor) price was set about 12–20 per cent below the target price, to reflect transport costs between the producing regions (Orleans–Ormes in France) and consuming regions. Public agencies were required to prevent market prices from falling below the intervention price by intervening and purchasing at the intervention price all quantities of grain offered.

Although the Community gave preference to domestic production, it decided to use world grain markets to stabilize the domestic market. If the EC system had been an autarky, domestic prices would have risen sharply because farmers in the EC6 could not produce enough food to satisfy domestic demand. The wheat regime was therefore designed to allow imports whenever domestic production was inadequate. The Community defined the entry (threshold) price so that wheat imports in the consuming region would equal the target price (i.e. the threshold price equalled the target price less the transport, handling and other delivery costs from the port of Rotterdam to Duisburg). When the world price was below the threshold price, the Commission set a variable levy (tariff) equal to the difference between the threshold and third-country offer prices (cif Rotterdam). The wheat regime also allowed exports of Community surpluses. The Commission set a restitution payment equal to the difference between the EC market price and world export price.

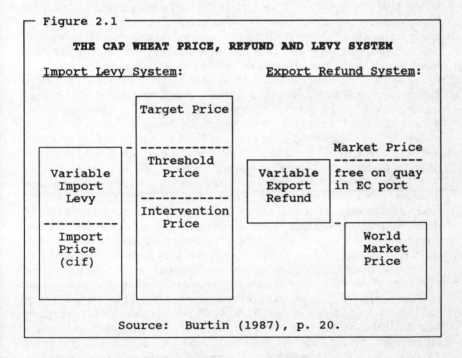

Figure 2.1

THE CAP WHEAT PRICE, REFUND AND LEVY SYSTEM

Import Levy System: Export Refund System:

Target Price

Threshold Price

Variable Import Levy

Import Price (cif)

Intervention Price

Market Price

Variable Export Refund

free on quay in EC port

World Market Price

Source: Burtin (1987), p. 20.

This system of protected internal markets and limited access to international markets suited both the national security concerns of the original six member states in the 1960s and the strategic goals of the US. The CAP was a 'cornerstone' of the security policy of Europe because 'a more unified western Europe could provide a stronger deterrent against further Soviet expansion, both because of its ability to organize a more coordinated military effort and because of its diplomatic weight.'[6] Keohane and Nye point out that the US government grudgingly accepted the CAP in the Kennedy Round of the GATT in 1963 because of 'concern about a communist military threat.'[7]

Security in the 1980s

During the 1970s, super-power politics began to shift towards discussion and mutual coexistence and away from confrontation. The US opened trade and diplomatic relations with the Peoples' Republic of China, withdrew from Vietnam and negotiated with the USSR a number of agreements to lessen the nuclear threat.

The Soviet invasion of Afghanistan in 1979 and election of Ronald Reagan as President of the United States in 1980 at first appeared to signal a return to cold war politics but changes within the Eastern bloc checked this tendency and subsequently accelerated disengagement. The economic troubles that plagued Poland beginning in 1980 started to appear in other Eastern bloc countries. Then, the death in 1982 of Leonid Brezhnev, General Secretary of the Communist Party in the USSR since 1963, opened the way for new leadership. When Mikhail Gorbachev gained power in 1985, he introduced sweeping reforms of Soviet politics, economics and international affairs. These efforts reached a peak in 1987–9 when the Soviet government introduced the economic 'perestroika' programme of market liberalization and the 'glasnost' political reforms, held contested elections for the Supreme Soviet, withdrew military forces from Afghanistan, pressed Cuba and Vietnam to resolve territorial disputes in Angola and Kampuchea, announced unilateral cuts in conventional military forces in Europe and negotiated agreement on intermediate range nuclear missiles. Then in May 1989, Soviet allies began to dismantle the 'iron curtain' security fence dividing Eastern and Western Europe and in November 1989 the Berlin Wall, the ultimate symbol of the cold war, fell, opening the floodgates to more rapid change in Eastern Europe.[8]

As United States strategic interests shifted, the US government re-examined its trade policy. Disengagement between the two super-power blocs and declining economic growth changed the balance between international and domestic concerns. Beginning in the 1970s in the Tokyo Round of GATT and continuing through the 1980s, the US government sought to open foreign markets to expand trade and enhance economic growth, which conflicted with the long-standing US policy of support for European integration. During the 1970s and 1980s, the world economy was transformed by the expansion of trade and the operation of large transnational corporations. The traded share of national GDP continued to rise in almost all national economies while many transnational corporations now often produce components of single products in different countries and only assemble them in the destination market (i.e. 'screw driver' plants). This production system depends critically on the continuation of trade and financial flows. As domestic concerns gained the upper hand, the official US policy shifted. In 1982, President Reagan announced the US would never again use food embargoes to enforce its other foreign policy objectives; farm exports would henceforward be driven exclusively by commercial concerns. Since then, the US has actively criticized European policies that limit trade and investment: the CAP wheat policy became the prime target.

EC strategic interests also changed. When the EC faced the threat of worldwide food shortage in the 1970s, policy-makers were initially comforted by their knowledge that Europe had nearly achieved temperate-zone food self-sufficiency.

But detailed study revealed that the CAP did not necessarily provide greater security from international developments. Livestock and dairy yields now depend critically on imported high-protein feeds from America and LDCs while the whole farm industry is heavily dependent on imported energy (used to operate machinery and embodied in the yield-enhancing fertilizers, pesticides and herbicides). The EC therefore has a strong reason to support and strengthen liberal trade and exchange rate systems.[9]

The reform of the CAP became a strategic goal of the Community after 1985. The CAP by then represented a major stumbling block in the pursuit of a stronger Europe. Debate over CAP reform frequently diverted attention from the domestic adjustments emanating from the 1992 policy while the EC position on farm policy reform threatened to derail the Uruguay Round of the GATT twice between 1986 and 1989.

The European Council in Copenhagen in 1982 had acknowledged that the EC economy compared poorly with Japan and the US and declared that it intended to complete the single European market within ten years. The Single Act was signed and enacted on 1 July 1987. The 'One Europe' policy of intra-Community trade liberalization is designed to create more dynamic pan-European corporations to compete on world markets, thereby boosting economic and employment growth in Europe in the 1990s. The Commission and most governments in the member states believe that the maximum benefits from the 1992 policy will only be realized when EC companies compete in a more open world marketplace – opening intra-EC markets will not be enough because they are mature.

Although primarily sold as an economic measure, the Single Market has a political dimension. As the cold war thawed in the 1980s, concern increased, especially in France, that West Germany could be enticed from the Western European alliance by promises of reunification of the two Germanies.[10] West Germans became less convinced that they needed either NATO or the US nuclear umbrella as East–West relations improved. France believes that if the internal market is completed, West Germany would find it increasingly difficult to turn from the EC towards either a neutralist or nationalist status, either alone or reunified with East Germany. France accepted that the CAP needed reform, so that resources could be redirected to implement the measures that would be required to complete the Single Market. Consequently, the CAP, regarded in the 1950s and 1960s as a cornerstone of the western security alliance, was by the 1980s viewed as a stumbling block in the path to a new Western European security structure.

Production structures

In the early post-war years and up to the beginning of the CAP, the typical continental farm was a 'small family undertaking employing only a few work units, usually members of the farmer's family.'[11] These small farms, generally overseen by old-time farmers, produced a wide range of products in much the same way as their ancestors had done since the agricultural revolution of the eighteenth century. They produced most of the inputs for crops or livestock (horsepower, fertilizers and feed) and consumed or processed a large portion of the output on the farm (feed, dairy products, vegetables and fruit) or sold directly to consumers. Meanwhile, world markets were dominated by production in the northern, developed countries.

Over the intervening thirty years, many farmers retired and were replaced by younger farmers or had their holdings consolidated into larger units. As a result, European agriculture emerged as a highly productive sector capable of competing in the world market. US economist William Cline has argued that for many industrial sectors 'comparative advantage is made, not given.'[12] The same is true for farming. Community policies on prices, finance, investment, taxes, trade, regulations and research have largely overcome the limitations imposed by the endowment of farm land in Europe, so that EC farmers are now competitive with the rest of the world. Although the majority of farm output is now produced on large commercial farms, there remain a significant number of small farms in disadvantaged regions.[13] At the same time, world markets have changed rapidly. Although wheat production has shifted from the West into the developing world, world wheat supply has not become more secure because production in new areas is more volatile and risky than in the older, more established growing areas.

Capital formation and production advances

The key change in the past thirty years was the surge in capital investment in farm machinery, structures and technologies in Europe. The EC farm sector received an above-average share of the new gross fixed capital formation following the beginning of the CAP. The German and UK farm sectors consistently invested about 25 per cent of their gross value added; in contrast, the national rate of capital formation generally peaked at only about 20 per cent. Although French farmers invested a smaller proportion of their value added in new capital equipment, the rate of investment was still generally higher than in the total economy.[14]

Much of the capital invested in farming was used for equipment, irrigation and land drainage, thereby helping to improve the productivity of the land. The most important change in farm practice brought about by this investment was the large increase in use of power machinery and equipment.[5] By 1985, virtually every farmer owned or had use of (through co-operative arrangements) both tractors and combine harvesters. As powered machinery replaced the horse, more land became available for cash crops. In 1968 farmers in the EC9 member states planted 3.7 Mha of oats (the main feed for livery animals). By 1987 the area planted to oats had declined to 1.3 Mha.

Farmers also moved their wheat production to their best land and invested heavily in irrigation for the less productive land. Irrigated land is not often used for wheat due to deleterious effects on quality of too much moisture, but it is satisfactorily used for growing other grains (e.g. maize). As a result, irrigation investment has made the non-wheat feed industry less weather dependent and more competitive with feed wheat.

The surge in real capital investment during the past thirty years changed cropping patterns and adoption of new high-yielding seeds (see knowledge structures) boosted the average yield of a hectare of wheat from about 2.2–3.1 t/ha in the 1954–8 period to more than 5.7 t/ha in 1983–7 in France and Germany and to more than 6.7 t/ha in the UK (Table 2.1). A group of particularly productive UK farmers have founded a 'ten tonne' club for individual farmers who have harvested at least that amount of common wheat from a hectare of land.

Table 2.1 Comparative wheat yields

t/ha	France	Germany	UK	USA
1904–08	1.38	1.79	2.24	0.88
1934–38	1.58	2.28	2.31	0.66
1954–58	2.24	2.90	3.10	1.45
1964–68	3.11	3.63	3.98	1.79
1973–77	4.33	4.38	4.35	2.03
1983–87	5.72	5.92	6.72	2.52*
Annual % change				
1906–36	0.4%	0.8%	0.1%	–1.0%
1936–56	1.8%	1.2%	1.5%	4.1%
1956–66	3.3%	2.3%	2.5%	2.1%
1966–75	3.8%	2.1%	1.0%	1.4%
1975–85	2.8%	3.1%	4.4%	2.2%

* 1983–86
Sources: Malenbaum (1953), pp. 236–9; IWC, *World Wheat Statistics*; Data from EC Commission

Recent studies show that cereals producers in both the UK and France are highly competitive in world terms (Table 2.2). The cost of the relatively greater use of inputs in Europe is offset by the significantly higher yields, so that Europe is competitive with dry-land farming in North America, Argentina and Australia. This is particularly true since 1985, because the sharp drop in energy costs make the energy-intensive farm system in Europe even more competitive. Thus, in both economic and financial terms, commercially-oriented UK and French farmers can compete.

Although the relative competitiveness of European farmers depends greatly on the ECU–US dollar exchange rate, data from the studies in Table 2.2 suggest that UK and French farmers should be competitive at even extreme exchange rates. The Stanton and Kansas City studies, for 1982 and 1987 respectively, show that even when the ECU was strong relative to the US dollar, UK and French farmers produced wheat at about the same or lower cost than US farmers.

A major factor limiting European farmers from competing freely with North American or Australian farmers is the relatively high cost of transporting grain to export position. In the early 1980s, it cost approximately US$33/t to move a bushel of wheat from the Paris Basin to the export port of Ghent while wheat could be moved from Minnesota to New Orleans (a distance twice as far) for only about US$12.50/t.[16] During the 1980s, however, the wholesale and distribution system was upgraded. Southampton, for example, was expanded during the decade so that it can now move as much as 10 Mt of grains in a single year.

Table 2.2 Relative cost of producing wheat in major exporting countries (US$/t)

Study	Year	Argentina	Australia	Canada	France	UK	USA
Total costs including land							
Stanton	1982	—	—	—	132.3	137.8	152.8
Cambridge Land Economy	1983–84	—	—	—	162.0	183.4	188.6
Stanton	1984	—	—	—	—	92.2	150.6
University of Guelph	1984	—	—	108.7	107.2	92.2	150.7
University of Guelph	1986	—	—	101.3	134.1	94.4	149.7
Fed. Bank of Kansas City*	1987	86.7	159.1	179.3	—	146.9	138.8
Total costs excluding land							
Stanton	1982	—	—	—	—	110.6	119.4
Cambridge Land Economy	1983–84	—	—	—	130.0	151.9	145.7
Stanton	1984	—	—	—	—	72.7	118.3
Fed. Bank of Kansas City*	1987	70.3	125.1	137.4	—	117.8	119.9
Yield (t/ha)	See note	2.3	1.3	1.9	5.7	6.7	2.5

* Central Plains, including Kansas

Yields: UK & France (1983–7); USA (1983–6); Canada, Argentina, & Australia (1980–4)

Sources: Murphy (1985), table 3.10. Barkema & Drabenstott (1988), p. 9. A. Sarris, 'EC–US Agricultural Trade Confrontations,' in Baldwin *et al.* (1988), p. 107. *The Globe & Mail*, 12–1–87

Consolidation and specialization

Another major change in Europe has been the marked increase in the size of the average farm and the specialization of commercial units. In the 1950s, the majority of continental European farmers produced and lived much in the same manner as their forebears in the nineteenth century or earlier. They produced cereal and vegetable crops on small, often widely scattered, plots of land, with minimal use of powered machinery (at least partly because powered machinery could not operate on many of the small holdings).[17] Horses, oxen and humans provided much of the energy on the farm, so a significant share of farm output was consumed rather than marketed.

After the Second World War, but especially after 1958, increased availability of financial resources allowed farmers to invest heavily in machinery and land. As a result, farmers were able to expand the size of their farms, to consolidate plots of land into larger areas that could be worked by power machinery and to shift their planting towards crops best produced and harvested by machinery. In the case of wheat, this allowed farmers to realize the production potential of their investment.

By 1986 farms with more than 50 ha of utilizable agricultural area (UAA) represented about 18 per cent of total farmers in France but cultivated almost half the land; this was up from less than 30 per cent of the land cultivated by the 5.5 per cent largest farmers in 1960. In Germany, about 5.5 per cent of all farms had over 50 ha in 1986 but they cultivated more than a quarter of the land in the country. In 1960, only 1 per cent of German farms were large and they cultivated about 10 per cent of farm land. The large farms in both France and Germany cultivated about 80 ha each in 1986. Meanwhile, UK farmers pointed the way to the future: by 1986 more than one-third of UK farms cultivated more than 50 ha of UAA and together accounted for almost 83 per cent of the farmland in the country. These large farms had an average 171 ha under cultivation in 1986, compared with only 110 ha in 1960.[18]

As they expanded, commercially-directed farms concentrated their efforts on production of a smaller number of products.[19] In 1970–1, about 46 per cent of European farmers (EC9) produced some common wheat: in Germany more than 61 per cent of farmers planted some wheat, compared with 48 per cent in France and only 15 per cent in the UK. By 1985, only 36 per cent of Community farmers (EC9) planted wheat: the number of farmers growing wheat dropped to less than 56 per cent in Germany and about 46 per cent in France and remained fairly steady in the UK. At the same time, the average area planted to wheat per farm rose a little in Germany and more than doubled in France and the UK.[20]

Specialization has been a two-edged sword. As the industry specialized and farmers improved their incomes, they became more exposed to the effects of policy changes and market fluctuations. The application of new technologies and the introduction of specialized machinery, equipment and structures make future adjustments more difficult. The new physical capital is not versatile. Specialized seed drills, combination harvesters, granaries and transportation equipment for wheat are not easily adaptable for other products. Farmers, therefore, are more exposed to consequences of shifts in markets than in pre-CAP days.

Nevertheless, farm incomes broadened and increased as farmers worked off-farm. Consolidation of holdings, specialization (e.g. cereals production alone without livestock rearing) and the introduction of labour-saving machinery reduced the labour required and left greater periods of the year available for off-farm pursuits. Many farmers have taken the opportunity to work off-farm to supplement the family income. In 1985 about 23 per cent of European farmers had other main gainful employment while another 7.5 per cent had other secondary employment. This varied widely over the Community, with about 42 per cent of German farmers, 32 per cent of French farmers and 21 per cent of British farmers working elsewhere to supplement their farm incomes.[21] The German government has encouraged this trend, implementing regional economic development programmes that assist industry to locate in rural areas to tap this source of manpower.[22] The move to off-farm work in the 1980s has been most marked in France, where the number of farmers holding other secondary gainful employment jumped to 19 per cent in 1985 from less than 5 per cent in 1980.

As a result, farm income statistics are unreliable indicators of farm family incomes. In addition to farmers themselves working off-farm, in many cases other members of farm families are also employed off-farm, supplementing the family income. Farm income statistics rarely report these figures. Gross farm income data also should not be used to make either cross border or farm versus non-farm income comparisons because the figures are not adjusted for the often very favourable tax treatment for farmers, they ignore imputed and realized capital gains from owning farm land and equipment and understate the imputed income available from the farm operation in the form of housing, transport and food.[23] At the beginning of the 1980s, farmers received roughly 2,500 to 5,000 ECU each in these forms of support.[24]

For the majority in the European wheat sector, therefore, the shift in production technologies and cropping patterns has narrowed the interests of individual farmers and broadened the income base for farm families. But at the same time, farmers have less opportunity to offset vulnerability in the product prices.

World production changes

The European wheat market does not exist in isolation. Developments in world markets have defined the physical and economic environment for European decisions and affect the commercial prospects for European wheat importers and exporters.

The major development in the world market since 1950 is the shift in production to the developing countries (Figure 2.2). Between 1950 and 1984 wheat production grew by more than 230 per cent in developing countries and 170 per cent in centrally planned economies but rose only 120 per cent in developed countries. Overall, total production increased by 150 per cent. The largest increases were recorded in Asia, where Chinese production rose six-fold and Indian output increased more than 700 per cent. Both China and India by the mid-1980s were judged to be normally self-sufficient. A crop failure in 1987 in India, which would in the past have caused widespread starvation, was managed without difficulty.[25]

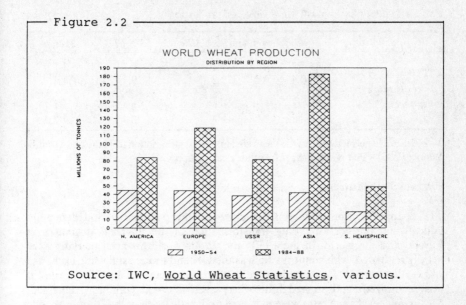

Figure 2.2

WORLD WHEAT PRODUCTION
DISTRIBUTION BY REGION

Source: IWC, <u>World Wheat Statistics</u>, various.

The changing farm policy in the Soviet Union is the other major factor in the world market. In 1953 the Soviet government ended Stalin's policy of maintaining wheat exports, regardless of domestic conditions, and allowed shipments to vary in line with domestic supply and demand. Although the USSR attempted to expand production and exports over the succeeding years, yields became more erratic and the Soviet government frequently had to adjust its export and import plans. The government expanded cereals production on to 40 Mha of new land in the semi-arid steppe region but its yields were highly variable because small changes in precipitation caused large swings in output. The increased volatility in Soviet production spilled over into the world market and caused wide swings in wheat trade prices during the 1950s and 1960s.[26] Then, in 1970, the Brezhnev government decided to expand livestock and milk production in the USSR, which necessitated a sharp rise in grain imports for animal feed. Since that time the USSR has been the largest single importer of wheat and feed grains. In the 1980s, agricultural reforms related to 'perestroika' reversed past policies in order to provide incentives for production increases. Some commentators predict the Soviet Union will regain self-sufficiency in wheat and other grains if the policy succeeds.

The combination of expanded production in Asia and the USSR made world wheat yields (and prices) in the 1975–84 period more volatile than in the immediate post-war period (Table 2.3). This volatility did not fully translate into wider production swings, however, because the US government used its farm programmes to encourage farmers to set aside large blocks of land to offset some of the instability in world markets. Consequently, instability in world wheat production actually diminished in the 1975–84 period compared with the 1946–55 period. The US ability to act as swing producer is diminishing, however, because each year it produces a smaller proportion of total production. Consequently, unless other producing and exporting countries join the US as swing producers, world production will follow the trend in yields and become increasingly volatile.

Table 2.3 Instability in world wheat yield and production

		World less USSR	USSR	World
Yield:	1946–55	3.1	8.7	3.5
	1975–84	3.2	9.4	4.4
Production:	1946–55	n.a	n.a	5.1
	1975–84	n.a	n.a	3.5

Note: Instability is measured as the mean absolute per cent variation from the fitted trend.
Source: IWC, *World Wheat Statistics*; author's calculations

Financial structures

The changes in the production structures in the post-war period depended critically on the corresponding transformation of the financial structures in Europe and the world. In the 1950s and 1960s world financial markets were heavily regulated, with countries such as the UK and France still using exchange and credit controls. Farmers, however, used little commercial credit (most of it was subsidized) and so had little worry even if credit conditions changed. Meanwhile, exchange rates were managed under the terms of the Bretton Woods system and capital flows were small relative to the flows of trade.

Changes in the financial system began in the 1970s but accelerated rapidly in the 1980s. Domestically, governments deregulated their financial systems, allowing farmers greater access to the financial capital that facilitated the reform of the production systems in Europe. When the governments attempted to use monetary policy more actively for macroeconomic purposes in the 1970s, they discovered that they were less able to control financial instruments. Meanwhile, international capital flows multiplied as the world financial system recycled the massive oil revenues accumulating in OPEC countries. In 1985 world capital flows reached US$84 trillion while trade flows totalled only US$2.7 trillion.[27] The combination of varying degrees of deregulation and large pools of mobile international funds strained the world financial system. As a result, in the 1970s the gold standard and the Bretton Woods system of fixed exchange rates were abandoned and in the 1980s both interest and exchange rates became more volatile.

Sources of capital

It is difficult to determine the exact causality of the changes, but it is certain that without the provision of capital from other family members, the commercial financial industry, governments and the farm supply business the dramatic shifts in production techniques and land holdings would not have been possible. In France, for example, agriculture was a net provider of funds to other sectors of the economy for most of the century prior to 1970. Since then, working capital has replaced labour employment, to the point where agriculture has been described as 'heavy industry'.[28] In France, the average farm had a debt load in

1985 of 44,369 ECUs or about 2.4 times the annual net value added per farm. In Germany it was 52,767 ECUs or about 2.8 times the net value added per farm and in the UK 63,043 ECUs, or about 1.6 times the average net value added.[29] In Canada, the average farm debt was 67,900 ECUs, or about 2.6 times the average net value added.[30]

Historically, the average German or French farmer inherited land holdings and equipment and the trend was for the available land and capital to be divided rather than augmented. Inheritance laws (in the Napoleonic Code which prevails in France and the Catholic states in Germany) provide each legitimate offspring with an equal share of any land. Thus, land holdings were perpetually being broken apart. Although the laws have not changed, the general economic boom in the post-war period provided for much greater movement from the farm into industrial employment. Now, when a farm owner dies it is unlikely that all the offspring will depend on income from sale of the asset. If there is a sibling who wishes to farm, the off-farm inheritors either continue to own a portion of the land, taking only a small share of the operating profits as their return or they sell the land to the sibling on a preferential basis. As a result, in France probably more than 20 per cent of the population, much of it urban, has an interest in farm land.[31]

The majority of the additional capital, however, has come from commercial sources. The revolution in financial services and introduction of more flexible loan terms have provided an opportunity for farmers to consolidate and expand marginal farms so they can realize economies of scale in the use of machinery, labour and human capital.

Farmers who used outside capital to rationalize and consolidate their farming operations now have larger and more efficient farms, but they must operate at or near physical capacity limits in order to service the resulting high levels of debt. In 1985, farm debt payments represented 23 per cent of German total outgoings, 28 per cent in France and 13 per cent in the UK.[32] Consequently, farmers are now significantly more exposed to variations in credit conditions than in earlier periods.

Commercialization of farming

Agricultural policy analysts often ignore the upstream and downstream industries that rely on farm production because of the artificial distinction in the national economic accounts between primary, secondary and tertiary industries. Ignoring the linkages between the farm and non-farm sectors in Europe may have made sense in earlier times when farmers supplied most of their inputs on-farm and consumed or sold directly for local consumption the large majority of their output. But the application of intensive crop techniques and the use of capital-intensive machinery and equipment has brought the northern European farm community fully into the economic mainstream.

As recently as 1958, German farmers purchased only about 30 per cent of their inputs from other sectors while French farmers bought just over one-fifth of their inputs from non-agricultural sectors. The average UK farmer, in contrast, purchased more than half of his inputs from non-agricultural sectors. With the rapid adoption of capital and intensive production technologies, French and

German farmers now are in line with UK practice (45–55 per cent of inputs purchased). Furthermore, outlays for capital depreciation, wages, land rent and interest accounted in 1986 for almost another 30 per cent of gross farm output in Germany, 26 per cent in France and almost 36 per cent in the UK.[33]

As a result, agriculture now plays a central role in the agro–industrial complex. The Commission estimates that less than half of the estimated impact of agriculture on European GDP is generated on-farm. In addition to the approximately 3.5–5 per cent of EC GDP and 7–10 million jobs contributed by on-farm value-added activity, input purchases by farmers supported an estimated additional 1.9 per cent of the total European economy while off-farm processing, distribution and marketing of the output contributed another 3.4–5 per cent of GDP and employed as many as 2.7 million workers.[34] In the cereals sector, where only feed grains are consumed in the raw form and many of the producers use intensive cultivation practices, the value added off-farm could be more than double the on-farm value added.

These strong linkages between cereals producers and upstream and downstream industries have created many opportunities for improved economic performance of the farm sector but have also opened it to two new market influences: credit conditions and inflation. Since 1958, the ratio of gross incomes to purchased inputs and costs, such as depreciation, rents and interest charges, has declined from over 3-to-1 to only 1.35-to-1 (and only 1.13-to-1 in the UK) in 1986. When farmers earned more than three times what they spent on inputs, large swings in prices had only a small effect on the prosperity and viability of the farm. Now, with small operating margins, farmers are much more vulnerable to inflation of their input costs, interest rate rises and small declines in producer prices.

One key result of these changes is that the price elasticity of demand for unprocessed wheat has declined. The average price of a commercially produced loaf of bread in Europe and North America now represents the value not only of the raw wheat (10 per cent), but also the costs and profit margins of the related transportation, milling, baking, packaging, distribution, advertising, wholesale and retail systems. As a result, changes in the price of unprocessed wheat have little impact on demand.

Changing international foreign exchange markets

The CAP system for wheat had a relatively smooth start once the question of price levels had been set. The common prices in Units of Account (UAs) were converted to national currencies at the prevailing fixed exchange rates and for eighteen months truly common prices prevailed across the Community. Then the financial base for the CAP began to crumble. In 1969 France devalued the franc by 11.11 per cent and shortly thereafter Germany revalued the DM by 9.29 per cent. In the absence of ameliorating measures, the target and intervention prices in France should have risen and those in Germany should have dropped. Neither government was willing to accept the political consequences and those adjustments were not made.

The Treaty does not require a single price for commodities at either the wholesale or retail level: Art. 40.3.3 states that the common price policy need only be based on common criteria and uniform methods of calculation.[35] A compromise system developed: common prices in UAs remained unchanged but the exchange rate used to convert the common prices to national prices deviated from the market rate. These 'green' rates of exchange are overvalued for devaluing countries, thereby dampening increases in domestic prices, and undervalued in revaluing countries, thereby sustaining prices in domestic currencies. The original green rates set in 1969 were expected to move quickly to the official exchange rates, thereby eliminating the discrepancy in prices (the gap between market and green rates is known as the 'monetary gap'). To ensure that intra-Community trade was not disrupted by different price levels in different Community countries, monetary compensatory amounts (MCAs) were created to equalize offer prices in all countries. MCAs were set equal to the difference between the market central rate for the currency and the green rate, minus a 'neutral margin' factor to avoid over-compensation. Countries with undervalued green rates (i.e. strong currency countries such as Germany) received subsidies (positive MCAs) to export while imports were taxed. The reverse occurred in countries with overvalued green rates (i.e. weak currency countries such as France).

The collapse in 1973 of the Bretton Woods system of fixed exchange rates caused exchange rates to move much more than previously (Figure 2.3). The Commission calculates that the average annual variation of the UA relative to individual member currencies in the 1975–8 period was as high as 17 per cent; currencies not conforming to EC monetary arrangements varied more.

Beginning in 1972 the Community attempted to control intra-EC exchange rates with the 'Snake' exchange agreement,[36] but had difficulty controlling currency swings because the UK, Irish, Italian and French governments would

Figure 2.3

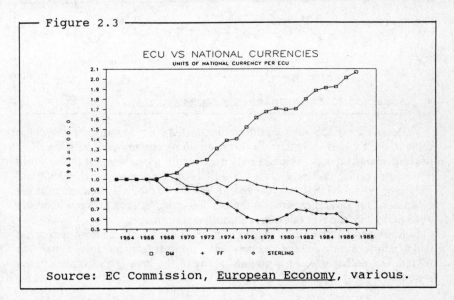

ECU VS NATIONAL CURRENCIES
UNITS OF NATIONAL CURRENCY PER ECU

□ DM   + FF   ○ STERLING

Source: EC Commission, *European Economy*, various.

not accept the loss of independent monetary and fiscal policy necessary to maintain stable rates. The UK and Ireland originally joined the Snake but dropped out in June 1972 when speculation drove their currencies outside the band. Italy joined but withdrew within a year. France joined in 1972, quit in 1974, rejoined in 1975 and quit for good in 1976 when the inflation gap between France and Germany and the rising current account deficit in France forced the French government either to deflate the economy or to devalue the franc.

The European Monetary System and the ECU were introduced in 1979 to replace the looser Snake. France became a full member but Italy had a wider band (6 per cent) and the UK refused to join. Even for those countries belonging to the system, green rates continued because diverging economic conditions in the member states caused the DM to rise and the franc and lira to depreciate. European exchange rates began to move less widely after 1983, when monetary and fiscal policies were more closely co-ordinated and inflation rates converged (Figure 2.4).

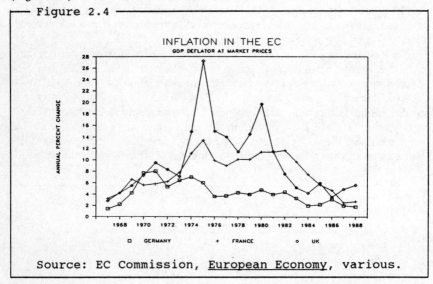

─── Figure 2.4 ───

Source: EC Commission, European Economy, various.

Concern over EMS rates was then superseded by wide swings in the dollar value of the ECU (Figure 2.5). Export restitutions vary inversely with the ECU price of wheat exports, which in turn depends on a combination of the world wheat price (in US dollars) and the US$–ECU exchange rate. Between 1980 and February 1985 the US dollar rose sharply relative to the ECU, reducing the net restitutions for cereals exports. As the US dollar depreciated between February 1985 and 1988, the cost of export restitutions rose sharply.

Since the end of fixed exchange rates in 1973, the European farm system has had to adjust to wide divergences between European exchange rates as well as a volatile US dollar, which has strained many of the long-term bargains in the system.

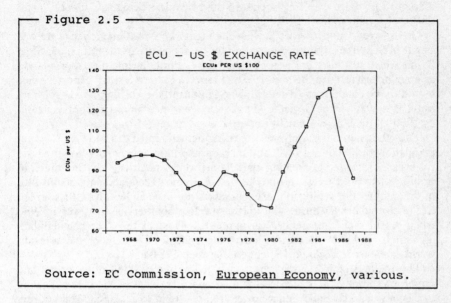

Figure 2.5

ECU – US $ EXCHANGE RATE
ECUs PER US $100

Source: EC Commission, <u>European Economy</u>, various.

Shifting wheat trade

International trade in wheat also changed significantly in the post-war period (Table 2.4). In the 1950s four traditional exporters – the US, Canada, Australia and Argentina – controlled about 90 per cent of the export market and developed countries still purchased 58 per cent of the wheat sold internationally. By the mid-1980s, the four traditional exporters shared less than 80 per cent of the

Table 2.4 World wheat market: import and export shares

	1934–38	*1949–54*	*1966–70*	*1980–84*
Exporters				
Argentina	23%	8%	4%	7%
Australia	20%	11%	14%	12%
Canada	33%	32%	21%	19%
USA	10%	39%	35%	42%
Other	14%	11%	26%	21%
–EC	na	na	9%	15%
–USSR	na	na	11%	1%
–Others	na	na	6%	5%
Importers				
Developed countries	80%	58%	29%	13%
Other	20%	42%	71%	87%
–Developing	na	na	49%	48%
–CPEs excluding USSR	na	na	20%	18%
–USSR	na	na	2%	21%

Source: IWC, *World Wheat Statistics*, 1985

market while more than 87 per cent of the wheat was being sold to LDCs and CPEs, especially to the USSR.

On the export side, the two key developments were the emergence of the EC as one of the three largest exporters and the cessation of exports from the USSR. Rising wheat surpluses in Europe pushed the Community into the export market as a major player after the mid-1970s (France had been a small exporter since before the Second World War). Equally significant, the USSR ceased exporting in the late 1970s when Soviet food policy concentrated on red meat production; by 1980-5, the USSR annually imported an average 20 Mt.

The other significant shift was the rising demand in LDCs and CPEs. Rapid population and income growth and marketing programmes to develop the taste for bread succeeded in creating markets for wheat in Africa, Asia and much of South America. CPEs apart from the USSR also now account for about one-fifth of the market. But selling to these markets is not easy. LDCs and CPEs, which had borrowed heavily during the 1970s, saw their debt service costs soar in 1980 when world monetary policy was tightened. Most of the debt rescheduling agreements in the 1980s require borrowing countries to cut imports; as a result, world wheat trade declined 15 per cent between 1984 and 1987.

The method of marketing wheat changed as the position of exporters and importers shifted. The 1972 'great grain robbery' highlighted the risks of dealing in this new market. Following a Soviet crop failure in 1972, USSR grain buyers negotiated with a number of grain merchants simultaneously and were thereby able to purchase the bulk of free world stocks before the news broke. Prices soared to record levels when the full dimensions of the new market situation were finally revealed. Beginning in 1975, the major exporters and importers used long-term framework agreements to prevent repetition of such disruptions. By the mid-1980s, Canada, Australia and Argentina had committed for export more than 60 per cent of their expected minimum annual exports.[37] The US had less than 20 per cent of its lowest annual wheat export volumes committed and the EC (France) had negotiated only one binding agreement. The FAO estimates that in 1979-82, between 42 and 56 per cent of the total world wheat trade was committed under agreements, with about 89-100 per cent of Chinese trade, 16 per cent of Brazilian trade and 31-50 per cent of Soviet trade under agreements.[38]

On the import side, the rise in the LDC and CPE markets reduced the market power of the exporters. By 1973-7 more than 90 per cent of wheat imports were purchased by state trading houses on behalf of the importing countries; during the 1950s only about 60 per cent of imports were controlled by state traders.[39] Competition has become increasingly intense because state traders in the importing countries use their market power to negotiate better terms from the exporters. The exporters can no longer play off one importing firm against another.

Knowledge structures

The application of additional physical and financial capital was necessary for the increases in production after 1958, but the gains would not have been possible without corresponding changes in the knowledge structure. The rapid changes in European farming in the post-war period were assisted by increased investment in education and farmer training as well as in the research and development of new wheat strains and new methods of cultivation. At the same time, farmers and farm policy makers face rising consumer demands for greater variety and higher quality output and pressure from environmentalists to reduce pollution which has accompanied the new, intensive production methods.

Education

Farmers in Europe, as in much of the world, usually received little formal education; most of their training was on-the-job, either on family farms or in larger commercial enterprises. This pattern of education was adequate when farming was largely a matter of having 'a strong back'. Now, an operator of a commercially-motivated wheat farm must understand: economics, so he can decide on the best mix of crops to take advantage of market conditions; plant and soil sciences, so he can choose the optimal time to sow and harvest and the optimal mix of and time to apply fertilizers, pesticides and herbicides; mechanics, so he can repair his increasingly complex machinery and equipment; accounting, so he can keep track of the cash flow and manage his debt; and, ideally, computers, so he can conduct the sophisticated analyses needed to keep the farm operating profitably.

At the founding of the CAP, production in the Community was limited by the low level of formal training among farmers and farm families. In France, for example, even as recently as the early 1980s only about 5 per cent of farmers had received any formal training in agricultural or agronomic practices.[40] German farmers are generally better educated but not necessarily in farming matters. UK farmers are probably better trained because of a comprehensive system of apprenticeship with larger farms and the availability of related university training.

France, in particular, recognized the problems resulting from poorly trained farmers and expanded training programmes for existing farmers during the 1970s. At the same time, the three north European governments expanded their extension programmes to inform farmers of new, more efficient farm practices. The combination of greater training for starting farmers, retirement of older farmers and the greater provision of extension services accelerated the adoption of new technologies and methods of production.

Biotechnical advances

The wheat seed, the critical factor in the production of wheat, was domesticated as early as 6000 B.C. but changed little until this past century. Seed developments late in the nineteenth century brought wheat production to the Canadian prairies, which radically transformed the world wheat market. Then in the 1960s and 1970s scientists developed new strains that have a shorter maturation period, resist fungal and bacteriological diseases (e.g. rust), give a desired protein level (either high for bread flour or low for feeds) and enhance yields.

The major breakthrough in wheat seed development in the post-war period was made by the Centro Internacional de Mejoramiento de Maiz y Trigo in Los

Banos, Mexico, where beginning in 1960 scientists released a succession of new wheat breeds suitable for moist growing areas, such as India, Brazil and Mexico. These new varieties, which provide a high yield of medium protein wheat with the application of proper amounts of fertilizer and irrigation, spread rapidly through the developing world and provided the foundation for the 'green revolution.'

Hybrids of the 'green revolution' strain of high yield and medium protein wheat arrived in Europe in the mid-1970s as enterprising farmers took advantage of the CAP wheat regime. In 1976–7, the Commission proposed and the Council accepted that the guaranteed price structure be modified to allow for a higher reference price to be paid for wheat of bread-making quality. The reference price for bread wheat, eventually supported by intervention buying, was set about halfway between the intervention and target prices for wheat. Although wheat had to satisfy higher quality standards to earn the higher reference price, Debatisse noted that 'the differentiation techniques between feed wheat and bread wheat has led to almost all wheat being considered bread wheat.'[41] Because bread-quality premiums were paid to some wheat that was not adequate for milling, farmers were encouraged to shift into those higher yielding, lower quality varieties which barely met the minimum standards.

Since then there has been a worldwide proliferation of wheat varieties. In the US, for example, in 1977 only eleven varieties represented the vast majority of all wheat planted in Kansas; during the 1986 crop year, forty-three varieties were planted. During the same period, wheat varieties representing 85 per cent of the acreage planted in Kansas in 1986 did not even exist in 1977.[42] The transformation was even greater in Europe. In the UK only one winter wheat variety used in 1975 (Maris Huntsman) was still used in 1987, when it was only planted on about 0.1 per cent of the wheat acreage.[43]

Introduction of new seed varieties into Europe has permanently changed production techniques. Each seed variety has characteristics that suit it to specific conditions, so farmers now generally purchase their seed annually, much as they buy other inputs. The new, high-yielding varieties also require large quantities of inputs – herbicides, pesticides, fungicides and fertilizers – to grow at all.[44] It would not be easy to revert to extensive production methods using existing seeds and the old, low-input, low-yielding varieties are now unavailable.[45]

Meanwhile, research continues. In 1973 the breakthrough of recombinant DNA (gene splicing) accelerated seed advancement. Governments world-wide are now funding research into the agronomics of wheat production with a view to improving yields or reducing costs of production. The Bureau Européen de Recherches reported in 1989 that breakthroughs in biotechnology could raise EC crop yields by another 10 per cent within ten years. Introduction of DNA–MAB probes into seeds, which would allow early detection of diseases, alone could increase output by 10 per cent.

Computers and the farmer

Development of computing programs and the dissemination of computers both among farmers and in the input and processing industries have significantly tightened the relationship between supply and demand.

Producers now have the computing power to calculate rapidly the relative profitability of differing price structures and input usage. Debatisse noted, for example, that 'the EEC animal feedstuffs industry uses highly sophisticated mathematical techniques of linear programming for optimising animal rations.' In effect, 'the computer directs purchasing in this sector.'[46] Consequently, feed lots and large cattle farms are able to calculate the relative merits of using forage, EC cereals and commercially mixed feed based on imported cereal substitutes (i.e. manioc, corn gluten).

Other developments in the livestock sector may have a major impact on the cereals sector. Computer technology has been introduced to the milking shed.[47] In 1987 a prototype computer-controlled milking and feeding dairy called 'Farm 2000' was tested. When cows enter the milking shed, a computer operates an automatic milker, reads a sensor on the cow's neck and prepares and presents a balanced meal of forage and concentrate to optimize milk yields.

In the cereals industry, computers are already being used in the fields to evaluate the quality and yields of wheat and make automatic adjustments to combining equipment. These, and other applications of computer technologies, will eventually optimize the use of cereals as feed and reduce the amount wasted as seed, feed and dockage.

Technological change in processing

Wheat demand has also been strongly influenced by changes in the processing sector. Bakers and millers have discovered that they can enrich medium strength European wheat with low-cost imported corn gluten to produce a stronger wheat flour suitable for pan breads. Commercial feed-lots also discovered that corn gluten could be used to extend and enrich feed for dairy and beef cattle. Because the EC bound the duty rate on such products at zero under the Kennedy Round of GATT negotiations, those products enter the Community tariff-free, which makes them highly competitive with low quality feed wheats.

More recently, the baking industry has discovered how to bake lighter-weight, air-pocketed pan bread without using high gluten or gluten-enriched wheats (most EC wheat has inadequate gluten to produce this style of bread using traditional baking processes). In the past, European millers mixed locally-produced medium strength wheat with imported high gluten wheats (often from North America). In the UK, where consumers overwhelmingly prefer lighter-weight pan breads, millers and bakers developed the Chorleywood baking process. The dough, enriched with extra yeast, fat and water, is continuously mixed using intense mechanical action to produce a higher yielding dough that bakes into a reasonable pan bread.[48] Consequently, the European market for higher quality wheats has declined.

Communications and information

The wheat trade has also been strongly influenced by the development of the 'global village'. The development of new technologies to gather and disseminate information has helped make information a truly public good. In earlier years, the big five grain trading companies generally had a monopoly on production information because only they had informants in each market. They were thereby able virtually to control the market and make large profits.

The Food and Agriculture Organization (FAO) pioneered the notion of free flow of scientific and crop information in the 1950s and 1960s but the practice only became common in the mid-1970s when new technologies had been developed.[49] The LandSat Satellite system, for one, can now scan and record crop progress in all parts of the world. No longer can any country conceal its crop results, as the USSR did in 1972. The US Department of Agriculture (with the help of the CIA), the FAO and the International Wheat Council now regularly acquire, analyse and report information on the current crop conditions and future prospects for the world market. This tends to tighten market relationships and ensures 'grain robberies' cannot happen.

The development of modern telecommunications has also spread a global conscience. Famines and chronic starvation have been common since the beginning of mankind, but now that television brings moving pictures of their effect into the living-rooms of the developed world, food aid has been conscientiously applied to the hunger problem.[50]

Consumers and research

World farmers ultimately depend on consumers purchasing their products. Recent medical research into biology and nutrition has shown linkages between low fibre diets and intestinal and stomach cancer and between red meat consumption and the incidence of high cholesterol, heart disease and strokes. Consequently, there has been a shift in the diets in many developed countries towards whole-grain and white meats and away from white bread flours and red meats.

On balance, the impact has been to dampen demand for both bread and feed wheats. Any shift to whole grains reduces demand because it only takes about 1.03 kg to produce a kilogram of whole wheat flour while it takes about 1.33 kg to produce one kilogram of white flour.[51] More importantly, it takes only about two kilograms of cereals to produce a kilogram of chicken meat whereas approximately five kilograms of wheat must be fed to a cow to achieve a gain of one kilogram of meat. Based on the conversion factors and the shift in types of meat demanded in Europe between 1980 and 1985, the annual demand for feed wheats in the EC10 has been reduced by about 0.8 Mt (approximately 4 per cent of the feed wheat use in 1985) compared with levels that would have been used based on 1980 tastes.

In the broader sense, consumers also are the ultimate arbiters of how the environment is used. During the 1970s and 1980s, scientists confirmed that intensive crop and livestock production techniques contributed to the degradation of the European environment. Nitrogen-laden run-off from wheat fields (as well as the effluent from feed-lots) is responsible for the algae bloom and oxygen starvation in many Northern European lakes while large feed-lots cause other air, water and soil pollution. Meanwhile, research has demonstrated links between some human illnesses and consumption of food produced using chemicals, herbicides and hormones. Recently, the European Council bowed to pressure from the EP, some national governments and consumer groups to ban red meat growth hormones effective from 1 January 1989, thereby creating a major trade dispute at the half-way point of the Uruguay Round of the GATT. Research on pollution and food chemicals, therefore, can create vast new pressures for the CAP to adapt.

Conclusion

Although the rise in European farm output and the development of exportable surpluses increased the pressure for farm policy reform in the EC, these are merely symptoms of fundamental changes that are pushing the system. The OECD concluded in 1982 that diverse changes in the underlying power structures have radically altered the farm policy environment. 'The increasing integration of agriculture within the economy has taken agricultural policy out of its purely sectoral context and policy formulation has been put within a wider context of general economic, social and environmental perspectives.'[52] The Community has spent the better part of the 1980s coming to grips with the new realities. The following chapters discuss the implications of these changes in the context of both domestic policy reform and international trade negotiation.

Notes

1. Kennedy (1983), p. 6.
2. See Tables 1.1 and 1.2.
3. Hendriks (1987), p. 35.
4. Tracy (1982), p. 232.
5. Pearce (1983), p. 147.
6. Taylor (1983), p. 301.
7. Keohane and Nye (1977), p. 47.
8. *The Economist*, 6–5–89.
9. Pearce (1981), p. 61.
10. B. Beedham, 'East of Eden: a survey of Eastern Europe', *The Economist*, 12–8–89, p. 18.
11. *Green Europe 217*, p. 55.
12. W. Cline in Rubin and Graham (1984), p. 26.
13. The EC has defined approximately half of all the farm area in the Community as 'disadvantaged'. Most of that land has natural disadvantages (e.g. hills and lack of moisture) or has a poor economic structure (e.g. land holdings smaller than economically viable).
14. Phillips (1989), p. 50.
15. Johnson (1973), p. 73, showed that the earlier movement from animal to tractor power in the US made possible the sharply increased level of production. He calculated that the maximum horsepower (hp) available if all land was used for feed would only be about 125 M hp; in 1970 the US farm industry required about 200 M hp to produce and harvest the crop. Thus, the current level of production usable off-farm could not be sustained without tractors and petroleum.
16. Insel (1985), p. 899.

17. Furtan *et al.* (1988), p. 105.
18. Eurostat, *Agriculture Statistical Yearbook 1988*, p. 70.
19. Bowler (1985), p. 114.
20. Eurostat, *Agriculture Statistical Yearbook 1988*, p. 46.
21. *ASC 1987*, p. T104–5.
22. Ardagh (1987), p. 131–2.
23. Howarth (1985), p. 30–4.
24. Commission of the ECs (1984), *Public Expenditure on Agriculture*, Study P.229.
25. *The Economist*, 2–7–88.
26. Johnson (1977), pp. 10–12, 20; OECD (1983a), p. 55.
27. Hiemstra and Shane (1988), p. 7.
28. Rosenfeld, Girling and Reid (1980), p. 46.
29. *ASC 1987*, p. 59.
30. Data for Saskatchewan.
31. *Financial Times*, 16–6–80.
32. *ASC 1987*, p. 59.
33. Eurostat, *Agriculture Statistical Yearbook 1988*, pp. 226–7.
34. *ASC*, 1980 and 1982.
35. Snyder (1985), p. 100.
36. The EC9 member states agreed in 1972 to limit the fluctuations in their currencies about central rates to a maximum 2.25 per cent band; the existing international agreement only held fluctuations to a 4.5 per cent band. This arrangement was called the 'snake' because exchange rates were allowed to 'snake' about within the bands.
37. Phillips (1989), p. 78.
38. R. Goldberg, 'Enhancing competitiveness: infrastructure and agriculture,' in Federal Reserve Bank of Kansas City (1985), p. 60.
39. Schmitz *et al.* (1981), pp. 7 and 25.
40. Duchêne, Szczepanik and Legg (1985), p. 95.
41. Debatisse (1981), p. 30.
42. Canadian Wheat Board, *Grain Matters* (Sept–Oct 88), p. 4.
43. Home-Grown Cereals Authority, *Cereals Statistics* (London, various).
44. Morgan (1979), p. 314.
45. Body (1984), p. 18.
46. Debatisse (1981), p. 26.
47. *The Economist*, 23–4–88.
48. Furtan *et al.* (1988), pp. 94–5, note that the new method also reduces the normal bread-making time by one-third to one-half, thereby reducing the labour input costs. Therefore, bakers might not be willing to return to their old baking methods even if the EC system ended.
49. Puchala and Hopkins (1983), p. 80.
50. Keohane and Nye (1977), p. 12.
51. The endosperm, used for white flour, makes up about 83 per cent of the whole kernel and the bran, included for whole flour, comprises another 14 per cent of the kernel; the germ makes up 3 per cent of the kernel.
52. OECD (1982), p. 103.

Chapter 3
Price policy directions

This and the next four chapters examine the fixing of wheat prices from 1973 to 1989 to illustrate how shifting power structures and changing bargains have directed the proposals, discussion and decisions. The analysis shows that prices are no longer primarily used to support farm incomes. At the beginning, the target price was set to meet perceived income requirements of producers in the food deficit regions of the EC. The lower intervention price reflected transport costs between there and the producing areas. In 1976–7 the target and intervention prices were separated[1] and by 1980 target prices were 'derived from the intervention price.'[2] Throughout the 1980s the Commission argued that 'a realistic policy with regard to pricing must be pursued, with the emphasis on the economic function of prices.'[3] Consequently, the debate has become focused on market rather than social concerns.

The price fixing process

There are three key stages of policy development: initiation, consultation and decision-making. Throughout the process, the Commission *initiates*, pressure groups at the Community and national levels as well as the official consultative organs of the Community (advisory groups, Economic and Social Committee and the European Parliament) *debate* the Commission's proposals and the Council *decides*. Consequently, this analysis follows the reforms beginning with the Commission and working through the European and national policy structures until a decision is made by the Council.

The Treaty of Rome gives the Commission primacy in the area of policy formulation. Article 155 authorizes the Commission to 'formulate recommendations or deliver opinions on matters dealt with in this treaty, if it expressly so provides or if the Commission considers it necessary.'

Although the Commission has the sole power to initiate, the decisive role of Council ensures that the Commission does not develop proposals in a vacuum. Between 1966 (the Luxembourg Accord) and the early 1980s the Agricultural Council decided on the basis of consensus, so the directorate general for agriculture (DG–VI) took 'full account of the interests of all member states in drawing up its proposals from the very beginning, and negotiate[d] first with them (in addition to consulting the technical bodies concerned), and later with the Committee of Permanent Representatives [COREPER], so as to give its proposals some chance of being adopted.'[4] The Commission also co-operated with COPA, the EP and the ESC to ensure maximum support for Commission proposals before they reached the Council. After the Agricultural Council re-introduced majority voting in 1982, however, the Commission discovered it had more leeway to set the agenda and less need to finesse its proposals. In spite of frequent high-level consultations between DG–VI and farmers, consumers and national governments, the official price proposals transmitted to the Council unquestionably reflect Commission concerns and goals.

Near year-end, the Agricultural Commissioner submits DG–VI's price proposals to the full Commission. Most years the Commission formally transmits the proposals (in a communication (COM)) to the Council of Agricultural Ministers between early December and the end of February. Formal consultation then begins. The ESC, EP and a collection of Community interest groups – including the official lobbies for farmers, industry, consumers and the environment – prepare and present critical opinions in an effort to influence the Council decision.

The price package should be (but seldom is) accepted by the Council before April 1, the beginning of the marketing year for most products. The focal point for all farm-related decisions is the Council of Agricultural Ministers: Article 145 of the Treaty of Rome provides that the Council has the 'power to take decisions'.

Once the Council has gathered all opinions, the President-in-Council convenes it as often and for as long as necessary to arrive at an acceptable compromise. With infrequent meetings over a span of weeks or months, the process is often open to influence by the national governments and domestic pressure groups. Although Eurogroups often attempt to influence the Council during its deliberations (e.g. COPA and the BEUC occasionally meet with the president of the Agricultural Council and frequently stage demonstrations outside the Council venue), generally they 'have had little success.'[5]

The Commission participates in Council debates under Article 149 which provides that 'where, in pursuance of this Treaty, the Council acts on a proposal from the Commission, unanimity shall be required for an act constituting an amendment to that proposal.' The Commission facilitates decisions by revising its proposals in line with the evolving Council debate; alternatively, the Commission can withhold approval in an effort to force the Council to accept Commission proposals. The Council, however, can override the Commission and enact any package it likes, provided it acts unanimously.

The Commission also has significant power to adjust the market system. Reg. (EEC) 2727/75, the main regulation governing the operation of the EC cereals market, authorizes the Council to set official prices and monthly increases and to establish the 'general rules' for intervention while the Commission is authorized to set the 'detailed rules' for regular and special intervention. Commission changes to the intervention system become law unless both the management committee for cereals and the Agricultural Council reject the proposal by a qualified majority within a time limit set by the Commission. The Commission also has the power, through general clauses in the Treaty of Rome and Reg. (EEC) 2727/75, to set prices in the absence of a Council decision (e.g. 1985 cereals prices). The Commission accordingly has significant power to control or to offset the potential outcome of any price debate.

The other decision centres in Brussels, including the Councils of Foreign and Finance Ministers, have had little impact on the price policy.[6] Council of Agricultural Ministers' decisions on prices (and the resulting expenditures) do not need to be ratified by any other Council or by the EP. Although farm issues may be passed to other Councils or to the European Council (heads of government), the farm ministers maintain a virtual monopoly on the information and bargains needed to finesse decisions in this complex policy area. Therefore the other Councils usually fail to resolve farm issues. The exception was at the 1988 European Summit where government leaders successfully concluded a historic package of reforms (with the support of their farm ministers).

Reform of the CAP wheat price policy

Reform has not come easily. The price fixing became increasingly complex and contentious as the basic farmer-based system began to unravel; in earlier periods the policy system could be characterized as a cosy, administrative arrangement between farm groups, the Commission and Council. The combination of a new world-security structure, increasing economic volatility and rising domestic production of most products, but especially wheat, caused strains in the system and a corresponding shift in the key bargains.

The shifting power structures and bargains created the conditions for reform of the CAP wheat pricing policy over the 1973–88 period. Since 1973 the guaranteed Community price has been sharply revised (Table 3.1). The biggest change was in the role of the target and intervention prices. In the early years of the CAP, the target price was 'the linchpin of the market organization' and was set at the beginning of each marketing year to reflect 'the farmgate price farmers should receive in consumption areas.'[7] As a result, it became the focus for much of the haggling in the Commission and Council. The intervention price, in contrast, was set about 12–20 per cent below the target price to reflect the transportation costs between the producing regions in France and the consuming region in Germany. By 1988, the system had been turned upside down, with the intervention price being set both conceptually and practically first; the target price was set largely to reflect Commission and Council concerns with the external market. As a result, in 1988, the Commission proposed and the Council accepted that the target price for common wheat for 1988–9 should fall 2.3 per cent because the cost of transport from Ormes to Duisburg fell to 26.90 ECU/t from 32.70 ECU/t in 1987–8. If the original intent for the CAP had remained, the intervention price should have been raised rather than the target price cut.

This change in the system evolved so slowly that it has been little remarked upon. In the early to mid-1970s, the price debate revolved around the price increase needed to sustain farm incomes, with the objective method providing a yardstick for all participants. Beginning in the mid-1970s the Commission worked to set the annual adjustments below the general rate of inflation and after

Table 3.1 Major changes in the EC wheat intervention system (ECU/t)

Year[1]	Common wheat intervention price	% Ch	Monthly increment	Buying period[2]	% Paid[3]	% Protein	% Water[4]	Cuts for feed[5]	Payment delays (days)[6]	Co-resp levy[7]	Max super levy[8]	Bread wheat price[9]	% Ch[10]
72	126.64	—	—	Aug–July	100	—	—	—	30	—	—	—	—
73	127.91	1.0	1.29	"	100	—	15%	—	30	—	—	—	—
74[A]	133.02	4.0	1.33	"	100	—	"	—	30	—	—	—	—
74[B]	139.67	5.0	1.33	"	100	—	"	—	30	—	—	—	—
75	152.24	9.0	1.69	"	100	—	"	—	30	—	—	—	—
76	140.24	–7.9	1.72	"	100	—	"	—	30	—	—	158.57	4.0
77	145.15	3.5	1.77	"	100	—	"	—	30	—	—	163.92	3.5
78	146.97	1.3	1.77	"	100	—	"	—	30	—	—	165.58	1.0
79	149.47	1.7	1.79	"	100	—	"	—	30	—	—	168.06	1.5
80	155.88	4.3	1.87	"	100	—	"	—	30	—	—	175.20	4.2
81	165.23	6.0	2.24	"	100	≥10½	"	—	30	—	—	192.72	10.0
82	179.27	8.5	2.44	"	100	—	"	—	30	—	—	209.10	8.5
83	184.58	3.0	2.57	"	100	—	"	—	120	—	—	215.29	3.0
84	182.73	–1.0	2.57	"	100	—	"	—	120	—	—	213.14	–1.0
85*	179.44	–1.8	2.57	"	100	—	"	—	60/90	—	—	209.30	–1.8
86	179.44	0.0	2.45	Oct–May	100	≥11½%	14½%	–5%	60/90	3.0%	—	183.03	–12.6
87	179.44	0.0	2.00	"	94	"	"	–5%	110	3.0%	—	183.03	0.0
88	179.44	0.0	1.50	"	94	"	"	–5%	110	3.0%	1.6%	183.03	0.0
89	174.06	–3.0	1.31	Nov–May	94	"	"	–5%	110	3.0%	3.0%	177.53	–3.0

Notes: [1] marketing years beginning August 1 (July 1 after 1986); [2] complete months; in 1987 buying-in was only activated when market prices dropped below the intervention price; in 1988 buying-in reverted to the complete period; [3] effective 1987, only 94 per cent of the intervention price is paid to producers; [4] for 1987 the moisture level was set at 15.5 per cent; [5] maximum cut in wheat payments for sub-standard wheat; [6] in December 1983 the maximum payments delay for cereals was extended to 120 days from 30 days; the remainder of the changes came at the beginning of the marketing years; [7] deducted from the intervention payment or market price when the product is sold to intervention or industry; [8] as for [7] except part of the levy is refunded if total EC cereals production is below 164.8 Mt; [9] in 1986 the reference price for 11.5 per cent protein wheat was scrapped and a 2 per cent premium (3.59 ECU in 1986–8; 3.48 ECU in 1989) was paid for wheat exceeding 14 per cent protein and meeting the other bread-wheat tests; [10] the percentage change for 1976 was from the basic intervention price while that for 1986–9 represented the changes in the new bread wheat price (14 per cent protein); * although the price for cereals was not agreed by Council the Commission implemented the cuts as a protective measure.

Sources: COMs, news reports, official publications, H-GCA.

1983 it attempted to cut both nominal and real prices. At that point, the Commission met strong resistance from both farmers and agricultural ministers in the Council. Council absolutely refused to approve direct price cuts. It proved willing, however, to accept 'camouflaged' and even automatic price cuts, as long as on return to their domestic constituencies the ministers could proclaim that they had not directly caused the price cut.

As a result, the power to direct prices shifted largely to the Commission from the Council. The Commission first tried to establish automatic mechanisms which would direct price adjustments based on the underlying economic conditions in the sector. The guarantee threshold system which operated from 1983 to 1985 forced a 1 per cent cut in the price increase in 1983–4. When the formula indicated a 5 per cent price cut in 1985–6 (because of the record harvest in 1984), the Council rejected the mechanism. (Council discovered that by using a three-year moving average production figure, they had designed a system that would also have triggered 5 per cent price cuts in each of the next two years.[8] After that failure, the automatic approach to price setting lapsed until 1988, when the Commission proposed and the European Council accepted the stabilizers system. In 1989–90, the first year of full operation of the new system, the intervention price was reduced by 3 per cent because cereals production exceeded the 160 Mt threshold. Between 1983 and 1989, automatic mechanisms forced a total 5.7 per cent cut in the official intervention price. If the stabilizers system is sustained, the nominal intervention price could drop by a further 8.7 per cent by the end of the 1992–3 crop year. The Council, after a bitter dispute, agreed in April 1990 to allow the system to cut prices again by 3 per cent for the 1990–1 crop year.

Although prices were reduced in both nominal and real terms after 1983, that is only part of the story. The Commission, largely with Council approval, changed its approach and used its own powers to effect 'disguised' price cuts. The first real attempt to reduce farm support through the disguised approach came at the beginning of the 1983–4 crop year, when the Commission announced that it would purchase only 3 Mt of bread wheat in the August–October period and would charge a 5 ECU/t security deposit on all intervention offers. Then in December 1983, the Commission announced it would delay intervention payments by four months for cereals producers, effectively cutting producer support by about 4 per cent.

The bulk of the camouflaged changes came in 1986 and thereafter. The bread wheat support system (i.e. reference price and corresponding intervention purchases) was replaced that year with a flat 2 per cent premium for wheat that had more than 14 per cent protein content. As a result, the effective support for bread wheat dropped by about 13 per cent. Meanwhile, the quality standards for basic intervention were raised, payments for lower quality common wheat were discounted up to 5 per cent and the value and number of monthly increments were reduced. In addition, the Council approved a flat 3 per cent co-responsibility levy on all cereals sold off-farm. In 1987 the Commission introduced a new buying-in system and opened intervention buying between October and May only when the average market price dropped below the intervention price. The Council also approved a Commission plan to pay farmers only 94 per cent of the basic intervention price, delayed by 110 days. In 1988 the Commission and Council adopted a 3 per cent super levy for cereals (refundable

Table 3.2 The impact of market changes on the effective support for producer feed wheat prices (ECU/t)

Year	Inter-vention price	Buying in rate	Monthly incre-ment	Incre-ments begin	Feed cuts %	January buying price	Impact of pay delays	Co-resp levy 1	Co-resp levy 2	January producer prices	% Ch
83	184.58	1.00	2.57	Sept	-	197.43	1.92	—	—	195.51	2.1
84	182.73	1.00	2.57	Sept	—	195.58	1.71	—	—	193.87	-0.8
85	179.44	1.00	2.57	Sept	—	192.29	1.68	—	—	190.61	-1.7
86	179.44	1.00	2.45	Aug	5	185.17	4.06	5.38	—	175.73	-7.8
87	179.44	0.94	2.00	Nov	5	165.70	3.57	5.38	—	156.75	-10.8
88	179.44	0.94	1.50	Nov	5	164.20	3.61	5.38	2.87	152.34	-2.6
89	174.06	0.94	1.31	Nov	5	158.85	3.53	5.22	5.22	144.88	-4.9
%ch	-5.7%	—	—	—	—	-19.5%	—	—	—	-25.9%	—

Notes: January buying price equals the basic intervention price, adjusted for the feed wheat quality and buying-in rate, supplemented by the cumulative monthly increment applicable for January 1 of the marketing year (i.e. monthly increment × the number of months of increments). The adjustment for the impact of payments delays was produced by COPA. The second co-reponsibility levy for 1988–9 is the actual net payment after the refund and for 1989–90 is the initial rate (subject to refunds if production for 1989 is less than 164.5 Mt).

Sources: Commission of the ECs (1988a), *Produits Agricoles: Prix et Montants Fixes*: COPA

if production did not exceed 164.8 Mt) and further reduced the value of monthly increments. In 1989, the Commission proposed a phased reduction of the period of open intervention over the following years and Council accepted for 1989–90 that the buying period be shortened by one month to November through May. As a result of these changes, the support for farm-gate prices was lowered by more than a fifth between 1983 and 1989, in addition to the straight cut in the intervention price (Table 3.2).

Consequently the intervention system now operates as a safety net rather than an alternative market. By 1989, the higher quality standards, delayed payments and a shorter buying period (November to May) had reduced support during the critical harvest period. Furthermore, the Commission suggested in 1989 that it was considering a cut in the number of intervention stores and lower subsidies to transport grain to the delivery points. Already by 1989, the UK intervention agency had raised the minimum quantities it would purchase to 500t from 100t, making it more difficult for small farmers to offer their grain to intervention rather than the market.

The adjustments in national currencies meanwhile became less troublesome. In 1984 the Commission and Council implemented a new agri-monetary system that eliminated the pressure for higher ECU prices resulting from the strong DM. As a result, EMS parity changes became less difficult because they were automatically accommodated in the green ECU system. (EMS parity changes, however, still present a major challenge to the Community as it attempts to remove the artificial differences in prices caused by the green rates.)

Changes in the intervention system between 1983 and 1989 allowed market prices to drop below the intervention price. Figures 3.1, 3.2 and 3.3 indicate that wheat producers in France, Germany and the UK no longer count on the market price lying somewhere between the intervention and target prices. Since 1982–3 average market prices in all three countries have consistently dropped below intervention prices.

Accompanying this shift in price policy was a reformulation of the CAP policy for improving the economic organization of the farm sector (that set of programmes is commonly called 'structural policy'). Marsh and Swanney note that EC agricultural structural policy underwent a radical shift in orientation during the late 1970s, coinciding with the period of significant reform in price policy. Structural policy, which was economically directed in the 1960s and 1970s, instead became a social safety net for small farmers and disadvantaged regions. This continued throughout the 1980s. In 1983, the Commission announced its 'intention that in future greater emphasis be put on long-term structural action, as opposed to market intervention and price support, to alleviate social and income problems in agriculture.'[9] In line with this new approach to structural issues, the Commission in 1986 permitted the less-favoured areas (LFA) designation and the corresponding support programmes, to extend to cover 48 per cent of the Community's agricultural land base, up from the 31 per cent allowed under the 1975 programme. As a result, 51 per cent of German, 38 per cent of French and 52.5 per cent of UK agricultural land is covered by the LFA designation. Then, in 1988, the Council approved a programme of extensification and direct EC and national income payments to support small farmers suffering declining revenues as a result of the reforms in the price system.

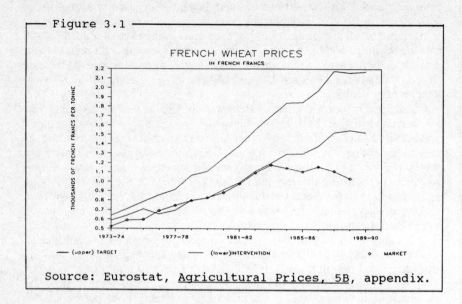

Figure 3.1

FRENCH WHEAT PRICES
IN FRENCH FRANCS

Source: Eurostat, _Agricultural Prices, 5B_, appendix.

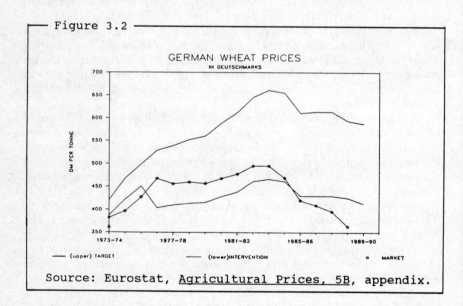

Figure 3.2

GERMAN WHEAT PRICES
IN DEUTSCHMARKS

Source: Eurostat, _Agricultural Prices, 5B_, appendix.

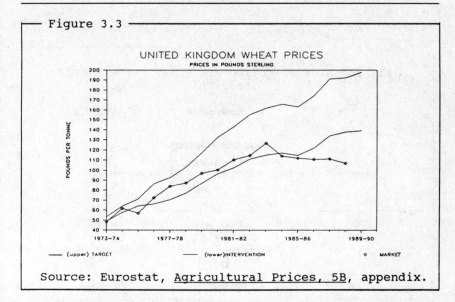

Figure 3.3

UNITED KINGDOM WHEAT PRICES
PRICES IN POUNDS STERLING

——— (upper) TARGET   ——— (lower)INTERVENTION   ◇   MARKET

Source: Eurostat, <u>Agricultural Prices</u>, 5B, appendix.

This change in the structures policy fits the evidence presented in this study. As price policy became market-oriented, it was quite natural that the 'justification of structural policy switched from economic to social criteria.'[10] Anything less would have been impossible given the political and economic bargains that support small farmers and disadvantaged regions.

The key bargains

Chapters 4, 5, 6 and 7 examine how the changing power structures discussed in Chapter 2 transformed the fundamental bargains in the system.

The founding bargain between the German and French government set the tone for the early price reviews. The respective national farm organizations co-ordinated their actions in COPA, so that it was able to present to the Commission a strong and united position on their price demands. Consensus at the national and international levels had a powerful impact on Commission and Council actions and dominated the debate. In the early years of the CAP and up to around 1979, the key bargains outlined in Figure 3.4 largely determined the scope and direction of policy.

As the rate of structural change accelerated during the 1970s, the critical bargains underlying the annual price review were strained. Some fundamental bargains strengthened: for example, the German Ministry of Agriculture and the Deutsche Bauernverband (DBV) farm organization tightened their alliance. Other bargains weakened; farm organizations had greater difficulty building a common position and, as a result, the price recommendations of COPA became increasingly general and lacked focus. Completely new bargains were also developed; for example, the Commission developed new consumer and environ-mental lobbies to counter the farmers (Figure 3.5).

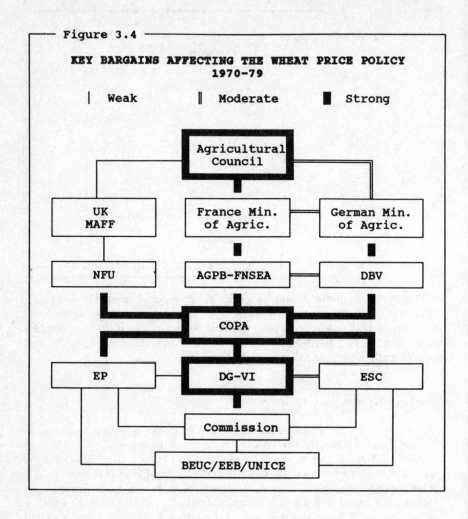

Figure 3.4

KEY BARGAINS AFFECTING THE WHEAT PRICE POLICY 1970-79

| Weak   ‖ Moderate   ∎ Strong

In 1988, a new factor entered the price review. The European Council in February 1988 reformed the farm budget so that it now incorporates all farm outlays, including depreciation allowances for intervention stores. As a result, farm ministers could no longer hide the true cost of farm support in off-budget areas. The flip-side of these changes is that the Commission now has authority to transfer Agricultural Council price decisions which appear likely to exceed budgetary guidelines to a special joint Council of Finance and Agricultural Ministers. The committee will then review and revise the prices to limit budget costs. If the system works, it would significantly open the decision process to non-farm influence at the highest level.

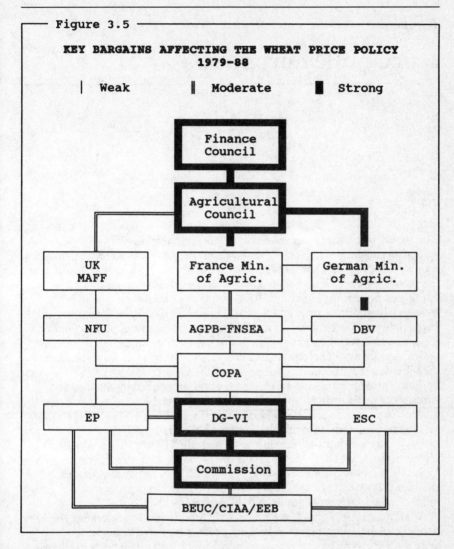

Figure 3.5

KEY BARGAINS AFFECTING THE WHEAT PRICE POLICY 1979-88

| Weak ‖ Moderate ▉ Strong

Finance Council

Agricultural Council

UK MAFF

France Min. of Agric.

German Min. of Agric.

NFU

AGPB-FNSEA

DBV

COPA

EP

DG-VI

ESC

Commission

BEUC/CIAA/EEB

Notes

1. *COM(75)600*, p. 55. All Commission price proposals (COMs annotated with an *) are listed chronologically along with the relevant opinions and decisions in Table B.1. All other COMS are listed chronologically in the bibliography.
2. *Green Europe Newsflash #44*, p. 5.
3. *ASC 1985*, p. 74.
4. Bieber and Palmer (1975), p. 311.
5. Averyt (1977), p. 3.
6. Neville–Rolfe (1984), p. 90.
7. Burtin (1987), p. 19.
8. Vasey (1985), p. 657.
9. *Bull. EC 9/83*, p. 27.
10. Marsh and Swanney (1983), p. 58.

Chapter 4

Price policy proposals

The wheat price proposals changed significantly during 1973–88. When the system began in 1967, Sicco Mansholt, the first Agricultural Commissioner, wanted prices to regulate production and structural policies to support small farmers. But the Farm Council never accepted his proposals. After pan–European farm riots in spring 1972, the new Commission found it had lost influence both with farmers and the Farm Council. In order to strengthen its role in the policy process and repair its relationship with the farm policy community, DG–VI developed the price system to support farm incomes.

The Agricultural Directorate had great leeway to manage farm issues during the following years because the president of the Commission was relatively weak; he was replaced frequently and his power was proscribed by the Council. The Luxembourg Accord, meanwhile, forced consensual decision–making in the Council and encouraged DG–VI to develop the expertise and contacts necessary to finesse proposals through the system. DG–VI, in collusion with COPA, thereby enjoyed unmatched power during the 1970s. This administrative legerdemain reached its peak in the mid–1970s with the operation of the 'objective method'. Farmers never got everything they requested but they did get significant price increases and were envied by other European lobbies as the most influential special interest group at the Community level.

As early as 1968, shifts in the power structures began to undermine the basis for the Commission's power. Changing production patterns began to make the price system less satisfactory, as output rose much faster than domestic demand, and new technologies threatened to exacerbate the problems facing both the intervention system and the Community budget. Meanwhile, international competition intensified and financial markets became more unstable, which created additional impetus for reform, as both farmers and the Community faced budgetary dilemmas.

By 1980, the Commission accepted the challenge to reform the domestic price system. First, it ended the objective method and then pushed for the domestic wheat price to respond to market imperatives rather than non–market concerns.

Key bargains at the policy initiation stage

The 'tenet of faith' in European unification created a bond among the original members of the Commission that lasted into the 1970s. In early years, leaders such as Mansholt and Walter Hallstein (the first President of the Commission) commanded great respect, which enabled them to override much opposition on the specifics of policy. In practical terms, the cadre of committed idealists[1] in the Commission ensured that the proposals from DG–VI were universally acceptable. Furthermore, French civil servants were always appointed to the key bureaucratic jobs within DG–VI that controlled cereals policy (i.e. the Director General and the head of the cereals division of DG–VI). As France generally set the standards for good Community relations, the cereals policy became a touchstone of Community spirit. In practice, this allowed DG–VI to prepare proposals and manage the CAP without input from the rest of the Commission.

Non–agricultural directorates have never had much influence on farm policy. In the 1975 Stocktaking an 'inter–service group' of officials from a variety of directorates recommended expansion of the 'horizontal dimension' of agricultural policy formulation. The group suggested that DGs I (External Relations), II (Economic Affairs) and XIX (Budget) should provide opinions on DG–VI price proposals and that the final price package should be approved both by the Economic Policy Committee of senior treasury officials and the Finance Council.[2] Neither proposal surfaced in the report on the Stocktaking (which was prepared by DG–VI). Farm policy therefore remained largely a monopoly preserve of DG–VI and the Agricultural Council until the special summit in Brussels in 1988 (see Chapters 3 and 7).

During the 1960s and 1970s DG–VI worked to bolster its position in the policy system by carefully cultivating relationships with farmers, the national farm organizations and COPA (Figure 4.1). Farmers had long been convinced of the value of a common market in agriculture. So, shortly after the Treaty of Rome was signed in 1958, the new European Commission involved farmers in the development of the new market systems. National delegations of farmers, food industry representatives and government leaders from the member states attended the Stresa Conference in July 1958 (convened under Article 43 of the Treaty) and established some guidelines for future CAP development. Mansholt then helped farmers to establish pan–European lobby organizations (COPA and COGECA).

The set of actors then increased sharply during the late 1970s. Most important, perhaps, were changes inside the Commission. As the Community expanded and policy became more complex, the Commission civil service grew, so that by 1976 there were seven times more bureaucrats than in 1958. The Commission also employed more specialists in a greater number of horizontal units. The European Commission inevitably became 'bureaucratized'[3] as the number of staff increased and the influence of the original, ideologically–committed Eurocrats waned (especially when many of them retired in the 1970s). As a result, informal cross–directorate contacts declined and technocrats came to run farm policy.

As the Community grew, the number of Commissioners also expanded, from nine in 1970 to 17 in 1986. Competing directorates (such as DG–XIX

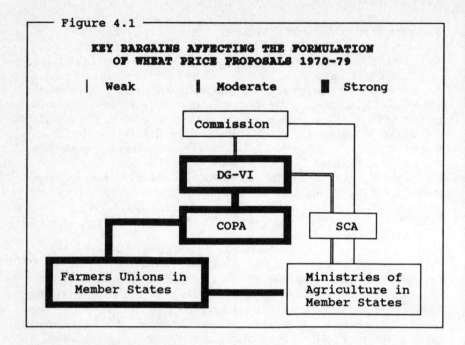

Figure 4.1

**KEY BARGAINS AFFECTING THE FORMULATION
OF WHEAT PRICE PROPOSALS 1970-79**

| Weak | Moderate | Strong

responsible for the Community budget) wcrc created. Table 4.1 shows that as the Commission expanded and the issues became more technical, consensus in the Commission began to break down. Although deliberations within DG–VI and the Commission are supposed to be confidential, the fact that disagreements have become public suggests the level of agreement has declined.

COPA also was pressed to accommodate an increasing number of views and interests. Changes in the production and finance structures caused the interests of farmers to diverge while the expanded Community added groups of farmers with new interests. As a result, COPA increasingly failed to develop specific policy proposals in time to have any chance of influencing the Commission proposals and thus forfeited any substantive role in the policy initiation stage.

The changing power structures and widening gaps among farmers and between COPA and DG–VI led the Commission to look to new areas for support (Figure 4.2). Some changes, such as a greater role for the SCA, were imposed by the Council; others, such as expanded contacts with farm organizations at the national level and with consumers and environmentalists, were deliberate attempts to strengthen the position of both DG–VI and the Commission in the policy community.

In the 1980s, those in DG–VI who wished to continue using prices to support incomes lost the ability to control the debate. Disagreements developed within the Directorate. The traders in DG–VI, who recognized the potential for wheat exports, sided with other Directorates (especially DG–I) and with the French government in an effort to optimize the commercial potential of wheat exports.

Table 4.1 Disagreements in the Commission and DG–VI at the initiation stage, 1973–88

Date	Issues/degree of split	Source
Lardinois 28-03-73	2 UK & 1 It. Commissioners opposed the DG–VI price proposals	*Agra Europe*, 513
Gundelach 25-01-79	Rumours of split in Commission; France and FRG Commissioners sought to replace the proposed price freeze with a 2% rise	*Guardian*
Dalsager 15-01-81	DG–VI proposed 5–6%; criticized; Commission proposed 8%	*Financial Times*
13-02-81	UK Commissioner (Budgets) unhappy with price increases	*Agra Europe*, 915
16-12-82	DG–VI proposed 5.5%; Commission changed to 4.3%	*Guardian*
03-03-83	UK Commissioner (Budgets) criticized price rises	*Financial Times*
30-07-83	2 UK, 1 FRG & Irish Commissioners voted against COM(83)500	*The Times*
Andriessen 26-01-85	DG–VI proposed 3.1% cut in cereals prices; Andriessen changed to -3.6%	*Financial Times*
16-06-85	FRG Commissioner voted against the *Green Paper*	*Financial Times*
05-07-85	DG–VI split; traders wanted price cut; majority wanted quotas and other options; Italian Commissioner publicly criticized the *Green Paper*	*Agra Europe*, 1140
11-02-87	Commissioners failed twice to agree on green rates and oils tax	*Financial Times*
08-01-88	Commissioners split on set-asides	*Financial Times*

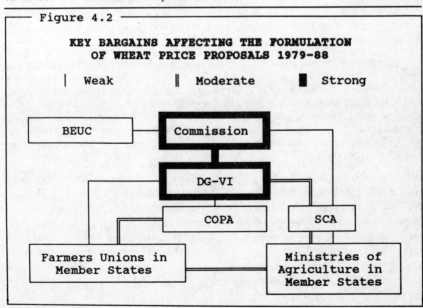

Figure 4.2

KEY BARGAINS AFFECTING THE FORMULATION OF WHEAT PRICE PROPOSALS 1979–88

| Weak   ‖ Moderate   ■ Strong

This created significant friction, as commercial concerns conflicted with social interests.

The remainder of this chapter examines the Commission price proposals during 1973–88 — and their focus on income support, agri–monetary issues, the budget and surplus production — to demonstrate how and why these bargains changed and ultimately to show the impact on the operation of the policy and price system.

The objective method and prices as income support

Although Mansholt wanted to use prices to regulate production, the Commission was forced to use them to support farm incomes when the Council failed to adopt the 1968 structural adjustment plan.[4] It transpired, however, that using prices to support incomes was generally consistent with the underlying security, production, finance and knowledge structures of the 1970s.

Mansholt nevertheless was unwilling to preside over such a policy. During his tenure as Agricultural Commissioner, the Commission proposed to freeze or marginally reduce guaranteed wheat prices in each price review. Prices in 1971, his last price review, were virtually unchanged from the levels set in 1965. But inflation, which accelerated after 1970 because of shifts in the financial structures, cut sharply into the real (inflation–adjusted) purchasing power of wheat. This change in the real wheat price galvanized the EC farm lobby into action. Farmers agitated for higher prices in spring 1971 but were too late to influence the Commission proposals. Council responded, however, with a modest 2 per cent increase for wheat and set the stage for rapid price gains over the next decade.

The Commission could no longer ignore the pressure from farmers and the member state governments. Petrus Lardinois, the new Agricultural Commissioner, responded and introduced what was called 'the objective method' to establish the Commission's annual price proposals. The Commission's *Memorandum: Agriculture 1973–78* stated that:

The Commission intends to formulate its future proposals more and more in the light of trends in the general level of prices on modern farms: these are the farms which, under the general farm price policy, should be ensured[5] an income comparable to that received from non-agricultural work, account being taken, on the one hand, of a satisfactory return on invested capital and, on the other hand, of trends in prices of the means of production and in productivity. However, as regards the prices of individual products, the Commission will, in its proposals, take account of the supply and demand situation on each of the markets concerned.[6]

Although the Council never responded either to the *Memorandum* or to a draft regulation, the Commission began to use the method with the 1972–3 price review. In short, the method entailed calculating the percentage increase in guaranteed prices necessary to keep incomes of 'modern' farms in line with non-farm incomes. On the cost side, national currency increases in the cost of farm inputs were calculated for each of the member states over the preceding few years and aggregated to provide a Community average. The reference or target income for the farm sector was then calculated based on the rise in the average compensation for non-farm wage labour. The Commission then derived the theoretical price increase required to offset the cost increases of the past few years and to maintain the ratio between farm and non-farm incomes. The Commission deducted first 1.5 per cent to compensate for the average annual productivity increase attributed to state investment and support for research and development[7] and then the value of past price increases granted through both official price reviews and via changes in the representative exchange rates. The remainder was the indicated Community average price increase.[8]

The objective method quickly became the focal point in the price fixing system, as both farm organizations and DG–VI saw its potential. The formula initially brought the Commission and COPA together to make the system operate effectively. Before 1974, relatively low rates of inflation in wage and input costs (averaged over three years) ensured that the gap between farm and non-farm incomes did not widen. Then in 1974 inflation and interest rates rose precipitously (at least partly due to changes in the underlying financial power structure), economic growth slowed and unemployment climbed. Farmers believed that they were bearing too large a share of the burden because European farm prices rose more slowly than either input costs or world prices (which soared due to the 'great grain robbery').

In spite of the price increases approved by the Council for 1974–5, COPA used the objective method to demonstrate that the accelerating wage and cost inflation warranted an additional price increase of at least 4 per cent. This was perhaps the high point of the influence of COPA. Although there was no provision in the rules for interim price increases, COPA successfully organized a series of protests that forced the Commission to accept the results of the objective method and present an interim price increase for 1974.

After that experience, the Commission recommended that the objective method be changed. It argued that the policy should be expected to provide a decent income only for farmers and farm labourers who work on agricultural holdings 'which are run on a rational basis and which are economically viable.'[9] As a result, the Commission decided to use target farms (as defined in Dir 159/72/EEC) rather than 'modern' farms (which included a wide range of small and uncompetitive farms in the calculation), to disaggregate costs further to increase precision of estimates, to set new weights for the member states and henceforward to use a movable 36-month period for calculations.[10] The Commission warned that the method only 'yields a general indicator, which the Commission uses in combination with other indicators (e.g. market situation, economic trend) to arrive at its proposals for increases in the general level of agricultural prices consistent with the efforts being made to ensure market equilibrium.'[11]

Swinbank noted that the experience in the 1973–8 period 'shows the ease with which the calculations can be manipulated behind a wall of secrecy' because 'the final calculated figure is critically dependent upon a series of arbitrary decisions taken with respect to the method of calculation.'[12] A good example was the 1977–8 price review. The NFU learned that the Commission proposed to use single-week exchange rate averages from the beginning and end of the three-year review period (i.e. first week of 1973 and last week of 1976), which indicated prices should decline in 1977–8. After lobbying, the Commission decided to use two-month averages at the beginning and end of the period, which indicated a 0.1 per cent price increase. If the average exchange rates for 1973 and 1976 were used, as requested by the NFU, the objective method would have indicated the need for a 6 per cent increase.

The Commission also made ad hoc modifications to the method so that it indicated price increases that fit with their other concerns (Table 4.2). In 1975 and 1976 Italy was excluded from the calculations (on the grounds that the lira was fluctuating widely in both years), which lowered the indicated increase for 1975–6 and raised it for 1976–7. Then in 1977–8, the Commission excluded from the formula countries not involved in the exchange 'snake', which yielded a higher rate and justified a higher increase. In 1978–9, the Commission proposed that prices rise only 2 per cent rather than the indicated 4.2 per cent, on the basis that as a moving average the formula overestimated need. Finally, in 1979–80 the Commission calculated but did not publish the indicated value. It simply stated that the general farm income situation would allow a price freeze and that 'the results of the objective method corroborate this conclusion.'[13] In short, history demonstrates that the objective method was seldom objective.

Table 4.2 The history of the objective criterion method for setting prices

Year	Objective method	Modified value	Changes to criteria	All prods	COM proposals Common wheat	Bread wheat
1972A	2–3.0%	–	–	2–3.0%	2.3%	–
1972B	5.0%	–	–	6.5%	4.6%	–
1973	3.0%	–	–	2.8%	2.8%	–
1974A	7.2%	–	–	7.2%	.0%	–
1974B	4.0%	–	–	4.0%	4.0%	–
1975	12.4%	6.5%	Excl Italy	9.2%	9.0%	–
1976	4.6%	9.1%	Excl Italy	7.5%	-5.8%	6.9%
1977	0.1%	5.1%	Snake Only	3.0%	3.0%	3.1%
1978	4.2%	–	–	2.0%	1.3%	3.1%
1979	n.p.	–	–	.0%	.0%	.0%
1980	n.a.	–	–	2.5%	1.8%	1.7%
1981	n.a.	–	–	7.8%	6.0%	4.0%
1982	9.0%	–	exchange rate	8.4%	6.6%	6.6%

Notes: Marketing years beginning with date given; n.p. = figure calculated but not published; n.a. = either not calculated or kept confidential; 1972A was withdrawn; the figure for the reference price for wheat of bread-making quality (bread wheat above) for 1976 is the percentage increase between the reference price in 1976 and the intervention price for common wheat for 1975.
Sources: Swinbank (1979), p. 305; *COMS of the EC

DG–VI then ceased using the objective method until 1982, when it presented a complete set of calculations, with indicated price increases ranging from 4 to 15 per cent. The declared average (9 per cent) was chosen largely to facilitate green rate changes and to buy acceptance of the new co-responsibility measure that would set future prices based on market conditions. When Council approved the Commission's proposed guarantee threshold system, the income-supporting role for prices effectively ended.

Changes in the power structures had combined to shorten the period of fixing prices using the objective method. Volatile exchange rates, tight budgets and rising surpluses, which did not fit within the objective method, increasingly influenced the Commission's price proposals.

Exchange rates and the price review

The agri-monetary system, developed in 1969, provided for fixed 'representative' exchange rates to be set during the annual price review and then to be left unchanged during the marketing year, regardless of international exchange rate movements. The Commission initially extracted agreement that the gaps between the green rates and market exchange rates would be reduced at the time of the price review (or, in exceptional cases, during the year at the request of a national government). Although green rates were expected to be short-term aberrations, the end of the Bretton Woods system caused wide fluctuations in exchange rates, so that few countries ever closed their gaps for long (Figures 4.3, 4.4, 4.5). Green rates became essential in order to maintain the common price system.

The Commission, however, was unwilling to accept the massive derogations from common prices that developed: at times ECU prices received in Germany and the UK differed by as much as 50 per cent. The Commission worked throughout 1973–88 to eliminate the monetary gaps. Occasionally agri-

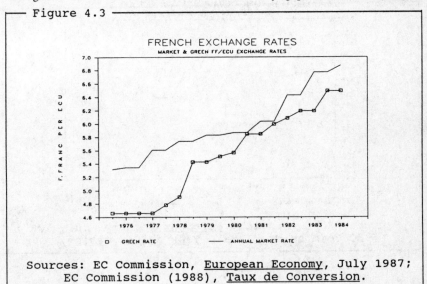

Figure 4.3

FRENCH EXCHANGE RATES
MARKET & GREEN FF/ECU EXCHANGE RATES

□ GREEN RATE   ——— ANNUAL MARKET RATE

Sources: EC Commission, *European Economy*, July 1987; EC Commission (1988), *Taux de Conversion*.

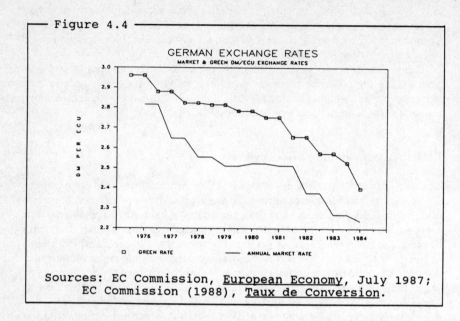

Sources: EC Commission, <u>European Economy</u>, July 1987;
EC Commission (1988), <u>Taux de Conversion</u>.

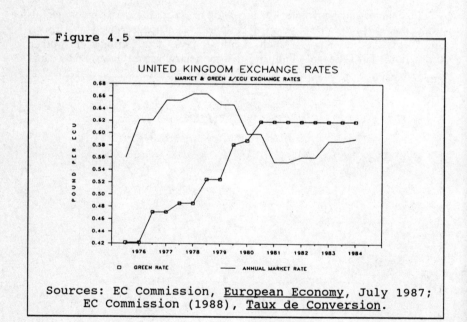

Sources: EC Commission, <u>European Economy</u>, July 1987;
EC Commission (1988), <u>Taux de Conversion</u>.

monetary reform overshadowed other issues and virtually determined the magnitude of the proposed price increases.

The Commission adopted two broad approaches to management of the system. First, the Commission worked to develop a more stable set of exchange rates in the Community. In 1972, the Community created the 'snake' but was still unable to offset wide swings in exchange rates (see Chapter 2). Meanwhile, the Commission sought adjustments to representative rates to close the monetary gaps at each price review. The Commission was strongly opposed to the continued use of green rates to circumvent the common price system and proposed in the 1975 Stocktaking that the Commission and Council adopt formal rules to set and dismantle green rates.[14] In 1976, Lardinois suggested that green rates be regularly revised every six months but Council did not agree.[15]

In the absence of Council action, the Commission proposed price increases for 1976–7 and 1977–8 that would allow the maximum dismantling of positive MCAs. Then in 1978, the Commission proposed a seven-year schedule for elimination of MCAs and alignment of green rates with market rates.[16] Each year one-seventh of the gap would be eliminated. Shortly thereafter, the Commission warned that the agri-monetary system's 'link with the "snake" draws common prices upwards and strengthens guarantees to producers.'[17]

The European Monetary System (EMS), developed during 1977 and 1978 to replace the ineffective 'snake', was designed to stabilize exchange rates and to forestall future monetary gaps. It almost failed to be implemented, however, because France insisted that it would only accept the EMS if the Council would adopt an automatic timetable to eliminate Germany's positive MCAs. The EMS began in March 1979 only after the Council agreed that new MCAs could be eliminated over two years provided changes in green rates did not cause nominal prices to fall in any member state (known as the 'gentlemen's agreement').

The 'gentlemen's agreement' limited Commission proposals over the next several years. The 1979 price proposals did not include any revaluation of strong currency green rates because the Commission did not plan to raise ECU prices and in 1980 the Commission was forced, in spite of market and budget pressures, to propose a price rise for wheat in order to allow a revaluation of the green DM. In 1981 DG–VI proposed wheat intervention prices rise 6 per cent in ECU terms (4 per cent for bread-wheat) to allow for a 5.3 per cent revaluation of the DM and a 5.8 per cent rise in the green pound. But Germany calculated that the revaluation would cause farm-gate prices to drop, which violated the 'gentlemen's agreement', and Council rejected the Commission package. Again in 1982 and 1983 the Commission proposed wheat price increases to provide room to revalue both the green DM and pound. By 1983 the Commission had had enough: the Commission declared that 'the "gentlemen's agreement" which attempted to define conditions for the gradual phasing out of monetary compensatory amounts has proved unsatisfactory.'[18] The Commission proposed to close the monetary gaps automatically by one-third at the time of the exchange rate change and one-third at the beginning of the next two marketing years; existing MCAs would be reduced as conditions permitted. Germany, and other countries revaluing green rates, would be permitted to compensate their farmers.[19] The Commission warned, however, that 'common prices expressed in ECU may be frozen or even reduced; and consequently that the Community support prices expressed in national currency may be reduced in nominal terms.'[20]

DG–VI then proposed for 1984–5 a freeze in the ECU wheat reference price and revaluations of 6.3 per cent in the green DM and 4 per cent in the green pound but the Council rejected the package and held the green DM and pound steady. The debate then moved to the Fontainebleau Summit, where the French President of the Council negotiated an agreement to introduce a green ECU system. The new system holds German farm-gate prices steady when the DM appreciates by setting the agricultural unit of account (AUA) equal to the real ECU multiplied by a 'correcting factor'. All other countries receive increases equal to the appreciation of the green ECU over the real ECU. The Commission proposed and Council agreed that existing positive monetary gaps for Germany and the Netherlands would be eliminated by the beginning of the 1987–8 marketing year.

Although the green ECU was not the Commission's preferred solution, it acknowledged that 'it is politically impossible' to expect national governments to allow currency changes to cut domestic prices, as normally happens with other traded goods in the EC.[21]

After prices were fixed for the 1984–5 marketing year and the new green ECU system was introduced, the Commission moved quickly to reduce the existing DM positive monetary gap. At the beginning of 1984–5, the new green ECU had been set 3.4 per cent above the real ECU to reduce the positive monetary gap for the DM. In July 1984 it proposed a further five-point reduction in the German monetary gap effective 1 January 1985, with German farmers compensated for losses in farm incomes. In 1985, Germany vetoed the cereals proposals and caused the Commission to forgo further agri-monetary changes until 1987–8. Then DG–VI initially published proposals to cut ECU wheat prices 2 per cent and hold the green DM steady but Germany protested and the Commission revised the proposal to include an ECU price freeze and a complete revaluation of the remaining 2.4 per cent positive DM monetary gap (which would have allowed Germany to compensate its farmers for the lower prices). Although Council refused to revalue the DM immediately, it eventually eliminated the remaining positive monetary gap (less the neutral margin) on 1 January 1989.

Once the Commission and Council agreed on this system of managing positive monetary gaps, the price proposals focused less on setting prices to accommodate exchange rate changes. DG–VI found the green ECU system reduced the upward pressure on ECU prices resulting from the positive DM monetary gap. (Between 1984 and June 1989 four realignments of the EMS boosted the correcting factor to 1.137282; without the green ECU, these realignments would have created significant pressures to raise ECU prices.) Consequently, the Commission was able to focus on the two problems looming on the horizon: budget pressures and production surpluses.

Budget pressures

Large price increases, application of financial capital and a proliferation of new, high-yielding crop and livestock varieties caused a sustained rise in production beginning in the 1970s. Increasing surpluses of wheat, at a time when world markets were becoming more competitive, compounded the costs of the CAP, thereby forcing budget concerns into the farm debates. The budget also became the focus of UK efforts to reform the CAP, so that many subsequent reforms of the wheat system were couched in budgetary terms. The budget, however, seldom directed Commission proposals. The non-farm directorates certainly attempted to force the CAP to live within budgetary limits, but DG–VI was unwilling to prepare the price proposals solely in the context of real or notional budget limits. Instead, DG–VI attempted to use the budget as a bargaining lever to get the Farm Council to adopt its proposals.

The link between the budget and CAP reform has been weak for a number of reasons. First, the budget ceiling is artificial because maximum revenues are set at an arbitrary percentage of the tax base. The Community demonstrated that the ceiling is flexible when it adjusted it in both 1984 and 1988. Second, the budget is out of step with the agricultural marketing year. The annual budget is drafted and usually adopted before the start of the calendar year while prices for the marketing year are seldom set before March. Consequently, each budget covers only six months (January–June) when wheat prices are known. Also, because the prices are usually agreed after farmers have made their production plans, the decisions have little impact on the volumes of product available. Third, budgetary rules require all outlays related to provisions of the Treaty of Rome — 'compulsory' spending, which includes EAGGF Guarantee Fund expenditures — be accommodated. Finally, the budget procedure which evolved during the 1970s does not allow the EP to change compulsory spending. It can control the farm budget only if it rejects the entire budget and forces the Community to operate under the 'provisional twelfths' rule.[22] The unrelated timing of the price fixing and budget and limited Parliamentary control of compulsory spending consequently reduces budgetary control over CAP.

Nevertheless, budget concerns certainly encouraged DG–VI and the Commission to look to other ways to support farmers. Shifts in production, technology and finance structures during the 1970s caused a sharp decline in the efficiency of using prices to support farm income. Table 4.3 shows that the average effectiveness of the price system — transferring funds to producers from consumers via both higher food prices and general tax levies — declined to about 50 per cent in 1985 from more than 70 per cent in 1976. This was particularly true for wheat, as the Community moved from approximate self-sufficiency in the 1960s and 1970s to a major export role in the 1980s. Marginal increases in prices were even less efficient. Price increases in 1980 were estimated to have raised farm incomes only by 56 ECUs for every 100 ECUs expended (vs. 67 per cent efficiency for the whole price system)

Although Mansholt's plan in 1968 was partly in response to rising costs, the Commission did little to combat increases over the coming years. Before 1979, the cost of the cereals regime ranged from less than 400 M UA to 1.1 B UA and total outlays for all EC programmes remained well below the available resources.[23] But capital investment, adoption of new technologies and farm consolidation throughout the 1970s boosted farm productivity and caused large production gains. The Commission recognized that these shifts would continue to raise the cost of the CAP (then about 75 per cent of the total EC budget), which would limit the resources available for non-farm rural and urban programmes.

Table 4.3 Budgetary efficiency of the CAP (EC9)

	Year	Costs to benefits	% Reaching farmers
Bale & Lutz	1976	1.39	71.8%
Morris	1978	1.32	75.8%
Harvey et al.	1980	1.50	66.6%
Thomson & Harvey	1980	1.77	56.0%
BAE	1983	1.16	85.6%
Tyers & Anderson	1985	1.88	53.1%
10% price rise (Harvey):	1980	1.79	55.9%

The cost-benefit ratio shows the number of ECUs taxpayers and consumers surrender to increase farm incomes by an additional ECU; conversely, % reaching farmers shows the proportion of money foregone which increases farm income.
Sources: Table 1.3; Harvey (1982), pp. 177–8

As a first step to control CAP budgetary outlays, the Commission in 1977 appointed a Budget Commissioner, who quickly became a powerful focus for discontent with the CAP.

In 1979, three factors caused the Commission to focus seriously on the budgetary aspects of the CAP. First, the 'own resources' system was finally put into effect. Before then, the Community depended on a combination of own resources and national contributions, which seriously limited the Commission's ability to develop new programmes. The Commission wanted to use the new resources available after 1979 to expand non-farm programmes, but there was little left after paying for the CAP. Second, the UK for the first time in 1979–80 bore the full costs and benefits of the CAP. The new Conservative government in the UK then began a five-year campaign to reduce its net expenditures; for tactical reasons it chose to link its EC budget demands with CAP reform. Third, members to the EP were elected in 1979 for the first time and immediately sought to change the budget to suit their priorities. While the farm lobby remained important in 1979–84, the expanded group of MEPs with non-farm interests wanted the Community to develop new programmes in non-farm areas.

In December 1979, the EP rejected the entire budget, forcing the Commission to propose prices that would not increase EAGGF outlays beyond the resouces available within the provisional twelfths rule. The budget limits, however, did not effectively bind that year because rising world prices and the rapidly appreciating US dollar reduced EC export reinstitutions. DG–VI had enough fiscal room to propose price rises and still keep EAGGF within the budget limit.

Even though the budget pressure did not seriously bind again until 1984, the Commission sought to limit the cost of agricultural programmes. It believed that 'the Community budget must also serve the development of new policies, the lack of which is often harmful to European agriculture.'[24] But DG–VI and the Agricultural Council did not enthusiastically support efforts to limit the cost of CAP programmes. Nor were they seriously pressed to do so: between 1980 and 1983 the appreciating US dollar caused the world wheat price in ECUs to rise, so that the Community budget was not strained by the increased volume of cereals exported. Nevertheless, DG–VI framed its next several price proposals in an effort to reduce the incentives to production, which would go a long way to limiting growth in EAGGF outlays (see following section). It had decided that the budget lever was perhaps an ideal instrument to get the farm ministers to accept the prudent price policy, to strengthen co-responsibility, to eliminate MCAs and to review the external protection system.[25] In 1983 the Commission unsuccessfully tried to convince the farm ministers to limit growth in CAP outlays to below the growth in 'own resources'.[26] DG–VI surely saw that this would give them significant power to control future Council decisions, because the Commission would be responsible for calculating the growth of own resources.[27]

At the end of 1983, the budget situation because serious. To conserve resources and to prod the Council into further reform, the Commission unilaterally announced that intervention payments to cereals farmers would be delayed by four months. The Commission subsequently proposed a wheat price freeze for 1984–5 because the budget for 1984 already equalled 0.997 per cent of the adjusted VAT base (the limit was 1 per cent). Then in March the Commission got the European Council to agree that the Finance Council should intercede in Farm Council price decisions if they were likely to exceed expenditures under Commission proposals. The price package for that year, however, was resolved without resort to such measures.

The Fontainebleau Summit in June 1984 appeared to take the pressure off farm policy and to allow farm ministers to delay reform: the Heads of Government reached a compromise on the UK budgetary problem and cleared the way to raise the EC spending limit to 1.4 per cent of VAT beginning in 1986, with supplementary support from member states in 1984 and 1985. Then, in December 1984, the EP rejected the 1985 budget by an overwhelming vote, forcing the Commission and Council to limit price rises. The Commission took the opportunity to propose wheat price cuts of 3.6 per cent. Although Germany invoked the Luxembourg Compromise and vetoed the price proposal, the Commission implemented a 'precautionary' 1.8 per cent price cut.

In 1985, the Commission's *Green Paper* firmly shifted the debate away from budgetary concerns toward a complete re-evaluation of the price system. Budget pressure continued, however, because accession of Spain and Portugal quickly filled the fiscal room provided by the 1984 Fontainebleau Summit. Without reform of the CAP, there was little potential for new programmes to capitalize on the Single Market.

By 1988 budget reform could not be ignored. The Commission pressed the Heads of Government at a special Summit in Brussels in February 1988 to adopt stabilizer levies and automatic price cuts for cereals and to limit EAGGF Guarantee expenditures (including provisions for depreciation of both old and new stocks) to grow no faster than the annual growth rate of the Community GDP. The Summit ministers, with the help of their farm ministers, went even further than requested and approved both automatic price cuts and a lower growth limit on outlays (80 per cent of GDP growth, excluding depreciation of old stocks). Perhaps most important, the Summit announced that 'if the Commission considers that the outcome of the Council's discussions on these price proposals is likely to exceed the costs put forward in its original proposal, the final decision shall be referred to a special meeting of the Council attended by

Ministers for Finance and the Ministers for Agriculture which shall have the sole power to adopt a decision.'[28] This provision provided the Commission with a powerful negotiating lever for future price reviews as it could threaten to take the decision out of the hands of the farm ministers. (The Commission certainly will prefer to threaten rather than act, because there is significant doubt that the special Council could resolve any disagreements; special Councils have seldom been successful.)

In summary, the Commission used the budget as a bargaining lever during the 1980s. Cottrell argues that the Commission never saw CAP spending as a burden; rather it usually talked in terms of a 'shortfall in resources'.[29] DG–VI, in particular, believed that the agricultural budget was small relative to both national budgets and the gross output of the sector. During the 1980s, DG–VI and the Commission employed the budget to support its other policy priorities. DG–VI sought to use it to force reform of the price system while the other DGs saw farm budget limits as the only way they could develop programmes to complete the Single Market. In a sense, the budget lever was used to justify price cuts in the same way as the objective method was used in the 1970s to justify price increases.

Production surpluses

The most important change in Commission proposals in the 1980s is the enhanced market role for prices. The Commission was forced after 1980 to examine alternatives to using prices to support incomes because of the surge in farm output (Figure 4.6). DG–VI had three alternatives. In order of administrative difficulty, it could implement production quotas and maintain price and intervention guarantees, cut purchase prices but maintain explicit intervention guarantees, or reform the guarantee system. After a clash with Council in 1985, the preferred middle option was rejected. Internally, DG–VI split into two opposing camps: the traders wanted a market approach while others wished to maintain administrative control over the farm sector. The market approach prevailed as the commercial components of the farm policy community (in DG–VI, France and the farm organizations) dominated.

Between 1972 and 1979, the Commission disregarded Sicco Mansholt's warnings that high prices would encourage surplus production. The Commission also apparently ignored the early indications that EC wheat production would soon rise significantly higher than demand. The Community had recorded modest wheat surpluses since the start of the cereals regime and by 1973 EC6 annual production exceeded total domestic use by 4.7 Mt and surpluses were rising by more than 1 Mt each year. About that time, academic researchers showed that the EC9 would soon be one of the world's largest wheat exporters, a dramatic change from the prevailing position as a large market for wheat imports.[30]

During the 1970s, the threat of world shortages (see Chapter 2) and the need for a stable system to allow farmers to adapt forced the Commission to continue to use prices solely to support farm incomes. Although the Commission in 1973 publicly acknowledged that it would adjust the prices indicated by the objective method if market conditions warranted, it only once tried to do so.

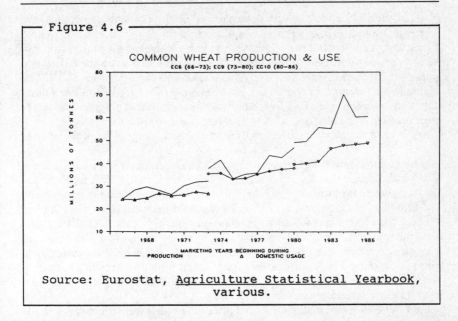

COMMON WHEAT PRODUCTION & USE
EC6 (66–73); EC9 (73–80); EC10 (80–86)

MARKETING YEARS BEGINNING DURING
—— PRODUCTION   △ DOMESTIC USAGE

Source: Eurostat, _Agriculture Statistical Yearbook_, various.

In 1975, DG–VI accepted the prevailing view that 'the tight situation on the world [cereals] market will probably not disappear in the near future.'[31] In this context, the Commission believed that 'further incentives should be given to producers of certain products for which there are acute supply difficulties [i.e., cereals].'[32] That view prevailed through 1978. The Commission proposed in 1976 that the Council realign incentives in the cereals market to encourage production of higher quality wheat suitable for milling and baking and to make lower quality wheats more competitive with both domestic and imported feeds. DG–VI was largely concerned with the distribution of production between grades of wheat and not at all about the absolute quantities produced. Then drought in 1976 cut EC wheat production, so in 1977 the Commission did not have to worry about wheat surpluses. The 'prudent' price policy introduced that year was explicitly targeted on sectors with structural surpluses, which did not include wheat.

During the next two years, the Commission accepted that the situation was changing. In 1978, it noted that cereals might be moving into surplus and consequently proposed that wheat prices rise less than indicated by the objective method. By 1979 the Commission accepted that the Community was self-sufficient in cereals and forecast that by 1985 the Community would produce 9 Mt more cereals than needed for domestic use (including 5–7 Mt of wheat). For the first time, the price proposals were directed toward limiting structural surpluses: the Commission proposed ECU guaranteed prices be held steady at the previous year's levels.

The Commission did not follow through with that policy in the following two years largely because the US export embargo of the Soviet Union in 1979 rekindled fears of world-wide shortages. Meanwhile, higher world market prices lowered the EC budget for cereals exports while the US embargo opened the Soviet market for expanded exports of European surpluses. In March 1980 the Commission announced that 'other sectors may exhibit some of the features of surplus production from time to time but none present a need for changes in policy in the same way that the milk, sugar and wine sectors do.'[33] The Commission therefore proposed to raise wheat prices for 1980–1 to allow adjustments in the green rates. But the Commission cautioned that in future 'the prices policy cannot on its own overcome the problems arising from the market situation and the need to maintain agricultural incomes, particularly those of the poorest farmers.'[34]

The Commission's *Reflections on the CAP* in December 1980 noted that the FAO had forecast that food shortages would continue in the foreseeable future so that the Community should have assured outlets for excess production. Nevertheless, the Commission decided that something would have to be done to control the expansion of both production and budget costs. DG–VI and the Commission were frustrated with the political imperatives of elections and pressure group politics that usually drove Council decisions.[35] By establishing rules and parameters for prices, the Commission sought to wrestle power from the Council. The market-based approach appeared to offer the greatest freedom from Council interference.

DG–VI concluded that open-ended price guarantees were unworkable in the long term because 'at the present state of agricultural technology it is neither economically sound nor financially feasible to guarantee price or aid levels for unlimited quantities.'[36] The Commission preferred 'producer co-responsibility above a certain level of production' as a permanent feature of the cereals market. Optimally this would be implemented via price cuts rather than levies because lower guaranteed prices would help EC feed grains compete with imported cereal substitutes.[37] The Commission hinted that if cuts in guaranteed prices proved impossible, similar reductions in farm-gate prices could be managed by the Commission unilaterally raising the quality criteria for intervention, limiting intervention buying to certain months, or reducing the intervention price for lower quality wheats.

The first full-scale assault on guaranteed prices came in 1981. Although the Commission did not publish a wheat forecast, it stressed that the sector faced both rising surpluses and costs. The Commission proposed a new 'fourth principle' for the CAP: in addition to common prices, common financing and Community Preference, producers should be responsible for the cost of disposing of production in excess of agreed quantities.[38] It argued that 'farmers should not be separated too far from market realities by guarantees that do not adequately reflect market realities.'[39] DG–VI wished to set separate basic quantities for durum, common wheat and all other cereals based on a three-year moving average of past production. Farmers would receive an initial payment when grain was sold into the market and any final payment would be adjusted to reflect the actual production for the year.[40] The Agricultural Council was willing to consider co-responsibility but disagreement about the proposed cuts in cereal prices in Germany and the UK (and the link with the UK budget debate) delayed the new system.

The Commission announced in June 1981 that farm income considerations,

Table 4.4 Commission forecasts of cereals production and surpluses (excluding durum)

Year	Forecast year	Domestic supply	Domestic demand	Exports/ surplus
1975–76 (EC9)	na	'acute supply difficulties'		
1976–77 (EC9)	na	food aid/crisis conferences		
1977–78 (EC9)	na	drought in 1976/no surpluses		
1978–79 (EC9)	na	cereals moving to surplus		
1979–80 (EC9)	1985	—	—	9
1980–81 (EC9)	na	US embargo of USSR cereal imports		
1981–82 (EC9)	na	cost of surpluses rising		
1982–83 (EC10)	1988	135	122	13
1983–84 (EC10)	1988	137	112–17	20–25
1984–85 (EC10)	1989	137	114	23
1985–86 (EC10)	1991	148	115	33
1986–87 (EC10)	1991	159	119	40
1986–87 (EC12)	1991	180	—	—
1987–88 (EC12)	1992	187	137–42	45–50
1989–90 (EC12)	1993	192	142	50

Sources: COMS of the Commission of the ECs

though important, would no longer be the sole reference point for fixing prices: the Community could not afford to continue unlimited guarantees for surplus commodities. The Commission concluded that 'prices must reflect market realities more than they have in the past.'[41]

Later in 1981 the Commission's *Guidelines for European Agriculture* marked the beginning of market-based planning for the cereals market. The Commission declared that 'decisions based on a horizon of one or two years are often inadequate.'[42] For the first time the Commission produced and published a detailed five-year outlook for cereals production, consumption and market opportunities, which showed the EC would have about 13 Mt of exportable cereals by 1988 (Table 4.4). The report concluded that the Community needed a 'programme of progressive reduction of cereals prices in real terms' to reduce EC cereals prices to about the support level under the 1980 US Farm Bill (Food Security Act, 1980). With strengthening world cereals prices, the gap between EC and US support prices was only about 20 per cent and price equality appeared attainable (see Figure 9.1). The Commission, however, categorically rejected using world market prices as a reference and cautioned that 'to avoid unacceptable consequences for production and incomes, such a programme must be gradual: one could not envisage a reduction in nominal terms.'[43] DG–VI was also not willing for the Community to reduce its share of the world export market: the 1988 production target (130 Mt) was based on maintaining the export volume of 1981.

The 1982–3 price review marked the end of the objective method system of setting prices and the beginning of market-based rules. The revised economic forecast showed exportable quantities would rise to between 20 and 25 Mt in 1988 (compared with an earlier forecast of only 13 Mt). The Commission prepared a detailed set of objective method calculations to justify an average 9 per cent price increase. In exchange for the price increases, the Commission wanted Council to accept a 'guarantee threshold' system for cereals that would cut price proposals in future years if the cereals crop (excluding durum) exceeded 119.5 Mt. For every full 1 Mt of production over the threshold, the price proposal for 1983–4 would be cut by 1 per cent, up to a maximum of 5 per cent. The Commission had bowed to pressure and revised its original proposal: prices under the new system would only be cut in a year following excess production and then only from a notional increase rather than in absolute terms.

When the Commission considered the 1983–4 marketing year, it was faced with a guaranteed threshold system even weaker than it had proposed. The system accepted by the Council compared the average production over the previous three years (rather than latest annual crop) with the threshold. The guarantee threshold also was raised by any amount of imported cereals substitutes over 15 Mt. If the Commission's threshold system had been accepted by Council, the 1983–4 wheat price proposals would have been reduced by 5 per cent rather than the actual 1 per cent cut.

Later in 1983 the Commission announced that it could no longer honour its 1981 commitment not to cut nominal prices. It cautioned that 'the common prices expressed in ECU may be frozen or even reduced; and consequently that the Community support prices expressed in national currency may be reduced in nominal terms.'[44] The Commission proposed that 'speeding-up of the narrowing of the gap between its prices and those applied by its main competitors should be an objective in its future proposals for common prices for cereals.' The Commission also hinted that 'if this objective is not attained by the prices policy, the Community will then have to consider, in spite of the administrative difficulties which such a solution would create, imposing a levy on cereals to cover all or part of the cost of exports.'[45]

When the Commission came to prepare the price proposals for 1984–5, it had little room to manoeuvre. Real farm incomes had fallen in 1983 in almost all member states and budget costs were forecast to jump sharply because both volumes and the per tonne refund cost of exports were rising (US dollar export prices were falling faster than the ECU was depreciating). The Commission proposed to freeze wheat ECU prices, to revalue the green DM and pound and to raise the quality standards for intervention purchases. Although Council rejected much of the Commission's package, it accepted, for the first time ever, a small cut to guaranteed ECU prices.

The Commission reciprocated in 1985 with its first proposal to cut ECU prices since 1970. The 1984 record cereals crop triggered a 5 per cent cut under the guarantee threshold system and, with exportable production of cereals (excluding durum wheat) forecast to reach 33 Mt by 1991, the new Commission decided to try to get a large cut in 1985. Frans Andriessen reduced DG–VI's proposed 2 per cent notional price rise to 1.5 per cent, which, combined with the 5 per cent co-responsibility cut, would cause prices to fall 3.6 per cent. Germany, which also faced a proposed 0.5 per cent revaluation of the green DM, invoked the Luxembourg Accord in Council and killed the proposal (see Chapter 7). With stalemate in the Council, the Commission implemented an interim set of intervention and reference price cuts.

The impasse in Council during the 1985–6 price fixing highlighted the political problems associated with the middle approach of cutting prices to slow growth in wheat production. Although the Commission cut real ECU prices for wheat between 1975–6 and 1985–6, production continued to rise. The ECU reference price for wheat of bread-making quality rose only 37.5 per cent between 1975–6 and 1985–6, resulting in a real decline in ECU prices. Even after adjusting for exchange rate changes over the period, price increases per tonne in national currencies were much less than inflation. But wheat yields rose about 3 per cent per annum, so that the gross value of wheat output per hectare rose at about the rate of inflation in Germany and exceeded inflation by about 8 per cent in France and 18 per cent in the UK.[46] Cereals producers in Germany and France also received significant direct income support during those years, compensating them for smaller price increases. Thus, for all the attempted restraint on the part of the Commission, the real returns from wheat were higher than in 1975–6.

In the summer and autumn of 1985, the new Commission concentrated on two priorities: the white paper on completing the internal market and farm policy reform. As discussed in Chapter 2, the two were inseparably linked in the eyes of the new Commission.[47] Although there was general agreement on the Single Market, different groups within DG–VI and the Commission disagreed over how to proceed with farm policy reform. The traders wanted to force the Council to cut prices while others in DG–VI wanted to offer a selection of soft options to supplement price cuts.

The resulting *Green Paper* warned that unless the Community gives 'market prices a greater role in guiding supply and demand within the agricultural policy, it will be drawn more and more into a labyrinth of administrative measures for the quantitative regulation of production.'[48] After consultations, the Commission concluded that it could not rely simply on price cuts. It proposed to continue the restrictive price policy, to reduce the intervention price for feed wheat and to impose a co-responsibility levy that would be adjusted annually to pay a specified share of the cost of surplus exports. The Commission cautioned that 'if the levy is to be effective as a guide to farmers, it must not be offset by artificial increases in institutional prices, as has sometimes happened in the past for milk products.'[49] Although the changes were widely accepted, the Commission was not united: the Italian Commissioner publicly rejected the new levy because it would hurt Italy as a deficit producer.

The 1986–7 price fixing proposals attempted to implement the conclusions of the *Green Paper*. DG–VI proposed to freeze ECU prices for wheat, to replace the special reference price for wheat of bread-making quality with a flat 2 per cent premium for wheat exceeding 14 per cent protein, to cut by 5 per cent the intervention price for common wheat failing the old bread-wheat quality standards, to reduce the maximum moisture content for wheat and to end intervention buying until after the harvest. This package was expected to cut the effective market price sharply because the reference price for bread wheat had generally acted as a floor for EC wheat prices. The Commission also proposed a co-responsibility levy that would be triggered whenever total cereals production in the expanded Community of 12 exceeded 149 Mt; production was forecast to reach 161 Mt in 1986–7. The Commission proposed a levy of 3 per cent for 1986–7, which represented about one-half the cost of disposing of the expected 12 Mt surplus. The first 25 tonnes each farmer delivered to the market or to intervention would be levy-free. The Commission announced the levy would need to be raised to 6 per cent in 1987–8 to cover the full cost of exports. A change in the marketing year to July 1–June 30 (introduced to accommodate southern Europe) would partly compensate northern cereals producers because the first monthly increment (worth 2.45 ECU/t) would be brought forward to August 1. Furthermore, the Commission offered to raise the target price for wheat (thereby tightening Community Preference), to devalue the franc to provide French wheat farmers with a small price increase and to delay any revaluation of the green DM.

In 1987, the Commission attempted to complete the reforms begun in 1986. The forecast for exportable production for 1992–3 was raised to a range of 45 to 50 Mt, which increased the sense of urgency in the Commission. Price cuts were ruled out. Instead of doubling the co-responsibility levy to 6 per cent as suggested in 1986, the Commission proposed to limit intervention buying to the February to May period and to restrict the monthly increments to the period of intervention. The changes to intervention, the most significant reforms for the wheat price system ever proposed, were designed to appeal to Germany. German farmers, who usually sell most of their crop during the harvest (July–September) because they do not have adequate on-farm storage, were not seriously concerned about reduced monthly increments after the harvest. The Council rejected that reform, however, and preferred the Commission's alternate proposal (offered during the Council negotiations) to reduce the buying-in price by 6 per cent.

The Commission, however, was not yet satisfied. DG–VI reviewed progress in the late summer of 1987 and decided that although budget savings had been made and real prices cut, both the EAGGF budget and cereals production were continuing to rise. DG–VI therefore proposed to tighten further the cereals system. The Commission formally transmitted to the Council in October 1987 its so-called stabilizers package. Specifically, DG–VI proposed a new co-responsibility levy to cut the intervention price by up to 5 per cent in 1988–9 and 7.5 per cent in 1989–90: if production exceeded a proposed 155 Mt threshold by more than 1.55 Mt (1 per cent), then a proportionate levy would be imposed when intervention opened on November 1. It warned that if the reforms failed to stem the rise of production, it would have to impose either land set-asides or quotas, which were not universally popular in the farm community.[50]

After hard bargaining at the Brussels European Council meeting in February 1988, most of the important measures proposed by the Commission were adopted (see Chapters 3 and 7). At least until 1992–3, prices would be set automatically, based on market conditions. Shortly after, the Commission proposed and the Council approved a new Community programme of direct income support payments, which would allow payments by member states. The Community also implemented a related set of programmes to encourage land set-asides and extensification of production. The structures policy was therefore redirected to support small and disadvantaged farms. With those changes, the price and structures policies had come full circle, back to where Sicco Mansholt had wanted them in the first place.

Conclusions

In February 1988, the new market regime for cereals was virtually complete. Over the preceding 15 years, the Commission had cajoled, prodded, threatened and bribed the Council into converting the price review from an administrative exercise into a market-based, semi-automatic process. When the language and logic supporting the price proposals in the 1970s is compared with that of the late 1980s, the difference is startling. Pearce noted founders of the CAP had decided that 'the policy's chief object would be to maintain farm income and . . . its principal instrument would be price support.'[51] That no longer holds. The Commission's latest price reviews have barely mentioned farm incomes.

DG–VI and the Commission recognized that the fundamental changes in the power structures required reforms in the basic operation of the CAP system for wheat. Consequently, it used its initiative power to focus the debate on issues and solutions that bolstered its position and interests.[52] If it had ignored the inexorable change in the power structures, DG–VI, and probably the whole Commission, would have remained master of the CAP, but would thereby have become increasingly irrelevant for the majority of the Community.

The reforms in the price system also changed the map of interlocking bargains the Commission requires to operate effectively. Perhaps most importantly, DG–VI lost significant power to influence farm policy and farmers' livelihoods as it substituted automatic formulae (green ECUs, quantitative guarantees, stabilizer levies and stabilizer price cuts) for purely administrative mechanisms (objective method, green rates, basic co-responsibility). In exchange, DG–VI developed two new and potentially more important relationships. First, throughout the 1980s DG–VI reoriented the cereals price system so that the EC could develop commercially-based export markets. As a result, by the late 1980s, it had positioned itself at the centre of the most vibrant part of the farm policy community. But DG–VI recognized that it would need to expand its offerings to the less advantaged parts of the rural sector. In 1989, it began to redeploy resources to develop the rural economy, in an effort to attract the interest and support of the increasingly important non-farm rural sector and thereby to maintain its dominance in the Commission.

Notes

1. Poullet and Deprez (1977), pp. 138–9.
2. Neville–Rolfe (1984), p. 247 and 346.
3. Poullet and Deprez (1977), pp. 138–9.
4. Pearce (1981), pp. 10–11.
5. *COM(74)2001*, p. 2, stated that prices should 'guarantee' modern holdings with an income comparable to non-agricultural earned income (* see Chapter 3, note 1).
6. *Newsletter on the CAP*, Special Issue, Nov. 1973, p. 11.
7. Veer (1979), p. 291.
8. *COM(77)100*, 28–2–87, shows further detail.
9. Veer (1979), p. 284.
10. *Ibid.*, p. 292.
11. *COM(75)100*, p. 43.

12. Swinbank (1979), p. 308.
13. *COM(79)10, p. 18.
14. *Newsletter on the CAP*, 3 (March 1975), p. 11.
15. Neville–Rolfe (1984), p. 275.
16. COM(77)482.
17. COM(78)20, p. 198.
18. COM(83)380, pp. 4–5.
19. COM(83)500, p. 38.
20. Ibid., p. 10.
21. COM(87)64, p. 3.
22. If the budget is not passed before the beginning of the financial year, Art. 204 of the Treaty of Rome provides for outlays equal to 'provisional twelfths' of the previous year's budget.
23. Phillips (1989), p. 133.
24. *ASC 1980*, p. 21.
25. COM(83)380, p. 2.
26. Own resources, defined by a 1971 agreement between the Commission, Council and the EP, include EC tariff revenues, agricultural import levies and miscellaneous charges.
27. H. Wallace, 'The best is the enemy of the "could": bargaining in the EC' in Tarditi *et al.* (1989), p. 197, argues that the Commission would benefit because 'the Commission's propositions set the parameters, condition the climate and define the timing of crucial phases of budgetary negotiations.'
28. *Bull. EC 2–1988*, p. 9.
29. Cottrell (1987), pp. 172–3.
30. Schmitz and Bawden (1973), p. 63 and Appendix E.
31. *COM(74)2001, p. 39.
32. Ibid., p. 4.
33. *Green Europe #170*, March 1980, p. 22.
34. *COM(80)10, p. 4.
35. Club de Bruxelles (1988), p. 1.23.
36. COM(80)800, p. 17.
37. Ibid., p. 20.
38. *COM(81)50, p. 2.
39. Ibid., p. 11.
40. This would work similar to the Canadian Wheat Board pooling price system.
41. COM(81)300, p. 13.
42. COM(81)608, p. 6.
43. Ibid., p. 24.
44. COM(83)500, p. 10.
45. Ibid., p. 24.
46. Phillips (1989), p. 151.
47. *ASC 1985*. p. 26.
48. COM(85)333, p. IV.
49. COM(85)700, p. 6.
50. COM(87)410, p. 19.
51. Pearce (1983), p. 147.
52. Petit *et al.* (1987), p. 115.

Chapter 5

Price policy debate

During the 1980s the official consultative bodies and miscellaneous pressure groups interested in European wheat policy were forced by changes in the traditional bargains in the Community to adjust both their approach to the price review and their positions on farm policy.

Key bargains in the system

Before 1979, the farm lobby dominated the system (Figure 5.1). Farmers through COPA largely defined the scope and timing of the debate and created the greatest pressures for change. The national farmer organizations supported the system because they gained from a strong pan–European presence in Brussels. Consequently, the Commission, EP and ESC all focused their consultative efforts on COPA.

Non–farm interest groups had virtually no part in the policy process. Consumers were not regularly represented at the European level until the Bureau Européen des Unions des Consommateurs (BEUC) established a permanent office in Brussels in 1973; environmentalists only got representation in 1974 when the European Environmental Bureau (EEB) was established; and the industrial lobbies remained on the sidelines through much of the early period of the CAP.

Beginning in the mid-1970s, COPA lost cohesion and by the 1980s was no longer at the centre of the policy process (Figure 5.2). When the Commission dropped the objective method and began to address more divisive issues, COPA faced dissension within its ranks as individual commodity groups and national organizations clashed over their demands from the Community. The needs of individual members of COPA diverged and in some instances conflicted. The national farm organizations moved into the vacuum with greater consultation with their national governments in an effort to maintain control of the farm policy. Consequently COPA was pushed to the margins of the European debate. Taylor noted that by 1983 COPA simply provided 'a forum for exchanging information and help[ing] national groups define positions to follow in relations with national governments or national representatives in Brussels.'[1]

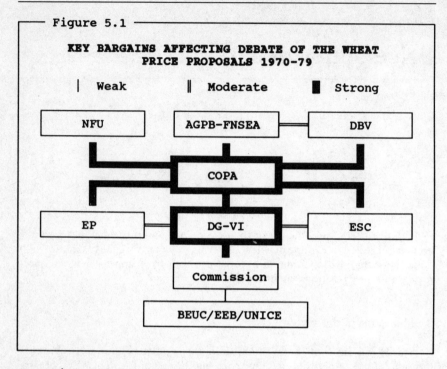

Figure 5.1

KEY BARGAINS AFFECTING DEBATE OF THE WHEAT PRICE PROPOSALS 1970-79

| Weak   ‖ Moderate   ▮ Strong

NFU   AGPB-FNSEA   DBV

COPA

EP   DG-VI   ESC

Commission

BEUC/EEB/UNICE

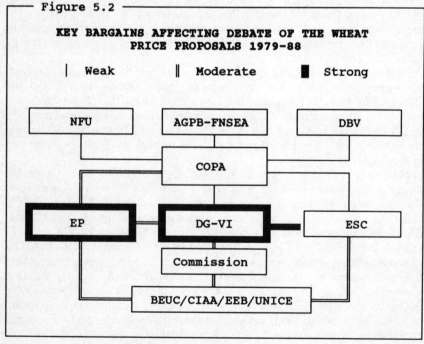

Figure 5.2

KEY BARGAINS AFFECTING DEBATE OF THE WHEAT PRICE PROPOSALS 1979-88

| Weak   ‖ Moderate   ▮ Strong

NFU   AGPB-FNSEA   DBV

COPA

EP   DG-VI   ESC

Commission

BEUC/CIAA/EEB/UNICE

The non-agricultural directorates in the Commission expanded contacts with the industry, consumer and environmental lobbies to increase their power and in effect to break the farm lobby's exclusive control of the price review. The EP and ESC followed suit, opening their processes to the concerns and interests of these other groups. The EP, especially after the 1979 election, sought to gain public favour and votes by courting consumer and environmental interests.

The following sections demonstrate how the shifting economic and political environment and Commission efforts affected the official consultative agencies and the special interest lobbies.

Economic and Social Committee (ESC)

The ESC was established in 1958 as a forum for elite accommodation among the leaders of labour, industry, farming and other interest groups and was given what looked to be a strong position in farm policy debates. Article 43 of the Treaty of Rome requires that the Commission 'consult' with the ESC on all proposals implementing the CAP. The Treaty (Article 47) also directed the ESC to create an agriculture section to prepare the draft opinion, which is presented to a quarterly plenary session of the ESC. During the 1960s and early 1970s farmers used the ESC to bolster their case for price increases. But the elite-dominated view of Community development rapidly lost favour, especially after the election of the EP in 1979, and both the Commission and COPA shifted their focus to the EP in Strasbourg. The ESC thereafter was forced to find a new role in farm debates or lose relevance. Gradually after 1982, the ESC developed as a forum for discussion of the soft options for reform; accommodations over prices were largely left to others. A consequence of this shift was that the ESC found itself more closely allied to the Commission in discussions concerning the reform of the price system.

Quite naturally, farm representatives were the most active members on the agriculture section. The pro-farmer draft opinions were often accepted by the plenary session because there was seldom enough time for the plenary session to discuss and amend the draft: between 1975 and 1988, the agriculture section had at least one month to deliberate and prepare the draft opinion (except in 1977) while the whole Committee had to debate, amend and approve the opinion during a two- or three-day session which always had a full agenda. As a consequence, the ESC strongly supported farmer demands for higher prices to sustain and increase farm incomes until well into the 1970s.

A number of factors then conspired to reduce farmers' influence in the ESC. After the farm lobby scuttled Mansholt's structural policy proposals in 1971, the Commission increased its direct links with COPA to improve its relations with the farm movement. Then, the objective method reduced the need for discussion and compromise: price packages were developed by technicians based on the objective criteria. As a result, COPA found that there was less to be gained by working through the ESC.[2] During the 1980s, when the Commission began to consult more frequently with the national farm ministries, COPA withdrew from directly lobbying the ESC and left the job to its members who were appointed to the Committee.[3]

The evolving membership of the ESC also weakened the farm voice inside the Committee. The number of farm representatives in the Committee held relatively steady during 1970–88, but the total ESC membership increased with the expansion of the Community. As a result, the proportion of farm representatives in the ESC declined to 10.6 per cent in 1986 from 17.6 per cent in 1970.[4] Furthermore, recent ESC appointees who joined the farm lobby (both from the original member states and from the new members) have been generally concerned with the interests of smaller farms and Mediterranean problems; the farm group is no longer dominated by Northern European members concerned with the problems of large, commercial enterprises.

Meanwhile, the environmental and consumer lobbies strengthened their position in the Committee, providing a counterweight to the farm lobby. Ten members (or 5 per cent of the ESC) in 1986 represented consumer interests, up from only three in 1970. Although there were no official representatives of the environmental lobby in the ESC in 1986–90, conservation issues were raised by many of the consumer representatives.

ESC opinions have evolved in line with the changing position of farmers in the Committee. Table 5.1 shows how the opinions changed. The Committee strongly backed the income–supporting role for prices adopted by the Commission in 1972[5] and during the following three years called for prices to be raised at least as much as indicated by the objective method. The 1976–7 price debate for the first time revealed 'deep divisions amongst members of the Committee.'[6] After three years when agriculture section drafts were accepted (at least partly because of the short time available for debate), the Committee had more than a month and a half to frame an opinion. As a result, the plenary session narrowly overturned the agriculture section recommendation that prices rise faster than proposed and approved the Commission offer.

The ESC plenary session then rejected the agriculture section draft opinions in each of the next three years. The plenary session stuck to the objective method calculations in each year, in spite of agriculture section pressure to vote for higher increases. Meanwhile, the non-farm members began to show more interest in the price debate. The farm lobby in 1978–9 narrowly defeated an attempt to amend the opinion to support the Commission's restrained price proposal (2 per cent) and in 1979–80 a group of consumers, trade unionists and industrialists attempted but failed to get a price freeze.

Following three years of defeat, the farm lobby triumphed in 1980 and the ESC opinion rejected many of the Commission's suggested reforms; it instead requested a large price increase. It strongly criticized the Commission for no longer using the objective method: it is 'a serious matter which could be construed as calling into question the common agricultural policy as it has been conceived to date if it turns out that the Commission has permanently abandoned the objective method — which the ESC has always supported — for its calculation in connection with the proposals for farm prices in the Community.' The Committee further rejected the budget argument because it was 'not in itself sufficient reason for not implementing economically and socially justified farm price increases.'[7]

The agriculture section prevailed for the last time in 1981. In 1982 the ESC was expanded and new members nominated. About the same time it also

Table 5.1 Commission agricultural price proposals and ESC opinions

	Commission average for all CAP products	Agriculture committee opinion	ESC plenary session opinion	Vote (F/A/N)	ESC minority opinion
1968–9	.0%	n.a.	n.a.		—
1969–70	.0%	n.a.	agreed; but no cuts		—
1970–1	.0%	n.a.	agreed; only wheat cuts		—
1971–2	>.0%	n.a.	agreed		—
1972–3 A	2.3%	n.a.	9.5%–10.5% spread over 2 yrs		—
1972–3 B	6.5%	n.a.	9.5%–10.5 spread over 2 yrs		—
1973–4	2.8%	n.a.	no opinion; too little time		—
1974–5 A	7.2%	n.a.	7.2% not enough		—
1974–5 B	4.0%	no opinion	no opinion		—
1975–6	9.2%	n.a.	9.2% inadequate	(41/22/5)	—
1976–7	7.5%	9.1%	accepts compromise	(30/23/20)	—
1977–8	3.0%	need upward adjustment	0.1% (objective method)	(66/17/16)	—
1978–9	2.0%	+4.7%	4.2% (objective method)	(48/42/6)	—
1979–80	.0%	3% increase	standstill for surplus products but reasonable rises for rest	(47/23/13)	—
1980–1	2.5%	n.a.	need higher prices; should use objective method	(55/14/13)	—
1981–2	7.8%	n.a.	7.8% quite inadequate	(47/27/11)	—
1982–3	8.4%	closer to 9%	8.4%	(60/50/9)	16.3% (20 members)
1983–4	4.2%	n.a.	4.2%	(53/25/39)	min. 7%; reject cereals co-resp.
1984–5	.8%	accept	limited rise	(70/21/19)	—
1985–6	0.3%	reject cereal price cut	rejected ag. section opinion; unable to reach an opinion	(42/52/9)	—
1986–7	.0%	n.a.	price freeze must be matched by structural policy	(84/10/15)	—
1987–8	−0.5%	accepted; for oils tax	accepted price and green rate changes; no to oils tax	(94/53/12)	supported oils tax
1988	Stabilizers	ok for 1989	only for 1989; want set-asides		

Sources: Neville-Rolfe (1984), pp. 248–51; ESC opinions in the *OJ* (see Table B.1).

instituted monthly consultations with the Commission (giving it advance warning of proposals), which allowed it to produce more timely opinions.[8] This change diluted the power and influence of the agriculture section because the non-farm interests had more opportunity to respond to the farm price proposals. In 1982–3, when the plenary session rejected the agriculture section draft opinion, a group of 20 'agriculturalists' in the Committee had little option but to issue a minority opinion calling for a larger price increase ('in accordance with the "objective method"' and equal to COPA's demands). The minority rejected the Commission proposals for prices and co-responsibility and wanted more strict Community Preference, strengthened producer guarantees and 'immediate implementation of a genuine, dynamic and on-going export policy for food and other agricultural products.'[9]

The 1983–4 debate was a carbon copy of 1982–3, except that the farm lobby lost further support. In 1984, Dalsager attended the plenary session to present the Commission's case for a low price increase and the ESC plenary session responded with an opinion that essentially supported the Commission proposals (and for the first time in several years, the farm group did not present a minority opinion). The ESC, deviating from past practice, spent some time examining a number of 'soft' options for the Commission to consider, including expansion of bio-energy and forestry to reduce surplus production and direct income payments to help small producers hurt by measures designed to bring structural surpluses under control. The ESC Annual Report that year noted that the agriculture section 'has unquestionably enhanced the ESC's prestige in the eyes of the Commission.'[10] This approach proved to be effective in building a new role in farm affairs.

In 1985 the ESC demonstrated that it no longer had any ability to resolve differences in the price negotiations. The draft opinion from the agriculture section rejected the proposed 3.6 per cent cereals price cut but the plenary session voted against it and the Chairman declared that 'this year, the Committee has been unable to take up a position on farm prices.'[11] After 1985 it was imperative that the Committee find a niche where it could do useful work, or it would become totally irrelevant.

Later that year the ESC examined the Commission's *Green Paper* and concluded that a cautious price policy for cereals was necessary but could not, 'in isolation, improve the market balance without entailing unacceptable social and political risks.'[12] The ESC, prompted by the environmental and consumer lobbies, called for the Commission to tighten the intervention system, expand domestic uses (e.g. starch and bioethanol), develop new international markets (e.g. food aid), diversify farm holdings into forestry and tourism, encourage organic farming and use land set-asides for conservation purposes. The Committee also agreed that farmers should be compensated for losses due to reforms of the CAP (taking into account total family income) provided they do not offset the efforts to reduce production.

The ESC in 1986, 1987 and 1988 generally accepted the Commission's proposals to freeze guaranteed prices and reduce intervention support. Although the farm lobby attempted a number of times to get the ESC to withdraw support for cereals co-responsibility, it was defeated each time. The new members in the ESC (nominated in 1986) generally showed more interest in supporting small and Mediterranean farmers than in helping Northern European farmers. Over that period the ESC worked to develop a new role as champion for the soft options. The opinions only obliquely referred to the price proposals (usually to accept the scope and direction of the recommendations).

In summary, after 1975 ESC opinions on prices increasingly supported the Commission, often at the expense of farm interests. When the farm lobby became isolated within the Committee (as new members with different concerns entered), the agriculture section built itself a fresh role as a forum for new ideas and as a proponent for alternative soft options for agriculture. Farmers, consumers and environmentalists discovered they could collaborate both in the section and in plenary sessions to develop proposals which provide new opportunities for farmers.

The European Parliament (EP)

The decision to elect the members of the EP, beginning in 1979, caused a fundamental change in how it dealt with farm issues. Before 1979, the EP, run by elites appointed by the member states, had an outlook that evolved in the same direction as ESC opinions as it sought to be the Commission's 'ally and partner.'[13] As a result, farmers were slowly losing support to non-agricultural members. Then in 1979 the Assembly was expanded and elected. Tugendhat argues that 'in modern Europe, only the ballot box can confer political legitimacy and all that goes with it; nothing else can.'[14] Farmers recognized that, and in the succeeding years increased their efforts to influence the EP. But, like most other legislatures, the EP balances farm sector demands with the concerns and needs of other groups in society. Consequently, the EP has a relatively fluid opinion on farm matters, at times siding with farmers, at times rejecting farm demands and looking at the larger picture.

The EP is part of the policy process because Article 43 of the Treaty of Rome stipulates that the Council can act only 'after consulting the Assembly'. Although the EP cannot block Community price decisions, its opinion has become important. Commissioners frequently state that their negotiating position with Council can be undercut if the EP votes for higher prices than proposed.[15] Furthermore, the EP has important budgetary powers which provide it with additional leverage. Article 203 authorizes the EP to amend the draft budget and, acting by a majority of its members and two-thirds of the votes cast, ultimately to reject the entire budget. If that happens, Article 204 provides the Community with interim resources equal to 'provisional twelfths' of the previous year's budget, which potentially disrupts all Community programmes.

Before the election in 1979, the well-organized farm lobby quite easily controlled the debate because the agriculture section of the EP had fewer than 20 members. Farmers also usually dominated the subsequent plenary session debates because MEP participation was uneven. Even though farmers represented a smaller percentage of the EP after 1979, they maintained significant influence for a number of years because only about 100 MEPs actively participated in the work of the EP and as few as 200 voted on average. Low participation and the need to develop a new majority for each vote tended to benefit farmers because 'those who have a clear "brief", such as agriculture, can be well informed and concentrate on single issues, whereas someone who attempts to deal with broader areas could have difficulty.'[16]

The EP agriculture working group, which prepares the draft opinions for the plenary session, largely determined the EP position on prices in the early years of the CAP. During the 1970s, it consistently proposed, and the EP approved, price demands greater than recommended by the Commission (Table 5.2). The farm MEPs accepted the objective method as a way of setting prices because it provided a mechanistic means to establish a specific price demand that impressed non-farm MEPs. This method also was particularly useful in arbitration between different farm demands in the committee stage.

Table 5.2 Commission agricultural price proposals and European Parliament opinions

	Commission average for all CAP products	EP agriculture committee opinion	EP budget committee opinion	Environment, public health & consumers	EP plenary session opinion
1968–9	.0%	n.a.	—	—	agreed; except butter
1969–70	.0%	n.a.	—	—	some increases; no cuts
1970–1	.0%	n.a.	—	—	increases for beef & cereals
1971–2	>.0%	n.a.	—	—	5.0%
1972–3 A	2.3%	'insuffisante'	—	—	withdrawn before opinion set
1972–3 B	6.5%	—	—	—	8.0%
1973–4	2.8%	4.0%	—	—	2.76%
1974–5 A	7.2%	'increase'	—	—	'substantial increase'
1974–5 B	4.0%	6.0%	—	—	6.0%
1975–6	9.2%	inadequate	—	—	'patently inadequate'
1976–7	7.5%	9.5%	satisfactory but inefficient	—	9.5%
1977–8	3.0%	at least 5%	3%; none for surplus prods	n.a.	3% is too low
1978–9	2.0%	5.0%	2%; none for surplus prods	2%	2%; no increase for surplus products
1979–80	.0%	at least 3%	0%	0%	3.0% except for surplus products
1980–1	2.5%	at least 7.9%	2.4%	2.4%	'stringent' ok but 2.4% not unacceptable
1981–2	7.8%	12.0%	7.8%	too high	12.0%
1982–3	8.4%	14%	8.4%	n.a.	14.0%, no production limits
1983–4	4.2%	at least 7%	acceptable	0%	no less than 7.0%
1984–5	0.8%	unacceptable	accept	0.8%	'noted' proposal; no figure
1985–6	0.3%	4.5%	accept	'noted'	3.5% in real terms
1986–7	.0%	no cereal price freeze	need direct income aids	unsatisfactory	no price figure set
1987–8	−0.5%	no cereals price cuts	endorses cuts	emphasis on quality	accepts price cuts and MCA changes
1988–9	Stabs	reject	accept	n.a.	accept stabilizers

Sources: Neville-Rolfe (1984), pp. 248–51; ESC opinions in the *OJ* (see Table B.1).

The pre-eminence of the agriculture committee was first challenged in the mid-1970s, when the EP restructured its committee system and created two additional committees to review and comment on the price packages. Although the agriculture committee remained responsible for drafting the opinion for the plenary session, the budget committee and the committee on the environment, public health and consumer protection (consumer committee hereafter) were given an opportunity to comment on the proposals.

Beginning in 1977, the agriculture committee was held in check by the new budget committee for two years. In 1979, the EP reviewed and commented on the 1979–80 price proposals before going to the polls in June. Although both the budget and consumer committees supported the Commission proposals, the MEPs compromised (at least partly because the election was just months away) and requested a price increase for all products not in structural surplus.[17]

Relations in the EP changed significantly after the election. During the first elected European Parliament (1979–84), the expanded group of electorally-minded MEPs were determined not to alienate potential farm voters. Consequently, they generally accepted the agriculture section opinions and concentrated on non-farm issues. Cottrell dubbed the EP the 'obedient servant to the farm lobby' for its strong support of farmers during this period.[18] The agriculture section regularly requested price increases well above what the Commission proposed and the EP accepted without amendment almost all of those draft opinions.

In 1982 the Presidents of the EP, Commission and Council clarified the budgetary practice related to compulsory and non-compulsory spending and largely removed the budget weapon from the European Parliament in future farm price debates. They agreed that EAGGF Guarantee outlays are 'compulsory'; as such, the EP can amend them only on first reading. If the Council rejects the amendments, the EP cannot amend them on second or subsequent readings. In exchange, the Presidents agreed that the EP can sustain amendments to all 'non-compulsory' outlays. The EP therefore lost some of its limited budgetary power over prices but gained ultimate control over non-compulsory outlays. Kirchner estimated that MEPs during the 1979–84 session spent only about 10 per cent of their time on agricultural and fisheries matters.[19] After 1982, EAGGF Guarantee outlays rose rapidly and left little fiscal room to expand programmes in areas the EP could influence. As a result, the non-farm lobbies made greater efforts to reduce agricultural outlays, which created increased friction between the farm and non-farm lobbies in the Assembly.

In 1984 the MEPs again went to the polls. The new EP included two fewer farmers and a much stronger contingent of consumer advocates and environmentalists. Consequently, there was considerably more interest in non-farm issues and MEPs were generally unwilling to approve agriculture section draft opinions that requested strong price gains. Meanwhile, membership of the agriculture section expanded in line with the larger Assembly (reaching more than fifty members by 1988) and farmers found that the committee which they had come to view as their monopoly preserve included many members with divergent viewpoints.

Meanwhile, all elected MEPs, including farmers, faced a greater variety of pressures which forced them to consider a wider array of interests and concerns during the plenary sessions in Strasbourg.[20] In particular, the relationship between MEPs and the national governments and parties in their home countries changed. Increasingly after 1979, national governments supplied their MEPs — both government and opposition party members — with information explaining their national policy positions. Moreover, the new MEPs belonged to political parties which had to reconcile support for farming with the need to appeal to a largely urban electorate. This competition for MEPs' support helped to balance the needs and concerns of farmers and the demands of other parts of the Community. Although the farm lobby remained strong after 1984, it could no longer dominate proceedings.

In 1985 the EP reached a stalemate when it attempted to develop a new position on CAP reform in response to the Commission's *Green Paper*. The Tolman Report produced by the agriculture committee recommended the Community end unlimited price guarantees (rather than implement 'drastic price cuts'), develop an active export policy and limit duty free imports of cereal substitutes. The budget committee disagreed; it wanted support prices to be fixed 'at a level close to international prices.' The committees on economic and monetary affairs and industrial policy, external economic relations and consumer affairs each recommended a variety of measures that were designed to reduce the cost of the CAP, reform the operation of the price system and develop new markets. In January 1986, the plenary session, faced with almost 200 often conflicting amendments, rejected the Tolman Report (114/168/56) because it was 'over influenced' by the farm lobby.[21]

Over the next several years the influence of the farm lobby continued to slide. In 1986 the agriculture section maintained that 'the market and price policy must remain the cornerstone for guaranteeing agricultural incomes in the future' and rejected the cereals price freeze and the 'feeble, emaciated, one-legged creature' of co-responsibility. The plenary session had difficulty reaching a compromise. Finally, Spain and Portugal helped swing the vote against the agriculture section draft opinion because they were concerned that higher prices might exhaust the budget and thereby reduce resources for regional and social programmes.[22]

Then, in 1987, interest in the Assembly increased because the EP was granted final say on all Single Market decisions. As a result, beginning in mid-1987 attendance at EP sessions rose sharply, so that more than 300 of the 518 MEPs regularly attended in 1987, which bolstered the non-farm contingent and further diluted the influence of farmer members.[23]

In 1987, both the Commission's price package and later the proposed stabilizers dissatisfied the farm lobby in the EP but the Assembly generally accepted the reforms. The agriculture committee for the first time since the early 1970s did not use the objective method to set its opinion (although COPA did); the section decided that the method had nothing to contribute to the new concerns over the market situation, food quality or the budget. Instead, the farm committee examined the specifics of the Commission package — payment delays, tightened quality standards, limited buying-in and co-responsibility levies — and rejected them because they might cut prices by as much as 15 per cent. The committee preferred a price freeze, combined with higher direct income support, set-asides, co-responsibility and the dismantling of the green ECU system. Nevertheless, the other committees endorsed the Commission proposals and the plenary session again accepted the Commission package. Later in the year, the EP allowed that stabilizers would be necessary to slow growth in production and to limit budgetary outlays, but said that they should be part of a larger package of land set-asides, extensification, diversification and assistance for feed incorporation.[24]

By the end of the 1980s, the changed composition and rules in the EP, combined with the renewed interest which flowed from the 1992 exercise, had radically altered farm debates in the Assembly. The agricultural committee, in particular, was forced to accept that the CAP was only one of many Community policies and therefore had to change: prices could no longer be the sole means of farm support. The committee after 1985 developed two parallel approaches to policy reform. The MEPs from the Northern European countries became strong supporters of the commercial farm sector and proposed development of an active export policy for wheat and other products in surplus supply. Meanwhile, the Southern MEPs forced the committee to review support for small and disadvantaged farmers and to promote the social dimension for the CAP, including a new structures policy, land set-asides and direct income payments. As a result, the EP was able to resolve the conflicts among farmers and between farm and non-farm interests.

Committee of Professional Agricultural Organizations (COPA)

Although there are more than 150 different European organizations with an interest in farm policy,[25] COPA certainly is the most senior and influential. Mansholt encouraged the national farm organizations to establish COPA in October 1958 because he believed that farmers would support further integration of agriculture and become a strong ally of the Commission. COPA did just that during the following decade. Farmers developed strong European ties through their Brussels office and found they could largely control the scope of farm debate. But as the power structures shifted and farm interests diverged after 1970, the Commission found it had to negotiate directly with the national governments, which forced much of the farm lobbying effort back to the national level. As a result of both economic and political changes, the farm lobby became less united and many farmers began to look for support more to special commodity groups and their national governments. Consequently, the underlying bargain between COPA and its member organizations weakened and the Council, Commission, ESC and EP no longer wait expectantly for COPA decisions.

In 1989, COPA was composed of 30 national farmer organizations from the 12 EC countries, including the Deutsche Bauernverband (DBV) from Germany, four large farm movements from France (including FNSEA) and three National Farmers' Unions (NFUs of England, Ireland and Scotland) from the UK. Although all farm interests theoretically are represented in COPA, the members of the Presidium have almost always been large (often cereals) producers because those individuals have been more able to find the time and money to be away from their farms. In 1976, most members of the Presidium operated farms that had more than 100 ha of land under cultivation[26] and little had changed by the late

1980s. As a result, the interests of commercial farmers were well represented at the expense of smaller, less-advantaged producers.

The Commission provides the key to the development and the survival of COPA. From the beginning it decided to meet and to work only with pan-European, multi-product farm lobbies. Consequently, farmers had to work through COPA to have any influence on the development of farm policy at the European level. During the 1960s COPA built upon this and developed three key services for its members. It established itself as a central meeting place to prepare detailed European positions that reflected the common needs of all farmers in the Community, as a central agency to organize lobbies or protests in support of common positions and as a set of eyes and ears in Brussels to inform national farm groups of developments and issues.

During the 1970s, COPA had good working relations with the bureaucrats in DG–VI (both through the advisory groups and via direct contacts), which ensured that COPA views were well understood and that the analysis that preceded the price review recognized farmer concerns. COPA used these contacts to gather information to review market conditions and to recommend an average price increase (and individual product increases before 1976) for the Commission to include in the price proposals. COPA was also given a preview of the Commission proposals before they were sent to the Council,[27] which allowed it to mobilize its support or opposition to the proposals. During the consultation phase, COPA completed its request for price increases in light of the Commission package and lobbied the Commission, ESC, EP and Council to explain, defend and promote its position. Kirchner estimated that COPA in 1973–8 devoted 35 per cent of its effort in the price review to lobby the Commission, 10 per cent on the ESC, 27 per cent on the EP and 28 per cent on the Council.[28]

Two important events in 1973 changed the direction of farm politics. First, the UK, Denmark and Ireland formally entered the Community and their respective farmer organizations joined COPA, which widened the interests and views of the organization. This, in turn, caused COPA in 1973 to provide for qualified majority voting on all decisions by the Presidium; until then all decisions had been unanimous. COPA had little alternative but as a result it no longer spoke for all farmers when it dealt with the Commission or Council; majority positions could be and frequently were contested by dissenting COPA members.

Second, Lardinois introduced the objective method for setting the Commission's price proposals and COPA rapidly adopted it. At first it looked to be an ideal approach for setting farm prices because it allowed technocrats in DG–VI and COPA jointly to develop the price proposals based on objective criteria, which had the potential of reducing the role for politicians. The Council, in COPA's view, was not always the best friend of farmers (and especially not in 1968–72).

During the 1970s, the objective method dovetailed with both the general inflationary psychology and the internal politics of COPA. Averyt noted that when 'inflation hit farm markets in the 1970s, agreement seemed to become easier: even if a national group desired only a 5 per cent increase, why not agree with other groups in COPA that are pressing for a 10 per cent increase.'[29] The objective method provided COPA with a convenient mechanism to set its price requests (Table 5.3). Before the method was adopted, COPA relied entirely on reports and comments from its member organizations to arrive at a differentiated set of price demands. The Presidium continued to prepare detailed price requests for the major commodities until 1976, but the focus rapidly shifted toward the average price rise. With the enlarged Community, COPA feared that farmers would fight among themselves and might move away from Community solutions, which would jeopardize the farm movement in the EC.[30] The objective method created a European focus for the farm lobby, which was viewed as necessary to solidify the influence of COPA.

Table 5.3 COPA price proposals

	Commission proposals	COPA price position on: all products	wheat	Objective method
1968–69	.0%	5.0%	n.a.	n.a.
1969–70	.0%	4–5.0%	n.a.	n.a.
1970–71	.0%	general +	n.a.	n.a.
1971–72	n.a.	5–10.0%	n.a.	n.a.
1972–73 A	2–3.0%	11–12.0%	n.a.	n.a.
1972–73 B	6.5%	11–12.0%	n.a.	5.0%
1973–74	2.8%	7.5%	n.a.	3.0%
1974–75 A	7.2%	16–17.0%	+8.0%	7.2%
1974–75 B	4.0%	8.0%	n.a.	4.0%
1975–76	9.2%	17.5%	15.0%	12.4%
1976–77	7.5%	10.6%	n.a.	4.6%
1977–78	3.0%	7.4%	—	0.1%
1978–79	2.0%	5.0%	—	4.2%
1979–80	.0%	4.0%	—	n.p.
1980–81	2.5%	7.9%	—	7.0%
1981–82	7.8%	15.3%	—	n.a.
1982–83	8.4%	16.3%	—	9.0%
1983–84	4.2%	7.0%	—	7.0%
1984–85	0.8%	3.9%	—	3.9%
1985–86	0.3%	4–5.0%	—	7.8%
1986–87	.0%	4.7%	—	4.7%
1987–88	−0.5%	n.a.	—	n.a.

Notes: — = not calculated; n.a. = not available; after 1982–83, the objective method numbers were from COPA, not the Commission.
Sources: Neville-Rolfe (1984), p. 248; Financial Times, various.

COPA's role in the price review changed in the 1980s. The critical negotiations were often conducted between bureaucrats from DG–VI and the SCA and between the Farm Commissioner and the Council of Farm Ministers; COPA could not easily influence either forum. COPA therefore decided to act as the eyes and ears of the national organizations. It now monitors both the Council and the SCA and meets regularly with Commission officials to provide member organizations with information to be used in the national capitals.[31] When it learns of an important meeting, it briefs representatives of the national farm organizations, who then make direct representations to their national farm ministries. During the 1980s, COPA also reduced its contacts with the civil servants in DG–VI and concentrated its lobbying efforts on the political level in the Commission (especially the Farm Commissioner and members of his cabinet). The civil servants in DG–VI therefore became less certain of the farm lobby's specific concerns, which reinforced their need to consult with the national representatives in the SCA. The Commission's frequent consultations with the SCA increased the opportunity for national farm organizations to become directly involved in the negotiations, which contributed to the distinctiveness of national groups[32] and highlighted the national differences among farmers. As a result, COPA found it increasingly difficult to find a common position among farmers.[33] The combination of events forced COPA to become more reactive and less influential in the price review.

COPA and its member organizations, however, continued to use the objective method to frame their demands. COPA's membership had become increasingly diverse during the 1970s, as the changed financial structures and increased incentive of high prices induced farmers to specialize and commercialize their operations. Then in the 1980s Greek, Spanish and Portuguese farm organizations joined. Consequently, COPA found it difficult to wean itself from the objective method. In 1985, COPA was persuaded by the northern European farm organizations to reject for the first time since 1972 the objective method result when setting its price demands. The method indicated that prices should rise 7.8 per cent but COPA only requested 4–5 per cent. But that decision was not universally accepted — farm union members in Italy, Greece and Ireland regarded it as a mistake[34] — and COPA returned to the objective method in 1986.[35] It ceased publishing the results in 1987, however, because the method indicated that intervention prices should fall. The formula could not reflect the significant changes being made to the intervention system (via changed quality standards, lower monthly increments, reduced buying-in rates and tighter quality standards). Henceforward, COPA focused on farmers' revenue situation to make case for higher prices.

As the Commission and Council used the price review to limit growth in production, to hold the line on budgetary outlays and to reduce the distortions caused by exchange rates, national farm groups began to have sharply different concerns.

The most common argument centred around the operation of the agri-monetary system. French wheat producers, in particular, disliked the agri-monetary system because it allowed real wheat prices in Germany to remain above French prices; French producers wanted Germany to be a large, protected market, not to compete with them.[36] When inflation was high during the mid-1970s, COPA was able to finesse agreement on incremental changes in the green rates proposed by the Commission because nominal prices did not have to fall in strong currency countries. But in the low inflation years beginning in 1980, German farmers faced price cuts at the farm gate whenever the Commission proposed to revalue the green DM. COPA was unable to resolve the differences. The only successful farm lobbies were bilateral. In 1979, for example, FNSEA and the DBV provided a resolution to the impasse over the introduction of the

EMS when they agreed jointly that MCAs could be eliminated, provided guaranteed prices increased sufficiently to ensure German farmers steady operating revenues. Mostly, however, national farm organizations lobbied their national governments. In weak currency countries, farmers lobbied for rapid devaluation of their green rates while in strong currency countries (i.e. Germany), farmers protested against changes that would cut farm-gate prices.

The issue of price cuts also divided the European farm community. With the largest 25 per cent of farmers receiving about 75 per cent of CAP support, the impact of price cuts would be distributed unevenly.[37] Buckwell estimated that a 5 per cent real price reduction in 1980 would cut absolute incomes on large farms by as much as eight times the amount for small farms.[38] Thus owners and operators of large farms, who are disproportionately represented in the cereals sector and in the national member organizations of COPA, have a strong incentive to fight against such a move. But when the cuts per worker are compared to income per worker, the losses for smaller farms in Germany represent a larger share (about 30 per cent) than for the larger farms (about 20 per cent). In France and the UK, both the smaller and larger farms would suffer in equal proportions. In all three countries, however, the absolute income per farm worker is significantly lower for small rather than large farms, so that even proportionate cuts would tend to hurt small producers more (i.e. it is easier for a high-income farmer to cut his cost of living than it is for a low-income farmer). Consequently, farm unions with more small farmers (e.g. the DBV in Germany), tend to be the most opposed to direct price cuts.

Although COPA rejected in 1981 the Commission's proposal to align EC prices with world or US prices, it grudgingly agreed that something would have to be done. In 1982 it accepted the guarantee threshold system and in 1985, when price cuts proved impossible, COPA accepted co-responsibility as the 'least worst' alternative, provided it was matched with tighter Community Preference, limits on cereal substitutes and an active export policy (wanted by French farmers). The co-responsibility system, however, exacerbated the already difficult relations with the NFU of England and Wales (which had probably always been the least 'communautaire' of the member farm associations) because a significantly larger proportion of UK farms were subject to the levy than on the continent (see Table 6.3).

One consequence of this 'renationalization' is that COPA has greater difficulty mobilizing farmers to support European lobbying efforts. Its ability to organize and plan mass protests across the Community peaked in 1974. The series of protests, which started in France in early July and spread throughout France, Germany and the Netherlands in August, culminated with more than one million farmers across the Community mobilized on September 17. Since then farm protests in Europe have either been small or limited to specific commodity groups or regions. In many cases the protests in one country have also been targeted against the interests of farmers in another part of the Community. Open battles have raged at times between competing producers in different countries (e.g. Italian and French wine producers in 1975–82 and French and UK sheepmeat producers in 1979–80), between producers of cereals and livestock (e.g. at the 1983 NFU meeting)[39] and between large and small producers (e.g. in Germany in 1987). COPA has not been able to solve the problem of diverging and conflicting demands from its member farmers.

In summary, COPA has been effectively neutralized in much of the farm debate. As issues became more complex after 1975, the Commission and SCA worked more closely together, which forced more of the lobbying effort back on to the national farm organizations. COPA also lost its ability to mobilize farmers to protest for a Community position. As it tried to compensate for its lost power, it developed more as an intelligence gatherer and educator, a valuable but significantly different role than envisaged in 1958. COPA, therefore, was pushed to the periphery of the policy debate in the 1980s.

Industry

The original bargain struck between Germany and its industrialists and France and its farmers has for the most part held firm and the industrial lobbies in Europe have not commented widely on any of the price-fixing packages produced by the Commission. The Union of Industries in the EC (UNICE) is generally vocal only when the Commission or Council examines reform of the CAP. In 1981, the agri-food committee of UNICE became independent: the Confédération des Industries Agro-Elémentaires de la CEE (CIAA) now represents 13,000 firms with about 2.2 M workers in the food and drink industries in Europe. The CIAA worked with the Commission throughout the 1980s to reform the CAP and, more recently, to implement the Single Market policy but has been 'comparatively ineffective' because it represents too many diverse and conflicting interests (ranging from feed suppliers to confectionery firms) to be able to develop effective bargains with the key agricultural policy-making bodies.[40]

Industry is formally connected in the farm policy area only with the Economic and Social Committee and the Commission. In the ESC, where one-third of the members are nominated to represent industry, the lobby works through the agriculture and budget sections and in the plenary session to counterbalance the farm lobby. The result, outlined above, is that the ESC has accepted that reform is inevitable. Industry also has contacts with the Commission directorates responsible for trade and industry, but they do not have access to the agricultural debate. Consequently, when industrialists present their views on farm issues, they are almost always ignored.

The industrial sector does not have any well-defined interest in the farm policy. Although the non-agriculture manufacturing sector as a whole has been hurt by the CAP (see Chapter 1), a significant part of the processing sector benefits from the operation of the policy. Rural industry, for example, often has a symbiotic relationship with farmers. Especially in industries where seasonal employment is the norm, employers have come to depend on their workers having the farm to fall back on.

Industries which process farm produce or provide inputs to the farm sector also do not have any clearly defined interest in changing the policy. Generally, the economics of farming ensures that most if not all sales to and purchases from the farm sector would continue under any of the options proposed by the European Commission. Price cuts and set-asides would tend to hurt larger producers more and are therefore least popular. But most analysts in the industrial sector acknowledge that the highly indebted, commercially-oriented farms which purchase most of the inputs and sell proportionately more into commercial channels could very well react to all other policy changes by increasing production and by farming more intensively in the short term. As a result, the industrial sector has little to win or lose.

At the same time, farm co-operatives control a significant portion of the agri-food industry. Consequently, farmers would lose doubly from any lower input usage or output. In France, for example, farmer-owned co-ops controlled 77 per cent of cereals storage capacity in 1977, owned and operated 30 per cent of combine harvesters in 1979 and provided 70 per cent of agricultural credit. With much of the up-stream and down-stream activity related to farming largely owned by farmers, the industrial lobby's opinions on farm policy are often muted.

Large and influential parts of the wholesale and distribution system also have strong reasons to maintain parts of the system. The agri-monetary system, for example, introduces arbitrary and speculative elements into intra-Community trade which the larger companies frequently exploit profitably. 'The complexity and seeming arbitrariness of the system impose[s] such significant costs on manufacturers and traders attempting to operate the system that they act as a barrier to smaller or traditionally-minded concerns, preventing them from engaging in intra- or extra-Community trade.'[41] Consequently, small actors are pushed out and the market is controlled by large multinational corporations which can afford the risks.[42] Some entrepreneurs also benefit handsomely from over-production and its concomitant problems. Cottrell points out that some of the new agri-millionaires in Europe are those who handle the surplus production.[43] Disposal of the mountains of grain and butter and lakes of wine and milk creates profitable opportunities for private traders as the surpluses are sold and transported to other markets.

Consequently, although the industrial lobby in the EC generally agrees that the CAP should be reoriented to the market, it seldom speaks with an authoritative voice during the critical stages of the wheat price review.[44]

During the 1980s, the European industrial lobbies recommended that the Commission should use production forecasts to set prices, that price guarantees and intervention buying should be limited and that trade policy should be adjusted to the needs of processors. In particular, they sought assistance for value-added exports and more opportunity to import commodities needed by processors but not adequately produced in the Community (e.g. hard bread wheat, durum and long-grain rice). In short, the CIAA wanted the demand side of the market to drive Community policy.[45] But this package masked major disagreements about the means of achieving the changes. There was no widespread agreement about how price discipline should be implemented or about how the difficult problem of cereal substitute imports could be resolved.

At times, the industrial lobby certainly helped focus the farm debate on some of the costs of the existing system and towards some savings. But it has failed to have any impact on decisions because it has neither a well-defined objective nor has it developed any significant bargains with any of the policy actors in the European farm system.

Consumers and the CAP

Analysis of food politics cannot be limited to the producer side. Consumers have a major interest in price, volume and quality of produce. Since 1973 consumers have earned a minor place in the price review by using contacts developed across the Community to push for the CAP to be transformed into a comprehensive food policy. Although the consumer lobby has developed a coherent and articulate programme of reform, it has been largely ineffective because it does not have access to the critical policy forums.

Although consumers are mentioned in Article 39.1(e) of the Treaty of Rome, they have never fully participated in the price review. Before 1973 they were shut out completely as proposals were prepared by functionaires in DG–VI assisted by COPA members, vetted by agriculture committees dominated by farmers in the ESC and EP, debated by farmers through COPA and set by farm ministers in the Agricultural Council. Since then the consumer lobby has expanded its level of contact and access. In 1973 the Commission helped the Community consumer associations open the Bureau Européen des Unions des Consommateurs (BEUC) office in Brussels and encouraged BEUC to work with other consumer and co-operative organizations through the Consumers' Consultative Committee. The consumer lobby really was launched in 1975 when the Commission developed a consumer programme.[46] Since then the BEUC has created close links with DG–XI (environment, consumer protection and nuclear safety), gained a seat on various agricultural advisory committees, developed contacts with the consumer representatives in the ESC (ten in 1986, up from three in 1970) and with the consumer committee in the EP and gained limited access to the Agricultural Council both directly and through the national consumer organizations. The consumer associations in the EC remain relatively powerless, however, because they are excluded from the decision-making process: farm policy decisions are still made almost exclusively by functionaires and ministers of agriculture.

In addition to poor level of contact, consumer associations suffer from a lack of public support within the Community. The strongest consumer groups in 1979 were located in the UK (750,000 members), the Netherlands (460,000 members), Belgium (395,000 members) and Germany (where the consumer association (AGV) has about eight million indirect members). In contrast, the two French consumer associations combined had only 48,000 members and countries such as Ireland and Denmark had less than 2,000 members each in their organizations.

The weakness of the consumer lobby is often a mirror reflection of public opinion on the CAP. Although a succession of studies has demonstrated that the CAP imposes significant costs on consumers (Tables 1.3 and 6.1), only about 22 per cent of the general public surveyed in 1987 thought the CAP was too expensive. In the three largest countries, about half of the general population thought that either too little or about the right amount of money was spent on farming.[47] When asked if the CAP was worthwhile, about half of all respondents in France, Germany and the UK agreed. The general acquiescence among consumers is at least partly the result of steady increases in labour incomes throughout the 1970s and 1980s and the declining portion of disposable incomes needed to purchase food. By 1986, the average European consumer spent only about 17.5 per cent of his income on foodstuffs and another 4.6 per cent on alcoholic and non-alcoholic beverages and tobacco.[48] In addition, the commercialization of the farm sector dampened the price elasticity of supply so that a 10 per cent increase in the guaranteed price causes retail prices to rise only by about 1 per cent[49]

The consumer lobby has partly compensated for its lack of contact and support by developing a coherent critique of the CAP and repeating it in every possible forum. The BEUC priority since 1977 has been to reform the CAP so that consumer interests are considered equally with producer interests. Although the consumer lobby agrees food security is essential, it believes that it has already been obtained. Now it wants to prevent permanent surpluses by separating income support from price policy. Since 1973 the BEUC has presented annual opinions expounding price restraint for all commodities and price freezes or cuts for surplus products. Only in 1982, when farm incomes were down sharply, did the organization allow that a price increase would be acceptable.

BEUC has not been overly concerned with the cereals sector, however, because the relationship between the producer support for cereals and the retail price for processed cereal products (e.g. flour and bread) is relatively small. Instead, it has concentrated its attack on the market regimes for milk and sugar where the producer price is a large proportion of the retail price.

During the 1980s, the BEUC recognized consumers' diminishing concern for prices and consequently shifted its strategy. Wealthier consumers, in particular, have become health and quality conscious and increasingly demand organically-grown produce and exotic vegetables and fruit. The BEUC consequently changed its primary focus from prices toward the examination of CAP structures and regimes to ensure that they provide the necessary incentives for farmers to adopt alternative crops or production methods.

After 1986, BEUC also concentrated more on the global issues of farm policy. In October 1986, the Council of Ministers resolved that consumer policy should be integrated with other EC policies and agreed that consumer impact statements should be attached to Commission proposals which affect price, choice or quality.[50] Although the resolution did not directly include farm policies, BEUC took the opportunity to expand its analysis and criticism of the CAP price system. After the Council resolution, it produced a series of detailed critiques of the CAP and proposed radical changes to the policy. In 1987, it examined food surpluses in the Community in the run-up to the debate over the Commission's stabilizers package. Its 'consumers' and taxpayers' 8-point plan for reform of the CAP' recommended the Community realign EC prices with world prices by 1992 and drastically reduce intervention support, abolish export refunds and cease destruction of food surpluses. BEUC proposed that co-responsibility levies and quotas (including those on imports of cereal substitutes) should be phased out as prices approach world levels and that the Community should redirect 20 per cent of the CAP budget to a comprehensive system of direct income payments to producers.[51]

The BEUC sought in the late 1980s a more certain role in the farm policy reviews, both through greater representation on the advisory committees (and consumer representation on the product management committees) and through formal acceptance of consumer impact statements into the process. By 1989, however, they had succeeded with neither goal. To compensate, BEUC attempted to build coalitions with other directorates and lobby groups in an effort to direct farm policy from the outside. Domestically, BEUC occasionally worked with the environmental lobby to develop a common position on the environment while at other times it attempted to attract support from the non-farm rural sector with proposals for the Community to develop a comprehensive rural policy. Meanwhile, BEUC made detailed comments on farm policy and the GATT in order to influence the EC negotiating position and thereby set limits to the future development of the CAP. In particular, BEUC recommended that the Community should work through the GATT to get international agreement to reduce farm support by 5 per cent in both 1990 and 1991. Furthermore, BEUC supports the US tariffication proposal,[52] knowing that if the EC binds its variable levy and agrees to reduce export subsidies, the Community will be forced to change the farm support system in the EC.

Nevertheless, in 1989 consumer influence remained limited by lack of access to the farm policy community, uneven membership and general public acceptance of the CAP. With its shift in emphasis from prices to CAP programmes, however, it had defied the odds and remained relevant in farm policy debates.

The environment and the EEB

As the farm sector has become more commercially oriented, Europeans have come to resent the sometimes unpleasant environmental impact of intensive farming practices. The increasing wealth and prosperity in Europe has provided conditions for the environmental movement to grow and prosper while the new information transmitted from research and environmental establishments has created pressures for change. The European Environmental Bureau was founded at the end of 1974 to press for sound environmental policies and since has worked to develop and expand its access to the policy process. But, like the BEUC, the EEB lacks effective and direct access to farm policy forums and has had to expend much of its energies to adapt to the constantly changing public mood to remain a viable, if peripheral, actor.

Since 1974, the EEB has developed a working relationship with the Commission through DG–XI and its Commissioner and built links with the environmentally concerned members in the ESC and the EP. Unlike the BEUC, however, the EEB does not have direct access to the Council of Farm Ministers or to a large body of supporters that can apply pressure to the national ministers. The environmental movement in Europe in the 1980s tended to be highly fragmented, with many single interest or umbrella organizations in each member state. For example, the EEB had 39 member organizations spread across nine countries in 1980, up from only 24 in 1974. In contrast, there were then only 22 (now 30) main farm organizations and 11 (now 17) national consumer lobbies.

Since its inception, the EEB has targeted agriculture.[53] It has consistently argued that the CAP must encourage environmentally sound extensive farm practices, which would include preservation of hedgerows and wild terrain, reduced use of fertilizers and pesticides, scaled-down livestock operations, regulation of laying batteries and conservation of energy. The environmental brief gained ground after 1980 as the EEB worked with the ESC and through the Rainbow Group of twenty MEPs in the EP. Together they worked to develop specific proposals that were environmentally sound and also helped to reduce production.

After 1985 the EEB acquired a new opportunity to comment on farm policy, which may increase its influence on farm affairs. The Commission and farm ministers now agree that the Community should conduct environmental impact assessments for major projects affecting the use of land (e.g. reparcelling, changes in water usage, roads, etc.). This does not open the farm price review to environmental concerns but, as the Community shifts away from using prices to support small farmers and towards a more active structures policy, more of the farm policy should be open to EEB influence.

By 1990, however, the agricultural community had only agreed to examine some of those options. As with the CIAA and BEUC, the EEB has been unable to sustain its positions because it has failed to crack the agricultural policy 'cartel.'

Conclusions

Shifting power structures have radically altered the policy debate in European agriculture since 1973. As the production, finance and knowledge structures created greater diversity in the farm and non-farm economies, the policy agenda expanded to include issues that pitted farmers against farmers and overlapped with non-farming jurisdictions. Consequently, COPA lost internal cohesion, which contributed to the erosion of its privileged position in the policy system. The process accelerated when the Commission opened the price review to new actors — including consumers, environmentalists and budget experts — and the ESC and EP debates shifted their focus away from the absolute price level, on which farmers generally spoke with a common voice, toward issues where farmers disagreed among themselves (e.g. green rates and quotas).

Other Eurogroups, however, have not filled the gap left by the weakened COPA. They have been unable to develop bargains with the key centres of power in the agricultural policy system — DG–VI and the Agricultural Council. Instead, the profusion of opinions at the European level has left DG–VI and the Agricultural Council with a greater opportunity to listen to national farm organizations and to act on their own concerns. Consequently, Eurogroups have increasingly become simply forums for exchange of information and agencies to help national groups to define common positions to follow in relations with national governments or national representatives in Brussels.

Notes

1. Taylor (1983), pp. 40–1.
2. Lodge and Herman (1980), p. 282.
3. Art. 194 of the Treaty of Rome specifies that ESC members must serve in a personal capacity in the ESC and 'may not be bound by any mandatory instructions.' But farm

organizations have always relied upon their members (who, after all, were appointed because they represent the farm sector) to work within the Committee to get an opinion which supports the COPA position.

4. Phillips (1989), p. 165.
5. *OJ* No. C 115, 28–9–74, p. 26.
6. *ESC Bulletin,* 1 (Feb. 1976), p. 2.
7. *OJ* No. C 182, 21–7–80, p. 35.
8. *ESC Annual Report 1983,* p. 9.
9. *Ibid.,* p. 7.
10. *ESC Annual Report 1984,* p. 11.
11. *ESC Bulletin,* 1985(3).
12. *OJ* No. C 330 20–2–85, p. 17.
13. Fitzmaurice (1985), p. 17.
14. Tugendhat (1986), p. 146.
15. *The Daily Telegraph,* 16–2–76; *Financial Times,* 1–4–81.
16. National Consumer Council (1988), pp. 92–3.
17. *Financial Times,* 16–3–79, noted that the EP was confused about the price proposals given uncertainty over the introduction of the EMS. As well as accepting a general price rise and freeze for surplus products, the EP also voted to use 'European Unit of Accounts' (which do not exist); if prices were denominated in ECUs, the average price level would have dropped 17 per cent.
18. Cottrell (1987), p. 28.
19. Kirchner (1984), p. 119.
20. For example, Lord Plumb, who was President of both the NFU and COPA in the 1970s, became a strong advocate in the EP for reform of the CAP in the 1980s.
21. *The Times,* 17–1–86.
22. *International Herald Tribune,* 21–4–86.
23. *The Economist,* 11–2–89.
24. *OJ* No. C 156, 15–6–87, pp. 127–8.
25. Fennell (1979), p. 62.
26. Averyt (1977), p. 75.
27. *International Herald Tribune,* 22–4–84.
28. Kirchner (1980), p. 111.
29. Averyt (1977), pp. 93–4.
30. *Ibid.,* p. 95.
31. Philip (1985), p. 56.
32. Averyt (1977), p. 90, reported in 1977 that the Commission consulted directly with national farm organizations. There is no evidence that the Commission during 1970–88 ever negotiated directly with any of the national farm organizations, except through the advisory committees. Rather, the Commission consulted with the SCA, whose members in turn talked to their national farm organizations. The impact was the same, however, because COPA was still cut out of the process.
33. Taylor (1983), p. 46.
34. *Financial Times,* 8–2–85.
35. *Financial Times,* 11–2–86.
36. *Agra Europe,* 606, 24–1–75, noted that Italy and France openly disagreed with Germany over MCAs at a COPA meeting.
37. Stoeckel (1985), p. 15.
38. Buckwell *et al.* (1982), p. 158.
39. *Financial Times,* 9–2–83.
40. Caspari (1983), p. 48–9.
41. Josling and Harris (1976), p. 67.

42. Debatisse (1981), p. 2.
43. Cottrell (1987), p. 66.
44. National Consumer Council (1988), p. 100.
45. Caspari (1983), p. 49.
46. BEUC (1985), p. 4.
47. *Eurobarometre*, 27, Table A.40.
48. *ASC 1988*, p. T/161.
49. *ASC 1977*, p. 102.
50. BEUC (1987), p. 3.
51. *Ibid.*, pp. 39–40.
52. BEUC (1989).
53. ESC (1980), p. 437.

Chapter 6

Price policy and national interests

Margaret Thatcher asserted in 1981 that in the Council 'there is no such thing as a separate Community interest; the Community interest is compounded of the national interests of the ten member states.'[1] These national interests are determined almost wholly within national policy frameworks as competing public and private interests use the system to advance their positions. National interest is not synonymous with the public interest; national interests reflect those private and public interests that are promoted by the explicit and implicit bargains that underlie the system. The public interest, in contrast, is the Pareto potential[2] for which economists long.[3]

After 1958, the national interests in Council reflected the private interests of farmers, as they had a virtual monopoly position in the policy system. But after 1973, the shifting power structures altered the fundamental bargains that determined the national interests of France, Germany and the UK, so that by the 1980s national interests seldom fully mirrored farm interests. In many ways, these new national interests present stronger pressures for reform of the CAP than the public interest of the Community.

Key bargains in the system

The national interest in each country depends initially on the balance of five institutional and economic factors: strength of national lobbies, relative benefits and costs of policy options, public interest, electoral system, and style of government.

Strength of national lobbies

Mancur Olson argues that, unless a group is small or there is coercion, 'rational, self-interested individuals will not act to achieve their common or group interests.'[4] Individuals quickly determine that their action alone has virtually no effect on the provision of public goods and they therefore act as free-riders in the system. Olson hypothesized that 'large organizations that are not able to make membership compulsory must also provide some noncollective goods in order to give potential members an incentive to join.'[5] The large farm organizations in France, Germany and the UK have to varying degrees done just that, offering technical advice, financial, market and production services and opportunity for personal political advancement. Farm organizations need an active membership as well as large numbers of members. The German farm lobby is probably the strongest because the DBV membership, which represents 90 per cent of all farmers, is active. In contrast, although the NFU of England and Wales represents more than three-quarters of the farm population, its membership is both numerically small and relatively inactive. France represents a middle case: the FNSEA membership is highly active, which makes up for the fact that it represents only about 44–65 per cent of French farmers.[6]

Relative benefits and costs

The impact of policy options on individual producers, consumers and taxpayers determines the passions that arise when change is mooted. Table 6.1 shows that at the economy-wide level, consumers and taxpayers in France, Germany and the UK pay a large cost to support farms in those countries. In per capita terms, consumers pay about 200 ECU in France and the UK and 280 ECU in Germany. But, because UK families have significantly lower disposable incomes, they pay relatively more than in France and about the same as Germany. In contrast, payments per farm holding in 1984 averaged 10,300 ECU in France, 15,400 ECU in Germany and 23,200 ECU in the UK. Farm operators therefore can be expected to fight harder to defend the CAP than the average consumer can be expected to fight for reform. 'Rational complacency' dictates that consumers are less likely to prevail than producers because changing the system is significantly more difficult than it is worth.[7]

Table 6.1 Estimates of the inter-sectoral transfers caused by the CAP (B ECU)

Ref. year	Author & date of study	Study coverage as in Table 1.1	Base prices	Consumer loss	Producer gain	Taxpayer loss
1976	Bale & Lutz (1981)	France	C	2.0	2.2	−0.6
		Germany	C	3.1	2.0	0.4
		United Kingdom	C	0.9	0.4	0.4
1978	Morris: IFS (1980)	France	C	4.8	5.5	1.1
		Germany	C	6.9	6.1	1.8
		United Kingdom	C	2.7	1.7	1.1
1980	Buckwell, et al. (1982)	France	C	5.4	5.2	2.0
		Germany	C	9.0	6.5	2.7
		United Kingdom	C	3.7	2.5	1.4
1984	Harvey & Thomson (1985)	France	C	8.2	10.9	3.0
		Germany	C	11.8	11.4	5.5
		United Kingdom	C	7.8	6.0	3.8

C = current year
Sources: Walters (1987), p. 23; Buckwell *et al.* (1982), pp. 49, 121, 124 & 130; National Consumer Council (1988), p. 255

The studies in Table 6.1 estimate the impact of all the measures covered by the CAP. The individual mechanisms also have differential impacts. Buckwell *et al.* showed that in 1980 a 5 per cent cut in real prices would have reduced German farm incomes by an average 540 EUA or about 10 per cent. In contrast, the same price cut would have reduced average incomes in France by about 450 EUA (6.5 per cent of net income) and in the UK by 510 EUA (only about 6 per cent of net income).[8] Veer demonstrated for 1983 that farmers in Germany would suffer a slightly larger cut in farm income due to a 20 per cent price cut than would farmers in France or the UK.[9] The agri-monetary system, in contrast, affects farmers differently. Veer estimates that French farmers would have increased their incomes by 5 per cent if the agri-monetary system had ended in 1983, while German farmers would have suffered a 15 per cent cut in income. With the strong pound at that time, UK farm incomes would have fallen 11 per cent; if the pound had been weak, UK farmers would have gained.[10]

Because price cuts would hurt German farmers relatively more than French or UK farmers, Germany has generally tried to avoid direct price cuts and instead preferred to make changes to the related mechanisms. After Germany vetoed the 1985 price package, it decided it would have to seek some way to protect its farmers from the inevitable realignment of prices. The co-responsibility system was the solution because it could be designed to distribute the cost of price cuts to suit Germany. Table 6.2 shows that with the levy applied solely on cereals marketed or sold into intervention (i.e. not on cereals consumed on farm) and with cash grants to compensate small farmers for the levy on the first 25t of cereals marketed, Germany wins. Farmers planting less than approximately 5 hectares (5ha × 5t/ha = 25t) or feeding a large portion of their cereals to their own animals are virtually exempt from the levy. As a result, only about 23 per cent of German farm holdings (mostly large) had to pay the cereals levy (more than 30 per cent of farmers cultivate less than 5 ha and almost one-third of wheat produced is fed on farms). In contrast, more than 50 per cent of French holdings and about three-quarters of UK holdings had to pay.

Public interest

The public interest can be viewed as the Pareto optimal set of measures for each country. In the farm case, this usually entails evaluating the costs and benefits of

Table 6.2 Application of the co-responsibility levy (1985)

	France	Germany	UK	EC
Production (Mt)	54.3	25.3	22.3	113.9
Subject to levy (Mt)	29.7	4.6	16.8	55.8
Production subject to levy (%)	55%	18%	76%	48%
Holdings subject to levy (%)	51%	23%	73%	41%
Note items (EC10):				
Avg. cereals ha/farm	13.9	8.6	42.3	8.3
% wheat fed on farm	12%	31%	5%	13%

Source: House of Lords (1986), p. 31

the CAP and summing up the gains and losses for each nation. It is assumed to be in the public interest of a nation to maximize its total economic welfare. This approach, adopted by empirical economists, assumes that a dollar (pound, DM or franc) lost is worth a dollar gained, regardless of who wins or loses. The studies cited in Table 6.3 demonstrate that it is in the public interest for France, Germany and the UK to end the CAP price system. On a national basis, the costs of the CAP are levied more heavily on the UK and Germany than on France. The UK gets a small share of the producer benefits because it has a small farm sector so, after the consumer and taxpayer losses are deducted, its net deadweight losses are large. Germany also has a large deadweight loss because its taxpayers pay a large share of the EC budget. France, in contrast, suffers a smaller deadweight loss because its producers get a large portion of the producer benefits.

Table 6.3 Estimated cost of agricultural support in France, Germany and the UK (B ECU)

Ref. year	Study author & date of study	Study coverage as in Table 1.1	Base for prices	Deadweight loss	Loss as % of GDP
1976	Bale & Lutz (1981)	France	C	0.5	0.16%
		Germany	C	0.7	0.19%
		United Kingdom	C	0.1	0.04%
1978	Morris: IFS (1980)	France	C	0.4	0.12%
		Germany	C	2.6	0.35%
		United Kingdom	C	2.1	0.81%
1980	Buckwell et al. (1982)	France	C	2.2	0.46%
		Germany	C	5.2	0.89%
		United Kingdom	C	2.7	0.69%
1984	Harvey & Thompson (1985)	France	C	0.3	0.05%
		Germany	C	5.9	0.75%
		United Kingdom	C	5.6	0.95%

Sources: As for Table 6.1

In 1980, Harvey estimated (Table 6.4) that the economic efficiency of the CAP was less in Germany and the UK than either in the Community as a whole or in France. On average, less than half the money given up by consumers and taxpayers in the UK was actually going to the farm sector. The rest was being dissipated through inefficient production and consumption. The policy was little better in Germany. In contrast, France found that more than 70 per cent of its effort reached its target. More disturbing to policy-makers, however, was that incremental price increases were an increasingly poor means of supporting farm incomes. Harvey estimated that the UK would have to give up more than £2.25 for each £1 that would be added to farm incomes. Germany and France also showed poor efficiency ratings for incremental price rises. Consequently, as prices rose throughout the 1970s, deadweight losses rose (see Tables 1.1 and 6.3).

Table 6.4 The economic efficiency of the CAP (1980)

		Efficiency ratio	Per cent efficient
Average efficiency:	France	1.42	70.4%
	Germany	1.80	55.6%
	UK	2.06	48.5%
	EC9	1.50	75.0%
Efficiency of 10% price	France	1.61	62.1%
increase:	Germany	2.20	45.5%
	UK	2.25	44.4%
	EC9	1.79	55.9%

The cost-benefit ratio shows the ECUs taxpayers and consumers surrender to increase farm incomes by an additional ECU; conversely % reaching farmers shows the proportion of money foregone which increases farm incomes.
Source: Harvey (1982), pp. 177–8

Of course, the operation of the CAP results in financial flows between the member states. Although the flows net to zero for the Community as a whole, flows into or out of individual countries represent significant gains or losses for member states. Koester estimates that France, in particular, gained about 9.2 M UA for each one percentage point increase in common wheat prices in 1975, which certainly provided justification for France pushing for higher common prices during the 1970s. In contrast, the UK opposed price rises because every percentage point increase worsened the already critical balance of payments deficit by about 4.7 M UA. The German economy lost only about 1.2 M UA from each price increase.[11] Higher prices after 1975 enlarged the inter-state transfers, eventually forcing a change in the budgetary rules. By 1985 the UK and Germany endured annual outflows that averaged about £1.8 B while France gained about £300 M annually. After the Council agreed to give the UK a rebate, the annual net UK financial loss from the CAP fell to about £500M while France began to experience financial outflows (Table 6.5).

Even when there was consensus that the CAP cereals price policy needed to change, there was little agreement about which mechanisms to alter. Veer's study of the 1983 systems (Table 6.6) showed that Germany and the UK would benefit most from price cuts while France and the UK would gain from the end of the agri-monetary system. In contrast, Germany would not benefit from the end of the MCA system. An earlier study, based on 1979–80 MCAs, estimated that Germany would lose about 51 M ECU if the agri-monetary system ended while France would gain about 1.2 B ECU.[12] The UK was estimated to lose more than 1 B ECU for two reasons. First, it had a large positive monetary gap at that time, which meant its farmers would have suffered relatively large price cuts. Second, the end of MCAs would raise the cost of operating the CAP because prices and production would rise in the many member states with large negative monetary gaps and the UK, as paymaster for the CAP, would bear a disproportionate share of those costs without getting the benefits. With UK budget rebates in the 1980s, the net impact on the UK would be less.

Table 6.5 Summary of estimates of the inter-state transfers resulting from the EC Common Agricultural Policy (£ million)

Ref. Year	Koester "(1977) 1975	Blancus #(1978) 1976	Rollo & Warrick *(1979) 1978	Cambridge (1979) 1979	Buckwell et al. '(1982) 1980	HM Treasury (1982) 1981	#1 EC auditors +(1985) 1985	#2 EC auditors +(1985) 1985	UK Govt (leaked) '(1987) 1987
France	+170	+272	+521	+734	-22	+597	+294	0	-195
Germany	+12	-122	-404	-671	-1041	-1750	-1826	-2061	-2018
UK	-79	-593	-818	-1123	-1150	-1422	-1767	-589	-536

Note: #1 EC Auditors is without the UK rebate and #2 EC Auditors is with the UK rebate. * With net effect on trade account measured using export restitutions. " Converted from units of account at 1 ua = £0.41667. # converted from US$ at US$1 = £0.55595. ^ Converted from EUA at 1 EUA = £0.598488. ' + Converted from ECU at 1 ECU = £0.588977. Converted from ECU at 1 ECU = £0.696027.

Sources: BAE (1985); Buckwell *et al.* (1982); Franklin (1988), p. 16; *The Economist*, 20–6–87

Table 6.6 Impact on national economies of a 20 per cent price cut and termination of the agri-monetary system (existing in 1983)

	Cut prices 20%	End MCAs
France	+0.26%	+0.04%
Germany	+0.42%	+ .00%
UK	+0.40%	+0.07%
EC10	+0.37%	+0.01%

Source: J. de Veer, 'National effects of CAP trade liberalization', in Tarditi *et al.* (1989), p. 108

Electoral systems

Politicians are often willing to support a specific sectoral interest even if it does not benefit the public interest, provided the perceived political benefits outweigh the economic costs. In the farm case, farmers gain or lose power to influence the government depending on the type of electoral system in the country. In first-past-the-post, single-member constituency systems (e.g. the UK), groups usually need a significant block of votes to have any serious chance of influencing policy through the electoral system. They must command at least as many votes as the victor's normal plurality during an election. In contrast, proportional representation often dilutes single interest voters' influence unless the group represents a large portion of the vote (e.g. farmers in France in the 1950s and 1960s) or unless it concentrates its vote on small or regional parties that can be dominated by interest groups (e.g. farmers in Germany).

Style of government

The style and form of government also critically determines whether special interests can influence policy. Coalitions are generally easier to influence because their survival usually depends on a few legislative votes which can be swayed by interest groups. Coalition governments sometimes compartmentalize policy to limit overlaps between policy areas, with the result that sectoral debates often are not open to counterbalancing lobbies. Presidential systems potentially are quite closed if elections are infrequent and the President does not need support from the elected assembly, but can be susceptible to pressure during or near elections if the vote is likely to be close. Finally, Cabinet government, as practised in the UK, can either be controlled by determined single-interest groups or open to wider concerns, depending on the concerns of the Prime Minister and the Cabinet.

In summary, the national interest reflects these different strains and opportunities as special interests use the various electoral and government systems to press for their preferred outcome. The following sections examine France, Germany and the UK to demonstrate the evolution of their national interests.

France and the CAP

Farm interests in France are considered by most people to be generally compatible with the French public interest.[13] France has been a wheat exporter since before the Second World War and by 1980 regularly exported more than half its annual production. President Valéry Giscard d'Estaing summed it up best in 1977 when he called agriculture the 'petrole vert de la France'.[14] As a result, farmers and the government have focused on the best way to keep the French farm sector competitive in European and world markets.[15] During the 1970s, farmers and the government were satisfied that they could improve efficiency and maintain their commercial interests within the existing price regime in Europe. The higher prices that were set to support farm incomes provided an ideal environment for farmers to expand production and exports. The Fédération Nationale des Syndicats d'Exploitants Agricoles (FNSEA), the major farm organization, had bargained its way into the public policy process in France, so that it commanded great power over the content of policy and was able to match farmers' commercial interests with their social concerns.[16]

The 'corporatist' relationship between the government and the farm lobby held until the Socialists won the 1981 election. By then the changed production and financial structures had strained the historically strong bonds between farmers and government. The new government no longer believed that the CAP price regime was consistent with France's public interest. The French farm lobby recognized that it could not expect to keep both high prices and the unrestricted right to produce and sell for commercial markets. As a result, the larger farmers led the French farm lobby to champion the realignment of prices towards world levels and the development of a commercial policy for wheat.[17]

FNSEA positioned itself at the centre of a powerful information and lobbying network after 1958. In contrast to Germany and the UK, French law (the 1945 Tanguy–Prigent Liberation Ordinance) prohibits FNSEA from providing non-collective services, such as insurance, which reduces its ability to attract members. At the start of the Fifth Republic in 1958, FNSEA entered a corporatist relationship with the newly strengthened executive government in order to solidify its position.[18] In exchange for support of the government, FNSEA got exclusive access to the policy system and was given responsibility for the operation of many important administrative agencies and boards that managed the farm modernization programme. FNSEA controlled, for example, the Sociétés d'Aménagement Foncier et d'Etablissement Rural (SAFERs), which buy land from retiring farmers and reallocate it to expanding farmers.[19] Because local FNSEA members effectively determined the viability of new and expanding farmers through these agencies, farmers had great incentive to join the organization. Furthermore, FNSEA got large subsidies from the government that allowed it to offer services to members; Keeler argues that without the subsidies FNSEA would not have survived.[20] Finally, FNSEA was the sole recognized voice for farmers in France. Although there are three or four other farm organizations, they generally had smaller memberships and, until 1982, were totally excluded from the policy system.

As in Germany, there are no effective non-farm lobbies to offset the power of the farm movement. Consumers, environmentalists and industrialists have had neither inclination nor means to influence policy. In 1987, for example, half of all consumers agreed that the CAP was 'worthwhile' while only 17 per cent disagreed.[21] This is a least partly because the average consumer and taxpayer pays less in absolute terms than in Germany and the cost of the CAP relative to average household incomes is lower in France than in Germany or the UK. The predisposition toward the CAP is also at least partly because benefits and costs are spread more evenly in France than in either Germany or the UK. Producer losses or gains are felt more widely than in either of the other two countries both because of the larger number of farmers in France (1.5 M or 7.1 per cent of total civilian employment in 1986) and because about 20 per cent of the French population has an interest in agriculture through land inheritance.[22]

Throughout the 1960s and 1970s, the high price policy also was almost fully consistent with the French public interest. Producer benefits were estimated to be greater than consumer costs and almost equal to the total of consumer and taxpayer costs (Table 6.1); the country was a net recipient of inter-state transfers caused by the CAP (Table 6.5); and every percentage point increase in guaranteed wheat prices raised inter-state flows to France by more than 9 M UA. As France had a sustained large current account deficit, even with the large net in-flows from the CAP, the nation benefited from any increases in institutional prices (Figure 6.1). Finally, agriculture was judged to be a key sector that would press for greater European integration, which suited France's security interests.

By the 1980s, however, France's public interest had altered, which created the conditions for change in the policy orientation in France. Using prices to support farm incomes became increasingly inefficient, so that the producer benefits of the CAP were less than the consumers' cost. Furthermore, expansion of the CAP to new Mediterranean products, the 1984 budget deal and the accession of Spain and Portugal in 1986 turned France into a net payer from its long-term position

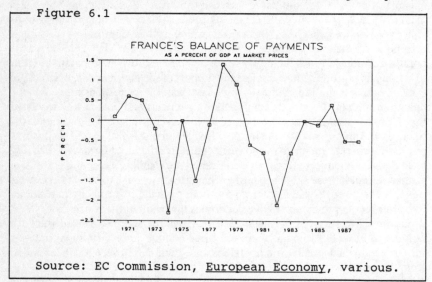

Figure 6.1

FRANCE'S BALANCE OF PAYMENTS
AS A PERCENT OF GDP AT MARKET PRICES

Source: EC Commission, European Economy, various.

as a net beneficiary of the CAP. Moreover, less than 8 per cent of the French population depended on agriculture in the 1980s, compared with 13.5 per cent in 1970 and 22.5 per cent in 1960. About that time France also reassessed its security interests and decided that the CAP impeded development of non-farm policies, thus potentially threatening the Western alliance (see Chapter 2). But agriculture remained important because it contributed a major share of national export revenues (12.6 per cent in 1986). The French government, and eventually the farm lobby, decided France could gain if the CAP was reformed to assist commercial farmers to maximize their production and export potential.

The key opportunity for farmers to influence policy through the electoral system comes at the septennial presidential election, when farm votes are carefully courted by right-of-centre presidential candidates. In 1966, the 'empty chair' confrontation in the European Council so angered farmers that they nearly defeated Charles de Gaulle in the primary election that year. Future right-wing candidates ensured they did not anger the farm sector at election time. In 1974, Giscard won the Presidency at least partly because Jacques Chirac swung the farm vote in his favour; the net one million farm votes (69 per cent) he gained offset his deficit in the non-farm vote. Below the Presidential level, farmers were also influential because of their strong connections at the local level, both through the Chambres d'Agriculture (dominated by FNSEA members) and through their 'notables' (local elected officials). A survey in the late 1970s showed that 94 per cent of farmers were acquainted with their 'notables' and 84 per cent had recourse to them if needed, which was the highest of all socio-economic groups.[23]

Consequently, agriculture was a key portfolio for ambitious politicians. A number of political leaders have used the post of agriculture minister in the French government or president of the FNSEA as a 'springboard' to French or European politics.[24] Both Jacques Chirac (1973–4) and Michel Rocard (1983–6) ultimately moved from minister to Prime Minister while two presidents of the FNSEA moved to greater prominence: Michel Debatisse first became a leading member of the European Parliament for the Gaullist party and then Secretary of State for the Food and Agricultural Industries in 1979; and François Guillaume was recruited as French minister for agriculture for 1986–8.

The 1981 election marked a turning point for farmers. Although 67 per cent of farmers again voted for Giscard, he lost because the declining farm population no longer had enough votes to offset Giscard's non-farm vote shortfall. François Mitterand, who had before the election prepared plans to break the compact between the FNSEA and the government, won the presidency. Immediately after the election, Edith Cresson, the new Socialist agriculture minister, granted official status to three competing farm organizations, in addition to FNSEA. Then in June 1981 Cresson announced new aid to the farm sector. Unlike in the past, however, FNSEA did not have any role in administering the programme.[25] Cresson also announced plans to review regulations on elections to the Chambres, to replace SAFERs with councils not controlled by FNSEA and to create new professional associations to replace those controlled by FNSEA. The government thereby hoped to undercut FNSEA's power base and to supplant it with sympathetic left-leaning farm organizations. Although SAFERs were not changed and FNSEA continued to have privileged access to the President, in the end FNSEA was faced with the reality that it no longer controlled the policy agenda.

Until 1983, the French government generally listened to and supported the farm lobby at least during the price review. The government was determined to forestall disruptive farm protests, which usually promised high prices. With the strong links between France and DG–VI, there was seldom much difference between their positions. They both accepted in the early 1970s that prices should be used to support farm incomes and, in the mid-1970s worked to introduce an automatic agri-monetary system that would force Germany to realign its under-valued green rate. Farmers supported this orientation and used their strong links with the government to extract maximum price increases through a combination of negotiation and protest. They were able to extract solemn undertakings from the French government (often from the Prime Minister or President) to support their demands in Brussels or, if that failed, to supplement inadequate price rises with national aids. Only for a short period during the tenure of Prime Minister Raymond Barre were farm interests partly subordinated to the national anti-inflation programme.[26] As recently as 1982, the French government fully supported farm demands and even threatened to force a majority vote for the price package to overcome a block in the Council.

Beginning in 1981, the government's opening position on the price talks shifted in line with the new public interest. France was increasingly concerned to sustain and improve the international competitiveness of French farmers.[27]

Consequently, after 1982 France supported Commission efforts to realign EC wheat prices with US target prices and to introduce an active export policy. When price cuts proved impossible in 1985, France worked with the Commission to develop the co-responsibility system that replaced the price and income policy of the 1970s and early 1980s. Farmers also accepted that the system required change; they could no longer hope to keep both high prices and unrestricted market privileges. Commercially competitive farmers, who dominated FNSEA,[28] disliked any scheme that would limit their production or output, such as compulsory land set-asides or tied income aid. As a result, FNSEA accepted that the CAP must change. The quantum approach of co-responsibility and thresholds became popular in the 1980s at least partly because it was similar to the system already administered by the Office National Interprofessionnel pour les Céréales (ONIC), where cereals producers paid a levy to develop domestic uses and export markets for French cereals. Provided the co-responsibility funds were used to expand market opportunities, that option would be acceptable.[29]

In summary, during the 1980s farmers faced the prospect of losing control of the farm policy network in France as the changes in the power structures forced apart the interests of farmers and the public. The new Socialist government, which did not depend on farm support, weakened the farm lobby after 1981 and seemed poised to bargain in Brussels for changes in the CAP. In response, the farm lobby moved to support reorientation of the price system and expansion of programmes to improve competitiveness and exports. Consequently, by the mid-1980s the French farm policy community was reunited, only now in support of reform rather than in defence of the old price system. France had become the driving force behind CAP reform.

Germany and the CAP

German history and the republican political system have provided German farmers with a unique opportunity to control the national position in European farm debates. Following the war, Germany actively supported farmers to promote food self-sufficiency and to sustain the population base in many war-ravaged areas. In the unsettled period immediately after 1945 and up to the mid 1960s, West German politicians (i.e. J. Ertl) regarded farmers — which represented more than one-quarter of the total West German population in 1950 and virtually all of the rural population — as a bastion against Communist agitation within the rural areas along the border.[30] At the same time, the government was pressed to develop non-farm jobs for the 12.5 M refugees from the East between 1945 and 1961 and took the opportunity to slow farm rationalization.[31] In return, farmers expanded output, integrated themselves into the rural economies and actively supported conservative governments. In 1955, the political bargain between farmers and the government was enshrined in the Green Law, requiring the government 'to enable agriculture . . . to offset the existing natural and economic disadvantages' in order to 'equalize the social situation of people working in agriculture with that of comparable professions.'[32] So by the time the CAP was created, farmers were well entrenched in German politics, with privileged access and significant influence over policy.

The German farmers' union, Deutsche Bauernverband (DBV), maintained its role at the centre of farm policy in Germany after 1958 because of its strong and loyal membership. The DBV is in practice the only key to the powerful lobby and farm service system. Through the Deutsche Raiffeisenverband (DRV), the co-operative movement markets more than half of the nation's cereals and 78 per cent of the dairy products, supplies 62 per cent of the fertilizers and 36 per cent of the machinery and provides 27 per cent of farm finance.[33] Although the DRV is legally separate, it markets DBV memberships, which are 'assumed by farmers to be a prerequisite for their [DRV services] obtainment.[34] At the same time, the DBV provides virtually the only access to government for farmers. Consequently, more than 90 per cent of all German farmers are members of the association. The DBV also remains active all year round — a survey of DBV members in North Rhine–Westphalia around 1980 showed 94 per cent of the members attended at least one meeting a year and more than 50 per cent attended regularly — so that it can mobilize the lobby during elections and key policy negotiations.[35]

The unity of the German farm lobby was severely tested but only partly damaged over the 1973–88 period. While the Napoleonic inheritance laws in Baden–Wurttemburg, Hessen and the Rhineland–Palatinate had led to farms being broken into smaller holdings, primogeniture in the North and much of Bavaria had facilitated farm consolidation.[36] Throughout the 1970s and 1980s, the shifting production and financial structures exacerbated these north-south divergences. Meanwhile, by 1985 the absolute number of farmers in Germany had dropped from more than five million in 1950 to about 1.3 M, half of whom work off-farm. The first challenge came in 1972, when the DBV, dominated by large-scale, full-time farmers, pushed the German government to prepare a 'Green Plan' that would provide support only for larger farmers. Small-scale and part-time farmers, comprising the majority of the German farm population, rebelled and formed a new association to lobby for their interests.[37] Although the new organization remained weak (because it did not get official recognition from the government),[38] relations in the farm lobby remained strained. As recently as March 1987, 10,000 small farmers protested against the domination of the DBV by large agri-business and called for the president of the DBV to resign.[39]

Despite internal disputes, however, the DBV successfully defended its power-base in the German farm policy community because it has 'no effective counter-vailing interest group.'[40] Although the consumer associations in Germany have more than eight million members, they are not influential because membership is spread across thirty-six various organizations and because the national consumer federation has no direct access to the farm policy process. The distribution of winners and losers under the CAP strengthens the farm lobby and weakens the consumer lobby. Predominantly small German farmers are heavily dependent on the CAP to sustain their incomes. On the other hand, although German consumers pay a higher total cost for the CAP than their counterparts in France and the UK, they have significantly higher per capita incomes, so that in Germany outlays on food, alcohol and tobacco comprise the smallest proportion of household expenditure of any member state. Germans also recognize related benefits of the CAP. Much of the German population views the CAP as the cost of belonging to the EC and not simply the cost of farm policy.[41] In a 1984 survey, 18 per cent of the respondents also liked the assurance of food supplies provided by the CAP while 11 per cent thought the country benefited from the trade advantages in the policy; only 5 per cent saw agricultural surpluses as a problem.[42] Furthermore, a majority of the population still lives in rural areas, so they see and accept the need to support farmers.[43] German town-dwellers have a romantic vision of farming,[44] which farmers have carefully cultivated. Consequently almost half of the German public surveyed in 1987 thought the CAP was on the whole worthwhile; only 22 per cent thought it was too costly.[45]

Economic interest (as measured by deadweight losses or financial flows) should dictate that Germans would want to change the basic CAP system. Bale and Lutz (Table 6.3) estimated that in 1976 the costs to consumers and taxpayers exceeded producer gains by about 0.7 B ECU and more recent studies show that the annual cost rose to almost 6 B ECU in the 1980s. As well, Koester determined that every increase in guaranteed prices raised the net payments from Germany to the rest of the Community. But Germany had relatively steady economic growth and a sustained balance of payments surplus over most of the period, so it could afford to ignore the negative effects of the price system and concentrate on the defence of those CAP features from which it benefited (Figure 6.2). The agri-monetary system, in particular, was popular with all the federal ministries[46] because MCAs provide higher domestic prices and stronger German farm incomes while dampening prices in other countries, thereby lowering potential EC production, surpluses and budgetary costs.[47]

The proportional representation system (with both single member constituencies and list voting) consolidates the power of the farm vote because the resultant coalitions need to court either the farm vote directly or the smaller parties that win with farm support. Individual farmers and the DBV generally support the Christian Social Union (CSU) in Bavaria and the Christian Democratic Union (CDU) elsewhere. In 1969, when the Social Democratic Party (SPD), which was not as pro-farmer as the CDU/CSU, governed in coalition with the Free

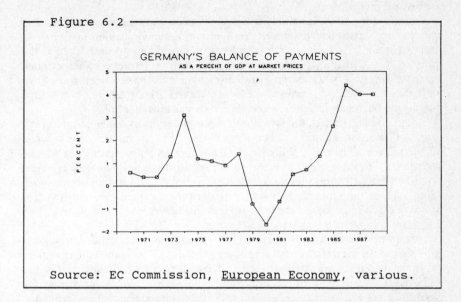

Figure 6.2

GERMANY'S BALANCE OF PAYMENTS
AS A PERCENT OF GDP AT MARKET PRICES

Source: EC Commission, <u>European Economy</u>, various.

Democratic Party (FDP), farmers fortuitously got support from Josef Ertl, a Bavarian FDP member appointed as agriculture minister. The SPD had little sympathy with the CAP but Ertl successfully exploited the coalition to support farm interests.[48] The FDP gradually became more receptive to farm interests and after 1980 it actively courted farm votes to ensure the party could get the 5 per cent minimum vote to ensure its parliamentary representation.[49] Ertl remained agricultural minister for fourteen years, strongly supported when policy disputes arose by the other three FDP ministers in Cabinet. After the 1981 election, the FDP shifted into a coalition with the CDU/CSU and Ertl resigned. The new agricultural minister, Ignaz Kiechle, was a CSU member and became another strong farm supporter. Throughout the period farmers kept pressure on the national governing coalition because the federal system ensured that there was seldom a period without either Länder or national elections. Governments in France and the UK, in contrast, generally have the comfort of three or four years between elections, which allows them greater freedom from special interest lobbies.

The federal system of government in Germany further strengthens the farm lobby. The federal Cabinet often has little opportunity to influence farm policy because the compromises and options have been finessed in negotiations among the department and minister for agriculture, the DBV, the Bundestag and the Länder. This 'sectorized nature of policy-making in the Federal Government places the existing [CAP] policy — and its protagonists in the ministry — in a strong position.'[50] Consumers, environmentalists and industrialists only have access to farm debates through other ministers in full Cabinet[51] and, therefore, are largely excluded from the policy debate. The DBV maximizes its impact in the system by working closely with the ministry of agriculture: key ministry officials 'usually come from' the DBV, so that there is a common view on the issues and prescriptions.[52]

The resulting set of interlocking bargains inside Germany ensures that farm interests dominate and determine the German national position in European farm debates. The German minister for agriculture almost always begins the price review demanding a set of prices that favour farmers, either through relatively low ECU price increases and no change in the undervalued green DM, or higher ECU prices to compensate for any green DM change. The bottom line has always been that DM prices and farm incomes must not fall.

In the 1973–6 period, the farm lobby faced two serious challenges to its high price policy: anti-inflation policy topped the SPD economic agenda while Ostpolitik was Chancellor Willy Brandt's key foreign policy venture. While the inflation policy was a greater immediate threat, any thaw in East–West relations would undercut the long-term security reason for Germany to support the CAP. Both policies, therefore, threatened farm prices and incomes. Nevertheless, Ertl used the coalition system to ensure that his government supported price increases for German farmers.

Then world commodity prices soared, Germany's terms of trade deteriorated sharply and the German current account moved into a significant deficit position, which triggered a major attempt to reduce farm support through the CAP (Figure 6.2). Ertl attempted to forestall the domestic reform movement during the second half of 1978 when as President in the Agricultural Council he declined to schedule time for debate of possible reforms. But in 1979 both Schmidt and his economics minister pushed for reform and in 1980 the SPD issued a study that proposed to end unlimited guarantees for surplus products and instead to introduce national income support.[53] Ertl held out, however, until the next election. When the SPD lost support in the 1981 election, the diminished FDP parliamentary wing shifted into a governing coalition with the CDU/CSU who were more sympathetic to farm interests.

Since 1981, the farm lobby has been solidly supported by Chancellor Helmut Kohl and the Cabinet. After 1983, when the Commission was pushing for reform, Kiechle was given Cabinet approval to take an unusually hard line in Council and reject any price cuts for cereals; he even was permitted to use the veto in the Farm Council in 1985. But the German veto proved ineffective (the Commission implemented the price cut anyway), as was Kiechle's rearguard action in the Farm Council in 1986 and his threat in 1987 to cut German payments to the EC if cereals prices were cut.[54]

The German farm policy community found it had to develop an alternative policy approach following the 1985 veto. The German government, prodded by the DBV, completely rejected direct price cuts but was willing to work with the Commission to reduce CAP outlays by implementing cuts in aids, ceilings on intervention and lower Community participation in structural programmes.[55] Germany had been willing as early as 1968 to introduce quantitative limits on intervention buying and stocks,[56] so it was only a small concession to accept the concepts of co-responsibility and stabilizers. As a result of strong German pressure, however, the new system affected less than one quarter of holdings in Germany (Table 6.2).

Because Germany had more non-competitive farms, it was also more willing than France to consider quantitative controls on production that would tie support to individuals. As early as 1986, Germany got the Community to provide funding for an experimental set-aside programme in one German state. When a Community set-aside programme was finally approved by the Farm Council in 1988, German farmers had the highest take-up rate in the EC.[57]

In summary, the German farm lobby is perhaps the strongest and most resilient in Europe. In spite of government efforts to undercut it during the 1970s, it maintained a dominant role in the national debates that formed the positions taken to the Agricultural Council. There seems little prospect of farmers losing that position to other lobbies, given the overwhelming sympathy and support from the population at large, the continuing absence of any effective countervailing lobby and the distinctive electoral and governance systems in Germany. Because the farm minister represents both his government and the special interests of the farm sector in the EC Farm Council, Germany has been a formidable player in the reform negotiations.

The United Kingdom and the CAP

The partnership forged during the Second World War between the NFU and the agriculture ministry did not survive the UK's accession to the Community. Before 1973 UK agriculture policy was invisible to most people. The ministry and the NFU had a monopoly on farm affairs; each supported the other in the policy process to exclude all offsetting lobbies.[58] The UK public interest coincided with private farm interest — at least as far as they were implemented within the particular UK political system. After 1973, however, the CAP strongly favoured farmers at the expense of both consumers and taxpayers, which was neither in the interest of the government nor the economy. The UK Cabinet, therefore, actively undercut the farm lobby, which ultimately provided the government with greater freedom of action to reform those parts of the CAP which harm the public interest.

The farm lobby in the UK faces difficult conditions. It is divided along regional lines, which reduces the movement's lobbying impact. More importantly, however, the NFU in England and Wales (the largest union) has neither a strong package of non-collective services to encourage farmers to join nor monopoly access to the policy system. Co-operatives market only about 17 per cent of the nation's cereals and have little to do with provision of the means of production, except insurance (through NFU Mutual). Until recently, the key benefit of joining the NFU was the advice it gave on how to get government assistance. When farmers were less educated and the government less active in extension work, this role ensured that farmers could not 'afford not to be a member of the NFU'.[59] Now that farmers are better educated and the government has a much more active extension system to inform farmers of technical and programme opportunities, this is less essential. UK financial deregulation also has increased competition in the insurance and finance sectors, reducing even those benefits. Consequently, the farm lobby now provides little in the way of non-collective benefits to attract and retain members. Meanwhile, consumers have direct access to the Ministry of Agriculture, Forestry and Food (MAFF), while industrialists and environmentalists have direct access to farm debates in Cabinet through other relevant ministers.

The farm movement also weakened as structural changes increased the diversity of interests. NFU annual meetings after the mid-1970s produced frequent disagreement over policy, with large farmers pitted against small farmers and grain farmers confronting livestock producers.[60] After 1980, divisions increased as the measures taken to control cereals and milk production hit larger producers harder. This also led the NFU at times to disagree strongly with its European counterparts. In 1980 the conflicts became so great that the NFU debated and passed a motion at the annual meeting calling for the UK to withdraw from the CAP and implement national support measures.[61]

In general, the public interest set the anti-CAP tone in the UK. The nation as a whole had the worst ratio of costs to benefits (Tables 6.3 and 6.4), the economy faced a large and increasing outflow of funds due to the CAP (Table 6.5) and each incremental addition to wheat prices raised the net outflow, which exacerbated the already large current account deficit (Figure 6.3). The UK government judged that those costs were excessive, given that the UK standard of living was below the EC average.

Majority-party rule and Cabinet and party solidarity generally limited farm influence on the system to voting times. The Cabinet keeps tight control on all European affairs through the European Section of the Cabinet Office, reducing the opportunity for farmers to sway the agricultural minister. Meanwhile, the first-past-the-post, single-member constituency system (with frequent boundary reviews to eliminate inconsistencies in ridings) and declines in the farm population, combined to reduce the electoral power of farmers. By 1981, there were only ten constituencies where the farm vote exceeded 15 per cent; in 1955 there had been 110. Furthermore, dependance on hired labour 'reduce[d] the strength of farmer's lobbies from that indicated by the total labour force proportions.'[62] Howarth concluded in 1985 that there was 'no danger whatever to the Labour

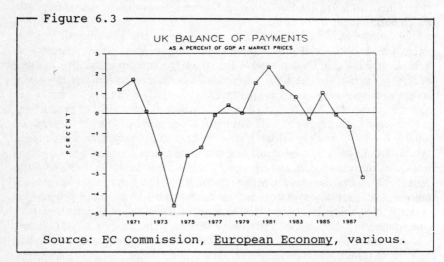

Figure 6.3

UK BALANCE OF PAYMENTS
AS A PERCENT OF GDP AT MARKET PRICES

Source: EC Commission, _European Economy_, various.

Party from losing whatever agricultural vote it has' and although in the past, Conservatives probably 'had some reason to fear offending the farmers' vote', now 'there no longer appears to be any electoral obstacle to the Tories adopting a radical stance on farm policy.'[63]

The NFU offset some of the decline in farm electoral significance during the 1950s, 1960s and early 1970s as it maintained political neutrality and developed a strong working relationship with officials in MAFF.[64] The Agricultural Act of 1947 provided the statutory right for farmers' representatives to be consulted by the government at the annual review of the agricultural industry and the NFU was accepted as the sole voice of farmers.[65] As a result, the farm sector was recognized as 'the one unequivocal example of an economic sector where an interest group has been officially recognized by the state and incorporated into the process of decision making, not merely to represent its members but to play a joint role in the political management of the sector.'[66]

The situation changed rapidly when the UK joined the Community. First, the farm lobby lost the Annual Review and the critical farm policy debate moved to Brussels. Then in 1974, the new Labour government opened the farm policy to other interests. Although MAFF at first 'staunchly resisted any move to open up the agricultural policy community',[67] it eventually accepted the change. The ministers for agriculture after 1974, who were usually both relatively junior members and non-farmers, were not much help because they were given a strong consumer-directed brief by Cabinet.

In line with its entente with the trade unions, Labour began in 1974 to favour consumers through an overvalued green pound and limited price increases. Higher prices, either from devaluations of the green pound or from higher guaranteed prices, would have exacerbated the wage-price inflation spiral the UK was attempting to combat through the social compact with unions. Higher prices also contributed to the balance of payments deficit, which eventually precipitated a payment crisis and opened UK policy to IMF influence. Meanwhile, UK wheat farmers were reaping windfall price rises as the CAP system was introduced in the UK. Consequently, the UK farm lobby did not get the government to support higher prices.

After 1978 the UK approach to the CAP changed. Beginning with the 1979 election of the Conservative government, the UK shifted emphasis in the price debate. The Foreign Office and Treasury advised the new Prime Minister, Margaret Thatcher, that there was no practical or negotiable way to reform the CAP to benefit the UK. North Sea oil, which also began to flow in 1979, quickly pushed the UK current account into surplus. From April 1980 to 1985 the green pound was overvalued, so the UK government could not use it as a bargaining chip in price negotiations. Furthermore, the rebates authorized under Article 131 of the Treaty of Accession ended in 1980, causing a sharp jump in the net cost of the CAP for the UK. The only solution was to squeeze the price system through the budget lever.[68] The UK government adopted a combination of budget demands and threats of vetoes to attempt to force change in the CAP. This approach, however, provided the UK with little influence over the content of the reforms. The UK agriculture minister neither had the support of the UK farm lobby nor of his fellow ministers. A number of times the UK farm minister appeared to be on the verge of agreement in the Farm Council, only to be undercut by the Prime Minister, Foreign Secretary or Chancellor of the Exchequer. In 1982, 1984 and 1985, for example, those ministers struck budget agreements that did not link directly to reform of the CAP. Therefore, the UK Agriculture Minister found the budget lever next to useless.

Because the agriculture minister and the farm lobby were unable to co-operate, few of the post-1985 reforms in the CAP were proposed by the UK. The UK government instead stuck to its demands for direct price cuts long after the rest of Council had begun to look at other options. Because the government and farmers could not agree on a common approach to EC debates, the resultant changes (including co-responsibility and stabilizer levies) generally were less favourable for UK farmers than almost all other alternatives. Even when the MAFF and the NFU agreed on basic direction, they failed to present a united front in European debates. In 1987, for example, both MAFF and the NFU supported the introduction of set-asides but they failed to agree about whether they should be voluntary and compulsory.

As the farm sector adjusted in the 1980s to the shifts in the underlying power structures, the ministry of agriculture — which is the only remaining sectoral ministry in the UK — sought new ways to justify its existence. The solution chosen, enshrined in section 17 of the Agricultural Act 1986, was to develop MAFF as the ministry of the countryside, in order to promote conservation, rural economic development and rural tourism, in addition to traditional farm interests.[69] This changed mandate challenges the ministry to balance farm and non-farm interests and should further diminish farm influence.

In summary, although the UK became one of the strongest proponents of CAP reform during the 1980s, it failed to influence the direction of reform because its weak farm lobby and peculiar budgetary approach often neutralized its position in the Council. As a result, the emerging cereals policy is not compatible with UK farm interests.

Conclusions

Farm organizations are able to dominate the national interests in Council as long as they maintain large and active memberships, strong bargains with the ministries of agriculture and electoral influence. When the relationships are strong, they can even overcome pressures for change that result from shifts in public interests. The German DBV has done just that. The French farm lobby nearly lost its position in EC policy debates in the 1980s when the French government rejected its historical support for high prices and opted to support the commercial aspirations of farmers. But the farm lobby quickly re-aligned itself behind the French government and thereby increased its influence over EC policy reform. In contrast, farmers in the UK lost their influence during the 1970s and the UK farm policy community entered EC debates divided.

France and Germany naturally came to dominate the farm reform debate because their positions in Council reflected bedrock support within both their governments and farm sectors. In contrast, the UK has not shown staying power in Council debates. The other governments recognize that the UK does not risk serious political backlash if it backs down in the negotiations because the UK position is usually not supported by the farm sector in the first place. Consequently, although the UK acquired greater freedom to set its policy position after 1973, it lost some of its influence in Council.

Notes

1. *The Times*, 3–2–81.
2. *The New Palgrave, V.3* says a Pareto optimal outcome is 'if there exist[s] no other productively feasible allocation which ma[kes] all individuals in the economy at least as well-off and at least one strictly better off, than they were initially.'
3. Frankel (1970), p. 39, argues that 'foreign policy is generally conceived as being based upon the concept of "national interest" which is deemed to represent the whole society and not to be a mere compromise between partial interests.' This concept of foreign policy revolves around national security and defence, which are both pure public goods. Commodity trade is not a public good and therefore the national interest in this area is not necessarily the same as the public interest.
4. Olson (1965), p. 2.
5. *Ibid.*, p. 16.
6. Keeler (1987), p. 265.
7. Zietz and Valdés (1988), p. 20.
8. Buckwell *et al.* (1982), p. 158.
9. J. de Veer, 'National effects of CAP trade liberalization', in Tarditi *et al.* (1989), p. 107.
10. *Op. cit.*
11. U. Koester in Buckwell *et al.* (1982), p. 63.
12. L. Mahé and C. Moreddu, 'Analysis of CAP trade policy changes', in Tarditi *et a'l.* (1989), p. 91.
13. Agra Europe (1983), p. 73.
14. Duchêne, Szczepanik and Legg (1985), p. 95.
15. Neville–Rolfe (1984), p. 104.
16. Keeler (1987), pp. 9, 12–13.
17. Neville–Rolfe (1984), p. 132.
18. *Ibid.*, pp. 51 and 55.
19. *Ibid.*, p. 112.
20. Keeler (1987), p. 167.
21. *Eurobarometre #27*, Table A40.
22. *Financial Times*, 16–6–80.
23. Hayward (1982), p. 126.
24. Petit *et al.* (1987), p. 46.
25. Keeler (1987), pp. 219–22.
26. Neville–Rolfe (1984), p. 131.
27. Franklin (1988), p. 30
28. Keeler (1987), p. 105, notes that votes in the lobby were based on dues paying members, who tended to be wealthy Northern cereals producers rather than poorer Southern farmers.
29. Neville–Rolfe (1984), pp. 17 and 132.
30. *Financial Times*, 8–11–78.
31. George (1985), p. 59.
32. Tangermann (1979), p. 243.
33. Foxall (1982), p. 54.
34. Keeler (1987), p. 262.

35. Andrlik (1981), p. 106.
36. Ardagh (1987), p. 129.
37. Andrlik (1981), p. 107.
38. Keeler (1987), p. 270.
39. *Walll Street Journal (Europe)*, 5–3–87.
40. Bulmer and Paterson (1987), p. 92.
41. Tangermann (1979), p. 249.
42. Bulmer and Paterson (1987), p. 149.
43. Philip (1989), p. 4.
44. Ardagh (1987), p. 141.
45. *Eurobarometre #27*, Table A40.
46. Petit *et al.* (1987), p. 56.
47. Tangermann (1979), p. 250–1.
48. Neville–Rolfe (1984), pp. 90–3.
49. Philip (1989), p. 11.
50. Bulmer and Paterson (1987), p. 72.
51. *Ibid.*, p. 105.
52. Edinger (1986), p. 192.
53. *The Guardian*, 20–10–80.
54. *Wall Street Journal (Europe)*, 5–3–87.
55. Neville–Rolfe (1984), p. 282.
56. Rosenthal (1975), p. 82.
57. Phillips (1989), p. 245.
58. Howarth (1985), p. 104.
59. *Ibid.*, p. 108.
60. *Ibid.*, pp. 109–10.
61. *The Times*, 13–2–80.
62. Harvey (1982), p. 183.
63. Howarth (1985), pp. 116–7.
64. Cox, Lowe and Winter (1986), pp. 188–9, says the relationship has been called 'clientelism', 'symbiotic' and 'proprietorial'.
65. Howarth (1985), p. 107.
66. Cox, Lowe and Winter (1986), p. 185.
67. *Ibid.*, p. 196.
68. *The Guardian*, 29–11–79.
69. *The Economist*, 10–9–88.

Chapter 7

Price policy decisions

Community farm policy decisions are heavily influenced by discussions leading up to the price debate among the farm ministers, but the key negotiations are always conducted within the Council itself. The main pressures on policy decisions arise either through the formal policy development process (Chapters 4 and 5) or from the national sources (Chapter 6). This chapter examines how the often-conflicting private and public and national and Community interests have been accommodated in the Council.

In the early years, the Commission advised, petitioned, cajoled and threatened the Council to adopt its proposals but had little success. The peculiar system of price, exchange rate and structural assistance in place in the 1970s enabled the Council, with or without Commission co-operation, to fashion price packages to satisfy virtually all the member states. But by 1980 changes in the power structures impeded Council efforts to strike bargains that satisfied all national interests. When renationalization of the CAP appeared imminent (see Chapter 6 on Germany and the UK in the 1970s), the Commission was forced either to relinquish control over the CAP or to reassert its authority and vision.

As early as 1977 the Commission tried to use its expertise to fashion a new role as a conciliator and bridge-builder in the Council. When that attempt failed, it used its power to propose as a bargaining lever. By 1984 the farm ministers had demonstrated that they were unable to manage the system either to their or the Commission's satisfaction, so the Agricultural Commissioner stepped in and used his own powers to manage the wheat market, to bargain with the Council and, in some cases, to override or offset Council decisions. As a result, the Commission dragged the Agricultural Council 'with much kicking and screaming' to reform the policy.[1] After 1984, real and, often, the nominal guaranteed ECU prices for average quality wheat dropped each year, while the Commission changed the intervention system (e.g. delayed payments, shortened buying-in periods and reduced monthly price increments) to reduce market prices. By 1988, the unlimited price guarantee for wheat was gone, official intervention prices merely represented notional prices that were often unattainable in the market, intervention operated as a buyer of last resort and prices were automatically adjusted based on market conditions. The system became significantly more market-directed and automatic than in earlier times. This chapter explains how the Commission managed this reform.

Key bargains in the system

The decision-making process revolves around the Council of Agricultural Ministers and the surrounding web of interlocking bargains. Council debate is usually proscribed and directed by the strong bargains between the French government and French farmers and among the German Ministry of Agriculture, the political parties and the DBV. In addition, the German and French governments have a loose bilateral relationship that at times transcends the Council chamber to form the basis for resolving policy impasses (e.g. the Stocktaking in 1975 and introduction of the EMS in 1979 and cereals co-responsibility in 1986).

COPA had its greatest influence during the 1970s, when it used its numerical might and access through the President-in-Council to influence policy decisions. Meanwhile, other pressure groups, which gained access to the Council only in the late 1970s, found that their generally weak and divided membership was no match for their adversaries or the issues.

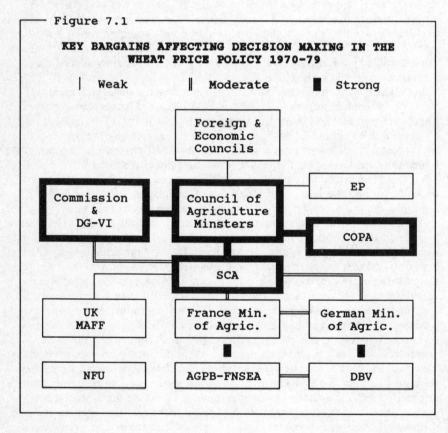

Figure 7.1

KEY BARGAINS AFFECTING DECISION MAKING IN THE WHEAT PRICE POLICY 1970-79

Relations at the decision-making level in Europe began to change about 1979. The inter-state bargains in the Commission, COPA, ESC and EP began to break down and the critical intra-state agreements — between the national farm organizations and the member state ministries of agriculture — became more important. The shifting production and finance structures weakened COPA and caused the farm interests in France, Germany and the UK to diverge. French farmers, anxious to expand and export, discovered they had less in common with smaller, less competitive German farmers. This strained the critical bargain between Germany and France in the SCA and Council. By 1979, the UK government had downgraded its bargain with the NFUs and became the key swing agent in the price review. Instead of developing any continuing bargains, the UK switched partners almost annually, alternately supporting its farmers, the Commission or just going it alone. Although this kept the UK in the middle of the debate, it did not contribute to its influence.

After 1979 the EP gained some influence through the budget and its agricultural section, but in the end found it could do little more than constrain Council options. Because the interests in the Assembly widened after the election, it seldom spoke with enough authority to impose its opinion. Furthermore, as the Commission's negotiating strategy evolved from 1977 to 1988, both the EP and ESC lost power to influence decisions because they were seldom consulted about the specific proposals.[2]

Pressure groups were also pushed to the margins during the 1980s. COPA, in particular, found that it had less impact on Council because it could neither produce influential opinions on issues critical to the debate nor organize lobbies that represented more than a single interest. Other Eurogroups, meanwhile, were forced to shift their focus toward non-price issues (e.g. food quality, structural programmes) and therefore found that they had little influence on the price review when they had their annual courtesy visit with the President-in-Council.

The Agricultural Council also lost some power. Increasingly during the 1980s the Commission or individual farm ministers placed farm issues on the agendas of the Budget, Economic, Foreign and European Councils. For most of the period this strategy did not harm the power of the Agricultural Council because the other ministers failed completely to solve the problems. But the 1988 European Council succeeded where the others failed. Now the farm ministers risk the Commission referring the price package to a joint Budget-Farm Council meeting if they exceed budget guidelines (Figure 7.2).

Last, and perhaps most importantly, the makeup of the Council affected policy decisions. In the 1970s the membership and voting rules that applied to other policy areas did not truly matter for agricultural affairs because all decisions were unanimous (after the Luxembourg Compromise of 1966). In 1982 the Council began to decide by qualified majority votes and the distribution of votes began to matter. As the Community grew in 1980 and again in 1986, the voting power of France, Germany and the UK (10 votes each) was diluted, so that now their interests can be overridden by the other countries (largely with Mediterranean concerns). After the 1986 expansion, it takes more than two of the three large wheat producers to block a Council majority decision (i.e. 23 votes out of total of 76 votes). Previously two of the countries working together could block a decision.

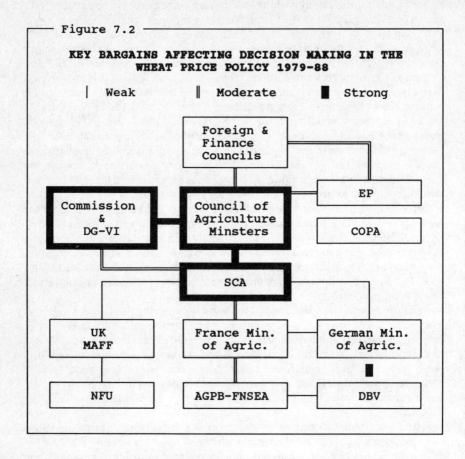

Figure 7.2

KEY BARGAINS AFFECTING DECISION MAKING IN THE WHEAT PRICE POLICY 1979-88

| Weak   ‖ Moderate   ■ Strong

Foreign & Finance Councils

Commission & DG-VI

Council of Agriculture Minsters

EP

COPA

SCA

UK MAFF

France Min. of Agric.

German Min. of Agric.

NFU

AGPB-FNSEA

DBV

Negotiations and outcomes (1973–9)

During the 1970s, national interests came to the fore and 'issue linkage and package broking rather than majority voting' became the means of conducting Council business.[3] After 1974 the 'growth of the new three-tier presidential-ministerial-civil service decision-making body ha[d] shifted substantially the balance of power in the Community.'[4] The national ministers in Council were able to fashion price packages that satisfied most national interests, often in conflict with Commission plans.

The Commission, however, remained integrally involved in the decision process. Commission President Roy Jenkins in 1977 characterized its role as 'conciliator and bridge-builder between member governments.'[5] In particular, the Commission courted support for its overall price goals formulated with the objective method by using its prerogative to propose ad hoc agri-monetary changes and differentiated product prices. At times this system seemed to work as the Council accepted the need for higher prices over much of the period.

At other times the national governments gained a tactical advantage in the negotiations as they alternately used the agri-monetary system to give their producers price increases in advance, established immutable bottom lines through their domestic processes or forced the debate into higher forums.

A review of the price fixings and related debates over the 1973–9 period demonstrates how these various strategies and tactics, combined with the underlying bargains at the national and Community level, yielded ad hoc price packages that generally favoured farmers.

Beginning in 1973, the new Commission, with Finn Gundelach as the Agricultural Commissioner, attempted to make the price setting more an administrative exercise based on the objective method formula and on automatic agri-monetary rules. If Council had adopted either, it would effectively have transferred power to the Commission, which would have seriously limited the ministers' ability to adjust the price proposals to suit their national interests. History demonstrated that the formula was not objective at all (Chapter 4) while 'any scheme to phase out MCAs would clearly remove a bargaining weapon which [the Agriculture Ministers] . . . found a very useful addition to their armoury.'[6] Council consequently never completely accepted either change. As the objective method completely failed to sway the Council, the Commission was forced to develop a new negotiating strategy.

The Commission then attempted to negotiate with the Council on the specifics of the price packages. As early as 1971 the Commission proposals to Council were less detailed than in the first years of the CAP; details were left to be completed during discussions with the national administrations.[7]

Price bargaining took two main forms. First, the Commission offered to negotiate different average price increases for all commodities. In 1977 and 1978 the Commission offered a higher overall price rise during the negotiation phase in an effort to sway the ministers.

Second, and perhaps more importantly, the Commission proposed and encouraged the Council to adopt differential pricing for products, so that deficit products or farm sectors with poor incomes would receive larger price increases. During the entire period of the CAP to 1986, but especially in the 1973–9 period, cereals farmers received least (average 2.3 per cent increase during 1968–86) while milk, beef and sugar producers received relatively more (average increases of 4.8 per cent, 5.5 per cent and 4.2 per cent respectively).[8] It was quite easy to bargain for these changes during the 1970s because there were few controls or restraints on any of the key products. As well, there were many small farmers who still produced a mix of products. Therefore, higher milk, beef or sugar prices could be used to compensate them for lower cereals prices. The Commission also found that it could finesse the price package with offers of differential prices for feed and bread wheat because the distribution of production of those two products varied by country.

Green rates provided the second major bargaining chip in the price review. Although the ultimate goal was the end of all monetary gaps, the Agriculture Commissioner was quite willing to negotiate differential pricing by country through ad hoc adjustments in green rates. The general tendency was to reduce the monetary gaps, but the speed and magnitude of change was largely a matter for negotiation. In 1973–9, France generally wanted to close its monetary gap faster than proposed by DG–VI (yielding higher farm prices) while Germany and the UK wanted to go slower (to protect higher farm prices in Germany and to prevent higher prices in the UK).

After 1976 the national governments and the Commission also allowed the diffusion of different representative rates for different products, so that national governments and the Commission together could tailor a specific set of agricultural prices to suit their needs. Countries tended to devalue green rates for products with short product cycles (e.g. milk, pigs and vegetable products) more rapidly and further than green rates for cereals. The Commission and Council used this in a number of years to facilitate successful bargaining.

Whenever Commission proposals were inconsistent with national interests, however, the farm ministers used the agri-monetary system to scuttle them. France, with a generally weak currency, had great potential to offset price restraint or to upset the price negotiations by devaluing its green rates and ensuring that its producers got a price rise. Meanwhile, the UK had room during 1973–80 to devalue its green rate (during 1973–8 the UK accession agreement also allowed it to accelerate or slow the rise of UK prices toward European levels). In contrast, Germany had a consistently strong currency and was unable to change its green rates to provide its producers with national currency price rises to offset Commission proposals.

Farm ministers also obstructed the Commission with appeals to national bargains. They could effectively stop a Commission proposal if they demonstrated unyielding national interests. Elections were the best excuse for not accepting a Commission proposal, but governments also made solemn promises to the farm lobby (c.g. France in 1975), got official Cabinet direction (Germany) or referred to parliamentary votes (UK) to sway the other farm ministers in the Council. Some member states also attempted to elevate farm debates to other European forums in the hope that farm interests could be overcome. The UK frequently tried to get the European Council or Council of Finance Ministers to decide farm policy. This tactic usually stalemated the process, however, because those forums lacked the expertise and contacts to fashion compromises. When these strategies were used, the Commission found it extremely difficult to salvage any of its proposals. Rather, it usually attempted to limit the damage from such a package.

As a result, the 1970s were not regarded as a successful time for the Commission. Neville–Rolfe argues that during 1973–7 'the locusts consumed.'[9] While farmers were still united at the European level and maintained dominant bargains with the German and French governments, the Commission found it had to make major concessions to farm interests to get its packages accepted in Council (see Appendix for Council decisions for wheat).

The 1977 price review heralded a change in the relations between the Commission and Council. The Commission posted a small moral victory because for the first time it did not compromise its original proposals. The Commission had proposed to complete the new wheat reference price system and to raise cereals prices by 3.0 per cent, to revalue the green DM and to devalue both the green franc and pound, but the farm ministers wanted to raise prices by 3.5 per cent and implement only modest green rate changes. The Commission refused to propose a 'compromise' different from its first proposal, which forced the farm ministers to act unanimously to enact the price package.

The negotiating pendulum oscillated during the 1978 price review and only swung toward the Commission proposals when it used its powers under Article 8 of Reg. (EEC) 2727/75 to establish a special intervention for bread wheat. The national governments outmanoeuvred the Commission initially by using the green rates weapon, but in the end the Commission finessed a lower increase in the wheat reference price (1 per cent rather than the 3.1 per cent originally proposed) with an offer to create a new special intervention for bread wheat of only minimum quality. This bit of legerdemain reconciled German demands for higher prices (by raising prices between August and October when 80 per cent of the German wheat harvest was usually marketed) while satisfying French and UK insistence on price restraint (which was desired to combat inflation).

The Commission in 1979 tried to build on its success by proposing a cereals price freeze and automatic realignment of green rates, but the price review was again upset by the national governments. Although the Commission was instrumental in resolving the differences that held up the introduction of the European Monetary System, it was ultimately excluded from the decision on the price package. The Commission accepted the 'gentlemen's agreement' of the eight members of the Agricultural Council (the UK did not participate) to dismantle MCAs 'pragmatically', provided that changes did not cause national currency price cuts that create 'economic difficulties for the member state concerned', but was unwilling to provide a price rise for cereals to facilitate a revaluation of the DM green rate. In the end, the Council rewrote the Commission package and raised the wheat reference price 1.5 per cent, devalued both the green pound and green franc and revalued the green DM 1 per cent.

Gundelach was angered by the Council decision to rewrite the 1979 price package.[10] A few days later the Commission concurred and unanimously denounced the farm deal. The Council decision in 1979 forced the Commission to rethink its tactics. It had failed to get Council to accept its approach to prices during the late 1970s, at least partly because its role as a conciliator in Council neutralized its own natural supporters. Eurogroups were increasingly ineffective because proposals revised during the negotiations were seldom publicized and never resubmitted to advisory groups (i.e. the EP, ESC, COPA and BEUC).[11] The Commission therefore could not call for support from those groups. COPA, when it found it could not work effectively at the European level, had little choice but to encourage its member organizations to work more closely with their national ministries of agriculture. The Commission recognized that unless it changed its approach, the CAP would slowly but surely be renationalized.

The system in transition (1980–3)

Between 1980 and 1983 the Commission seriously tried to implement automatic pricing (via the guarantee threshold system) and an automatic agri-monetary system in order to reduce the role for political gamesmanship in the price reviews. It offered a combination of differentiated prices, ad hoc green rate adjustments and, in 1981, 1982 and 1983, 'monetary events' to win support for its proposals, but found that the Council was not receptive.[12] The farm ministers and government leaders seemed interested only in their national problems. Economic recession, high inflation, rising unemployment and disgruntled voters encouraged national governments to press for greater farm support.

The 1980 price review was typical of the situation the Commission faced. The UK demanded and got a 5 per cent devaluation immediately before the review and then announced that it wanted both a price freeze and a budget rebate. When the newly-elected EP rejected the 1980 budget and called for a 'stringent' price policy, the Commission responded with proposals for restrained prices and a higher co-responsibility levy for milk. But France and Germany both faced general elections soon and wanted price rises. They noted that higher world prices and a weaker ECU ensured that resources provided by the provisional twelfths rule were sufficient to allow greater price increases.

The debate ebbed and flowed and the farm ministers only slowly developed a price package. When Farm Minister Peter Walker was directed by the UK Cabinet not to accept the price package until the UK got a satisfactory budget rebate, Giscard, who saw a presidential election on the horizon, threatened to pay FF 5 B to French farmers as income support if prices were not set by June 1. The French foreign minister also threatened that the other eight members would proceed if the UK blocked the developing price package. In the last week of May the farm ministers sent the dispute to a Summit without success. Finally, on May 30 (one day before the French deadline), the General Council agreed on a UK budget rebate for 1980 and 1981 and the UK lifted its veto on the price package.

The May 30 deal also gave the Commission a 'Mandate' to review the CAP to find ways to restrain costs and control surpluses. The foreign ministers of France, Germany and the UK generally agreed that CAP outlays should be restrained and both Germany and the UK thought the Commission was going in the right direction when it proposed co-responsibility as the fourth principle of the CAP. Gundelach fully intended to pursue this approach when he was reappointed Agricultural Commissioner, but he died a few days into his new term.

Before Paul Dalsager, the new Agricultural Commissioner, had a chance to release the price proposals for 1981, France demanded a 10 per cent price rise for 1981–2 and announced it would pay special grants worth FF 4.1 B to support French farmers. President Giscard, who sought re-election in 1981, was concerned about farm incomes in the face of the 1980 bumper wheat crop. Germany and the UK, in contrast, called for the 1 per cent VAT ceiling on Community outlays to remain, which appeared to rule out any price rises.

The Commission, nevertheless, pushed ahead and proposed to introduce a guarantee threshold system for cereals. Then world prices began to rise, so that by early January EC prices could rise 5 per cent without breaching the 1 per cent VAT limit and by the end of January even higher prices would be possible. The Commission proposed that prices rise an average 8 per cent (bread wheat by 4 per cent) in an effort to gain acceptance of the guarantee threshold system and its proposed significant revaluations for the green DM and pound.

Germany generally agreed with the Commission proposals because industrial unions in the Federal Republic were settling for 5 per cent that year, but the UK was unhappy with the price cuts being forced in the cereals sector (it did not accept that the UK should be the only country to face lower prices) while France wanted even higher farm prices. In March the Commission proposed a technical fix to the ECU to solve the conflict. When the Community introduced the European Currency Unit (ECU) for the CAP in 1979, it created the potential to change individual monetary gaps by realigning the central EMS rates. In practice, only the pound and lira central rates could be adjusted to suit agricultural interests (without affecting other sectors) because they were not linked closely to the EMS. The Commission offered to have the Standing Monetary Committee revalue the notional central EMS rate for the recently strong UK pound by 22.74 per cent and devalue the perennially weak Italian lira by 6.4 per cent, which would effectively revalue the ECU and narrow the German monetary gap by 2.5 per cent. This resolved the green rate negotiations because, in addition to the reduction in German MCAs, it eliminated the UK positive monetary gap (without affecting UK farm prices) and provided France with a new negative monetary gap (that allowed for a 2.8 per cent devaluation immediately before the presidential election).

The Commission appeared to have Council approval for cereals co-responsibility without any compensatory price increase when the EP resolved that prices should rise by 12 per cent. The Commission declared its position had been undercut and promptly gave way. The price package, set before the French presidential election, provided for a generous price rise (10 per cent for bread wheat) but merely approved co-responsibility in principle (implementation was delayed until 1982–3). The Council, however, did allow the Commission to introduce the first of what was to be a series of adjustments to the minimum quality standards required for intervention purchases. The intervention agencies henceforward would not purchase bread wheat that did not have at least 10.5 per cent protein content.

In June 1981 the Commission's final report to the Council on the Mandate confirmed that it wanted co-responsibility for surplus cereals production in addition to restrained pricing. At the Luxembourg Summit the Commission convinced the heads of government to delegate debate of the reforms to a special ambassadorial-level committee mostly of Committee of Permanent Representative (COREPER) members, not the SCA, to keep it away from the farm ministers. The committee reviewed the proposals during the following months and reported to the 1981 London Summit, where for the first time in many years agricultural matters were handled by other than agricultural ministers. But the heads of government failed to agree on CAP reform and the debate returned to the Agricultural Council.

Negotiations in 1982 opened badly. Mitterand announced a FF 5.56 B farm support package for 1982 and demanded that prices in France rise by about the rate of inflation (14 per cent). Prime Minster Pierre Mauroy also refused to accept any link between farm prices and the UK budget rebate, which was back on the agenda. Meanwhile, UK Foreign Secretary Peter Carrington threatened to veto the price package until a new budget deal was set. The Commission then produced a comprehensive package which introduced the guarantee threshold system for cereals and revalued both the German and UK green rates. The Commission again attempted to finesse the green rate changes by revaluing the theoretical green central rate for the pound by 8.27 per cent. Combined with devaluations of the central rates for Belgium and Luxembourg, the net effect was to revalue the ECU by 0.3 per cent, which reduced the German monetary gap by a corresponding amount. But Germany rejected the remaining green re-valuation. Meanwhile, France continued to press for prices to rise at least 12 per cent and threatened to force majority voting in Council to override any UK veto; the Commission agreed that it would support majority voting.

The Commission reopened negotiations in April and eventually accepted the Council President's proposals. The final package raised wheat ECU prices by 8.5 per cent, implemented a smaller green DM adjustment and introduced a modified guarantee threshold system. At the insistence of France and Ireland, the system compared three-year average production levels with the threshold level, adjusted for any imports of cereal substitutes over 15 Mt. The price cuts (in the succeeding year) would be in steps of 1 per cent for each full 1 Mt of over-production.

In May, before a UK budget deal was agreed, the Council put the package to the vote and the UK, supported by Denmark and Greece, refused to participate. Nevertheless, the vote passed. The Council refused to accept the UK veto because it was simply a negotiating measure and not a matter of the content of the package. The UK was unable to do much about it because it also at that time sought EC support for its embargo against Argentina during the Falkland War. The Commission subsequently offset some of the price rise when, at the beginning of the marketing year, it raised the medium quality standards for bread wheat. To receive the full reference price wheat had to have 11.5 per cent protein, as well as pass all the other quality tests.

The Commission tried to make a significant reduction in the EC-world price gap in 1983. The newly implemented guarantee threshold system dictated that wheat prices should be cut and CAP outlays for 1983 appeared set to exceed the budget (even without price increases for 1983–4) because of a record harvest in 1982. After a difficult internal debate, the Commission finally offered a 4 per cent increase for wheat, reduced by 1 per cent because production in 1980–2 exceeded the guarantee threshold by 1.4 Mt. Prices in Germany and the UK would be further reduced by green rate revaluations. In March, the EMS currencies were again realigned, which created a record 13 per cent positive monetary gap for Germany and an even greater negative gap for France. Germany rejected the proposed 2.8 per cent revaluation in the green rate (because ECU prices were proposed to rise only 3 per cent). Kiechle as President-in-Office toured the capitals and then reconvened the Council to present a slightly altered price package. The UK accepted neither a proposed 2.5 per cent revaluation of the pound (added by Kiechle to win Irish support) nor any increase in ECU prices. The Commission also refused to modify its proposals in line with Kiechle's compromise, which stalemated the Council because it could not agree unanimously to change the package. In May, with the marketing year already started for many products, Germany reconvened the Council and recom-mended the theoretical central rate for the pound be revalued to the market rate (which effectively revalued the ECU by 1 per cent); the UK agreed, provided France and Germany would accept the Commission package. In the end, the Council quickly concluded the price package, with ECU prices unchanged from the Commission proposals — the first time ever — and national currency prices only slightly higher than proposed.

After the Council agreement, the Commission got the cereals management committee to accept two reforms that cut the effective support for wheat. The Commission decided to limit special intervention purchases of bread wheat to 750,000 tonnes in each of August and September and 1.5 Mt in October and imposed a 5 ECU/t non-refundable security deposit to be remitted as part of any intervention offer.

Agriculture was near the top of the EC agenda for the last six months of 1983 but little was done. Both the Stuttgart and Athens Summits failed to resolve any issues.

Council-Commission relations had reached a turning point. The Commission knew that it could no longer manage the price review using only moral suasion or manipulation of price offers. The Commission strategy for negotiations with the Council was thwarted by changes in the economic environment throughout the 1970s and early 1980s. The strategy of 'buying' price restraint on some products (such as cereals) with offsetting improvements for other products was less tenable by the mid-1980s: other products had come under tighter market regimes (e.g. by 1977 there was a co-responsibility levy on milk) and new production technologies were becoming more product-specific, which made it difficult for (especially large) farmers to change their production plans. The Commission recognized that it was unable to manage the system by operating as a 'conciliator and bridge-builder'. In each year that the Commission attempted to bargain using only adjusted price packages, the Council took everything offered and more. The Commission so far had offered what the Council could do on its own.

But Council successes during 1980–4 masked significant change in the member states. During the early 1980s the government-farmer bargains in the UK and France were continually changing. The time was ripe for reform.

Price reform (1984–8)

The Commission finally began to achieve genuine reform after 1983. During the 1980–3 period, the Commission had pushed to make wheat pricing more market directed, at first through the annual price review and then with the operation of the guarantee threshold system. By 1983 it appeared the system might work, but the 1984 and 1985 price reviews demonstrated the difficulty with that approach. Price bargaining had proved ineffective and the 'monetary event' was impossible once the pound weakened in 1985.

Beginning in 1986, the Commission took the initiative and used its market management powers to push through a series of reforms that made prices more automatic and less open to the influence of individual member states. The Commission began to offer changes in market structures (called related measures; Table 7.1) and permit national income supports to finesse its reforms. The Commission consequently was able to set the agenda and force real reform during 1984–8.

The fundamental shift in some of the key power structures (especially in the financial markets and production systems) assisted the Commission. First, higher interest rates throughout Europe during the 1980s placed a higher opportunity cost on delays in payments for intervention. Because most farmers in the

Table 7.1 Related measures enacted by the Commission under Reg. (EEC) 2727/75 and impact on prices

Year	Measure	Impact	Used
Art. 7.5:	**Intervention (Commission sets specific rules)**		
1981	Minimum protein set at 10.5% for bread wheat	n.a.	yes
1982	Bread quality for bread wheat raised to 11.5% protein	n.a.	yes
1983	Delay intervention payments by 4 months for cereals	−4.0%	yes
1985	Shorten delay in payments to 3 months for cereals (2 months for small farmers)	+1.0%	yes
1986	Limit intervention to Dec. 1–Ap. 30	n.a.	no
1989	Reduce value of transport subsidies and number of intervention stores	n.a.	no
Art. 8:	**Special intervention (Commission sets specific rules)**		
1978	Begins for minimum quality bread wheat (continues to 1985)	n.a.	yes
1983	Limited purchases to 0.75 Mt in Aug.–Sept. and 1.5 Mt in October and levied 5 ECU/t security fee	n.a.	yes
1984	Same limitations as in 1984	n.a.	yes
1985	End of minimum quality bread wheat intervention	n.a.	delayed
Art. 9:	**Carry-over payments and other (Commission sets rules)**		
1986	Proposed cut in carryover payments	n.a.	no
1987	Threatened to change cereals rules to cut prices	n.a.	no

Sources: *COMs, Financial Times, Agra Europe, ASC,* and H-GCA (various), *Marketing Notes*

1980s borrowed heavily, each month of delay in payments equalled a 1 per cent price cut. Second, after 1979, EC wheat producers grew and marketed more wheat than was consumed in the Community, so market prices would have dipped below the intervention price without the operation of the intervention agencies. Delays for intervention payments, limits to intervention buying, or adjustments to special intervention rules and carry-over payments, therefore, all had a direct impact on market prices.

By 1984 the situation was ripe for change. All the major countries had completed their elections and for the first time the Community faced a real budget constraint. The Commission estimated that at current prices the EC budget would reach 0.997 per cent of VAT, just a shade lower than the 1 per cent limit. Even before the Commission presented its proposals, it announced that it would use its authority under Reg.(EEC) 2727/75 to delay all cereals intervention payments after January 1 by four months (the usual delay was one month), which effectively cut the real value of support by 3–4 per cent.

The Commission proposed in 1984 to freeze wheat prices, to revalue significantly both the green DM and the green pound and to allow only a modest franc devaluation. Germany balked and threatened to veto the large devaluation. The

UK was more concerned with getting a new budget agreement than with the actual price level while France adopted a conciliatory attitude (as President of Council). Mitterand served notice to the French farm lobby that he would not tolerate protests in support of their 4 per cent price request and threatened to prosecute any farmers who damaged public buildings. Then in Council, France proposed a new price package that would actually cut wheat prices by 1 per cent and reduce MCAs by even more. Germany, under pressure from the DBV, proposed instead a green ECU to replace the existing ECU-based agri-monetary system. The Agricultural Council eventually agreed in March that the wheat price would be cut 1 per cent, that the green ECU would be introduced and that Germany could introduce after 1 January 1985 a 3 per cent VAT refund to compensate farmers for the deflationary effects of the reduced DM monetary gap (the Commission had contributed to the solution by approving German plans to provide national direct income support). Existing monetary gaps would be dismantled in three stages: at the start of the 1984–5 marketing year, on 1 January 1985 and completely by the start of 1987–8. The package was put in jeopardy in May, however, when the Commission denied permission for the German government to pay farmers a 5 per cent VAT refund beginning in July; Chancellor Kohl had requested permission in an effort to improve CDU prospects in the EP election. Meanwhile, the EP withheld the UK's 1983 budget refund and the UK government retaliated by withholding formal approval for the package.

The heads of government met at the Fontainebleau Summit at the end of June and resolved all the outstanding disputes. The European Council agreed to give the UK a rebate worth 1 B ECU in 1984 and rebates equal to 66 per cent of its net contribution in future years, to give Germany a smaller but still significant rebate from the future cost of the CAP and to raise the VAT limit to 1.4 per cent, effective 1986 (with interim measures until then). The government leaders also overruled the Commission and approved Germany's request to pay a 5 per cent VAT refund effective 1 July 1984. Furthermore, the Summit gave the Finance Council authority to veto future price packages if outlays looked to exceed the average growth over the past three years.[13] Although the Commission was forced to concede the size and timing of the aid for Germany, it played a critical role in the negotiations, because as guardian of the Treaty, it had the authority to challenge national aids in the European Court of Justice.

The 1984 decisions on the budget and the agri-monetary system set the stage for further reform. The Fontainebleau agreement ensured that the UK share of additional spending was to be only 7 per cent (rather than 20 per cent) while Germany's share was reduced marginally. As a result, the UK had less interest in budget-saving reforms and the Commission lost a key ally.[14] But the redistribution of the burden made France a major contributor to the budget, which affected the way in which it looked at Community policies in the following years.[15] Also, the new green ECU system, initially resisted by the Commission, eventually enhanced the prospects for reform. Although it raised guaranteed prices in weak currency countries with each EMS realignment, it largely removed the pressure for ECU prices to rise to accommodate green rate revaluations. The new system also firmly established the validity of national income aids to support particularly disadvantaged producers or countries. Henceforward, ECU prices could be set based on market conditions rather than social concerns.

Hans Andriessen, the new Agricultural Commissioner in 1985, was immediately presented with an ideal opportunity to cut prices. The record cereals crop in 1984 had pushed the three-year average production more than 5 Mt over the guarantee threshold and triggered a 5 per cent price cut. The EP further strengthened the Commission position when it rejected the 1985 budget and forced the Community to operate with provisional twelfths. DG–VI proposed an average 2 per cent increase in prices, but the Commission instead voted 12 to 2 to raise prices only 1.5 per cent. When the 5 per cent guarantee threshold penalty was assessed, wheat prices would fall 3.6 per cent. In addition, the Commission pushed for further revaluation of the green DM, which would force German wheat prices down 4.1 per cent. At one extreme, the UK pushed for a flat 5 per cent ECU price cut while, at the other extreme, COPA demanded that prices rise 4–5 per cent (which was a concession because the objective method indicated prices should rise 7.8 per cent). Germany rejected the complete proposal and instead called for tighter quality controls, termination of intervention buying for feed–grade wheats and a freeze of institutional prices.[16] Perhaps the greatest surprise was that France sided with the Commission against Germany. It saw the price cut as a 'precondition for the continued expansion of the cereals sector' and viewed the German stand as a threat to the long-term commercial prospects for French cereals farmers.[17]

Kiechle promptly raised the stakes and promised German farmers that cereals prices would not be cut in DM terms. When the CDU lost some of the vote in state elections in North–Rhine Westphalia, the German cabinet backed Kiechle: Kohl appealed to the Commission not to push for the price cut while Josef Strauss, the Premier of Bavaria and a CSU leader, publicly supported a veto. The Agricultural Council reconvened in mid-May and approved by a qualified majority the 1985–6 prices for all products except cereals and rapeseed. The Commission then offered to moderate the cereals price cut to 2 per cent and finally to 1.8 per cent. But, when the issue was again put to the Council in June, Germany formally vetoed the prices. With the marketing year fast approaching, the Commission announced that it would adopt the 1.8 per cent price cut as an 'interim precautionary measure'; it interpreted the failure to take a decision as leaving it free to choose how to regulate the market. Kiechle threatened to compensate German farmers directly, which the Commission vowed to contest in the European Court of Justice. The Commission and Kiechle finally reached a compromise in June: Kiechle accepted the price cut in exchange for a reduction of one month in the EC delay in payments for cereals intervention (and approval for Germany to provide funds to reduce the delay further by one month for small farmers) and for extension of the special intervention for 3 Mt of bread wheat. Germany was placated as those measures allowed German farm-gate prices to remain relatively constant but it certainly was not in favour of further reform.

The Commission remained determined to press ahead. It released in July (against the wishes of one German Commissioner) the *Green Paper*, which proposed alternative policy options for the cereals sector, including a new co-responsibility levy in place of the guarantee threshold system, set-asides, support for alternative crops and export development and direct income payments. France accepted the general outline of the proposals but the UK preferred direct price cuts and Germany insisted that price support was essential to maintain farm incomes. The consultative bodies examined the report and provided opinions but little consensus developed. Before the year ended the Commission decided that guaranteed prices could not be cut directly because of German opposition. Instead, DG–VI prepared a detailed plan to rationalize the cereals sector by use of a new co-responsibility levy and a realignment of feed and bread wheat prices.

The Commission's 1986 price package proposed to implement DG–VI's plan. The reference price and special intervention for bread wheat were to be eliminated, feed wheat prices were to be cut, co-responsibility was to be introduced and intervention was to be closed until after the harvest. When the CDU lost support in German state elections in April (and feared losses in a state election in Lower Saxony in June which could have threatened the majority of the CDU/CSU/FDP coalition in the upper house), Kiechle promised to provide German farmers with up to DM 1 B direct income support if the prices were inadequate. When 50,000 German farmers protested against the price package, Kiechle got Cabinet support to veto the Commission package. Meanwhile, the EP and the UK sided with the Commission.

When the Council next met, the Commission regained control of the negotiations. By the end of the meeting the ministers had agreed by a qualified majority to implement most of the reforms: feed wheat prices were cut by up to 5 per cent from the common wheat intervention prices; co-responsibility was introduced; intervention buying was only open October to May (September 1 with an additional month payment delay); the reference price for bread wheat was replaced with a 3.59 ECU premium for wheat with more than 14 per cent protein; quality standards for intervention were raised to the old bread wheat standards; the monthly increments were cut 4.7 per cent and delayed until the shortened buying-in period began in October; and the green franc and pound were devalued 1.5 per cent. The Commission overcame German resistance by tailoring the co-responsibility system to German needs. It was levied only on cereals marketed (Germany uses a higher proportion of its cereals on farm as feed) and small farmers were to receive aid to offset the levy on the first 25 tonnes marketed. As shown in Table 6.2, that ensured that only about 18 per cent of German farm holdings were affected by the levy. The Commission also approved German plans to provide its farmers with DM 500 million in direct aid. Andriessen thus successfully introduced co-responsibility and tightened the intervention system for wheat through a judicious use of technical fixes, national aids, direct EC payments to small farmers and devaluations.

The 1987 price package was first delayed by the German federal election in January and then by disagreement in the Commission. Finally, in mid-February the Commission released proposals to freeze bread wheat prices, to cut feed wheat prices, to eliminate the green DM agri-monetary gap and to tighten intervention rules. Kiechle retorted that the proposals amounted to a 'declaration of war'.[18] The Commission in an unprecedented meeting between the seventeen Commissioners and the German cabinet offered to provide direct income payments from the EC budget in an attempt to persuade Germany to accept the package. But when German farmers protested in Bonn and Brussels, the German cabinet threatened to veto the price package. A Council meeting of farm and finance ministers failed to break the deadlock and debate dragged on through June. The Commission then threatened to make technical changes within its authority to force lower cereals prices.[19] Eventually, the Council and Commission compromised. The Commission withdrew its proposals to cut feed wheat prices, but Council cut monthly increments by 18 per cent, imposed a 6 per cent cut in intervention payments (offered by the Commission as an alternative to a cut in the intervention price) and allowed the Commission to implement new intervention rules that closed buying except when market prices dipped below the official price. Germany accepted an expansion in the MCA franchise to 1.5 per cent (equivalent to a 0.5 per cent revaluation) and agreed that the remaining effective DM monetary gap for cereals would be eliminated at the beginning of the 1988–9 crop year. In exchange, the Commission agreed to standardize the delay in payments at 110 days and allowed Germany to pay its farmers compensation of DM 1.1–1.2 B beginning in January 1989.

The Commission pressed forward during the autumn with proposals to remake cereals intervention into a safety net and to introduce automatic price cuts in proportion to over-production (either by higher co-responsibility or by shorter intervention). The Commission proposed that every 1.55 Mt (1 per cent) of cereals produced in excess of a 155 Mt cereals threshold should trigger a 1 per cent price cut, to a maximum of 5 per cent in 1988–9 and 7.5 per cent in 1989–90. The Commission would automatically implement cuts based on production figures, without reference to the Council. In an effort to provide the basis for a compromise with Germany, the Commission also proposed a voluntary set-aside programme to remove up to 20 per cent of land from production. Nevertheless, Germany rejected the package. Meanwhile the budget resurfaced as an issue. The EP rejected the 1988 budget and forced the Community to operate on provisional twelfths; the expected outlays for 1988 exceeded the resources available under the 1.4 per cent VAT ceiling.

The Commission opened negotiations with an offer to raise the threshold to 158 Mt and to exempt small producers from the new stabilizer levy on the first 20 tonnes of cereals marketed, provided they set aside 30 per cent of their land. Germany countered with proposals to set the threshold at 160 Mt and to cut prices by a 3 per cent maximum in 1988 and 2.5 per cent in future years. The UK rejected those changes and threatened to veto the budget solution being worked out in the Finance Council unless there were price cuts (it wanted a 155 Mt threshold); Germany responded by threatening to cut the UK annual rebate. The Council could have deadlocked over the issue, but Chancellor Kohl, as President-in-Office, wanted to get the CAP issue resolved so the Single Market project could proceed.[20]

When a special Brussels Summit convened in February, both sides backed down. With the help of their agricultural ministers, the heads of government negotiated a compromise on the stabilizers package. Germany accepted the new 3 per cent stabilizer levy (payable in advance but refundable depending on production) on top of the existing 3 per cent co-responsibility levy and the UK accepted the 160 Mt threshold in exchange for budgetary guidelines which limited growth in CAP outlays to less than growth in total outlays. The Summit even went further than the Commission proposed. First, the ministers adopted cumulative automatic price reductions for cereals whenever EC production exceeded the 160 Mt threshold; the Commission had only proposed non-cumulative reductions. Second, they agreed to set a ceiling on CAP expenditure growth of 80% of GNP growth (including new stock depreciation); the Commission had proposed a 100 per cent growth rate, provided depreciation of both old and new stocks was included. Finally, they empowered the Commission to challenge Agricultural Council price decisions and refer them to a special Finance and Agriculture Council meeting which would have power to revise the decision. As a result, they were able to conclude a new budget system (based on GDP and not the VAT) that can provide new resources to implement the programmes to make a success of the Single Market.

Conclusions

Thus, by February 1988, the Commission and Council had reformed the wheat price system. The reforms of 1984–8 were only possible because the Commission prepared a consensus package and then negotiated bilaterally with the dissenting members, using a combination of threats (of further technical changes to market mechanisms, such as reduction in the number of designated intervention delivery points and in the subsidy to transport grain to the intervention store) and enticements (approval for national aids). As a result, the 1988 and 1989 price reviews progressed relatively smoothly along the path laid out by the Commission in earlier reports and by 1990 the price and intervention system had developed closer links between producers and the markets.

The European Community, with a new market system for wheat in place, was well positioned to take a major role in the Uruguay Round negotiations of the GATT after 1988. The system in 1989 was neither perfect nor complete, but a major step had been taken toward having a market system in place in the 1990s that can produce exportable quantities of wheat at competitive prices, without prohibitively large budgetary costs.

Notes

1. Franklin (1988), p. 65.
2. *EP Doc 579/77*, p. 83.
3. Henig (1980), p. 29.
4. Bieber and Palmer (1975), p. 318.
5. *The Observer*, 16–1–77.
6. Fennell (1979), p. 100.
7. Taylor (1983), p. 82.
8. Phillips (1989), p. 266.
9. Neville–Rolfe (1984), p. 264.
10. *Financial Times*, 22–6–79, quoted him as exclaiming outside the Council meeting that 'I am deeply depressed but I have not yet been raped.' He said his comments had been poorly translated but the sense of frustration remained.
11. Philip (1985), p. 58.
12. The Commission in 1974 had proposed a 'monetary event' (devaluation of the lira and revaluation of the Snake currencies in the UA) to allow for a 2.76 per cent reduction in the German monetary gap, but Ertl vetoed it.

13. Bureau of Agricultural Economics (1985), p. 61.
14. Harvey and Thomson (1985), p. 14.
15. M. Butler (1986), p. 86.
16. Because it was based on a three-year moving average, the formula would also trigger 5 per cent price cuts in 1986 and 1987, which frightened German farmers even more.
17. Vasey (1985), p. 659.
18. *International Herald Tribune*, 2–3–87.
19. *Financial Times*, 19–6–87.
20. *The Globe & Mail*, 30–12–87, quoted an EC diplomat as saying that 'if [Germany] fails, this could go down as the worst EC presidency in history.' Another EC official said that being the president probably helps moderate the German position because 'they now have the opportunity to tell their clientele back home afterward that they had no other choice but to compromise.'

Chapter 8

Trade policy in the 1970s

The EC agricultural trade policy has generally been dictated by the stage of development of the EC farm sector. German economist Stefan Tangermann observed in 1983 that 'policy makers in the Community have never really taken any interest in agricultural trade; . . . in CAP thinking, trade is a variable that is dependent on domestic policies, but not an instrument variable or an objective in itself.'[1] This introspective orientation conformed during the 1970s with the power structures (Chapter 2) and with the pressures in the food policy system (Chapters 3 to 7): farmers, the Commission, most of the European consultative bodies and the national governments believed that the price system was the most important tool to protect EC consumers and to support incomes of small farmers.

The domestic orientation left little opportunity for an active export policy. Support for the domestic wheat price forced the Community to exclude low-cost imports from North America and Australia and, although the EC produced some wheat in excess of domestic needs during the 1960s and 1970s, the Commission and Council believed that EC wheat was not commercially viable. Consequently, excess output posed a problem of 'surplus disposal'. Henri Nouyrit of the French Confederation of Agricultural Co-operatives noted:

For exports there is no real policy. So called 'surpluses' are disposed of as the opportunity arises. There is no plan for exports, no medium term policy. Exports have become a sort of undesirable adjunct to intervention. Financial preoccupations over export restitutions have inhibited a proper commercial policy involving an effort to establish permanent trade flows, to seek out new markets and to develop commercial instruments such as credits and long-term contracts.[2]

The Community concentrated on finding the cheapest way to dispose of surpluses. In particular, it encouraged alternative uses, donated food as aid, stored surpluses in Community intervention stocks or simply concluded one-time export sales.

The CAP's domestic orientation also severely circumscribed the EC's approach to the Tokyo Round of the GATT because the EC sought to defend the mechanisms of the CAP. EC negotiators were unable to pursue international agreements that would allow the EC to take advantage of its emerging export interests.

This chapter examines how the price and export policies interacted and supported each other during the period and reveals the roots of the new policy orientation that developed in the 1980s.

Prices and trade

The EC wheat trade policy before 1979 was an ad hoc response to the surpluses that resulted from the domestic orientation of the EC wheat price system. During the 1970s, the objective method criterion was developed and prices were set based entirely on domestic needs. The Community used the threshold price and variable levy systems to protect the intervention system from competition from virtually all non-European wheats.

The Commission's 1960 price proposals had divorced domestic pricing from international market influences for two reasons that remained relevant during the 1970s. First, European farms were generally smaller than in the US, Canada and Australia, so that EC producers would not be able to compete with those producers. Second, and more importantly, the EC believed that the world wheat market could not be relied upon to produce either fair competitive conditions or adequate supplies at reasonable prices. In the 1950s and 1960s world trade in wheat had become largely a matter of competition between governments, so that world market prices seldom reflected real market or production conditions. Furthermore, domestic programmes in the major producing and consuming nations exacerbated the uncertainty in world markets (see Chapter 2). During the 1970s more than half of the world grain market (including the EC) was insulated from international market conditions. Although EC policy contributed to price volatility, a significant portion was due to agricultural and trade policies in other countries.[3] Also, in the 1970s, the Bretton Woods system of fixed exchange rates ended and all major world currencies began to fluctuate. Because most trades in the world wheat market were expressed in US dollars, a fluctuating dollar-ECU exchange (or its equivalent) rate forced changes in offer prices for exports and imports in EC currency terms even in the absence of any change in the world wheat price. During the 1970s, the swings between the US dollar and the European currencies would have exacerbated the volatility of domestic European prices if the variable levy had not protected the domestic market.

The Commission and Council, therefore, set the threshold price and variable import levy so that imported wheat would be priced at the target level in the food deficit regions. Figure 8.1 shows that the world price (represented by the Gulf offer price for US #2 Hard Winter Ordinary Wheat converted to ECUs) swung widely during the 1970s but the Community price system insulated both European consumers and producers from these gyrations. The Agricultural Council generally adjusted domestic prices in line with the objective method criterion, which reflected production costs, net farm income changes and economy-wide income growth.

After 1976, Community protection against imports was increased through adjustments in the price system (Figure 8.2). The Council implemented the reference price system for bread wheat and cut the common wheat intervention price. As a result the gap between the target and intervention prices expanded

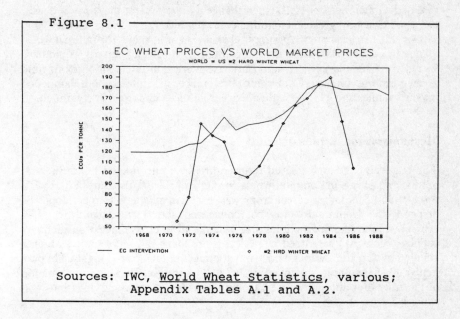

— Figure 8.1 —

EC WHEAT PRICES VS WORLD MARKET PRICES
WORLD = US #2 HARD WINTER WHEAT

—— EC INTERVENTION   ◇ #2 HRD WINTER WHEAT

Sources: IWC, <u>World Wheat Statistics</u>, various;
Appendix Tables A.1 and A.2.

from about 10 per cent in 1975 to more than 30 per cent in 1976. Between then and 1985, the gap increased to more than 40 per cent as intervention prices rose.

The successive expansions in protection served two purposes. First, increasingly after 1976 France demanded greater Community Preference to ensure that imports did not cut into its domestic market (which was shrinking as production

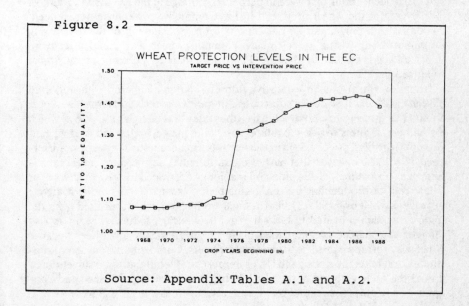

— Figure 8.2 —

WHEAT PROTECTION LEVELS IN THE EC
TARGET PRICE VS INTERVENTION PRICE

CROP YEARS BEGINNING IN:

Source: Appendix Tables A.1 and A.2.

rose in the other member states) in exchange for approval for the rest of the price package. Second, greater Community Preference helped the Commission support the market system. As supply grew ahead of demand, the internal wheat market price dipped down to the intervention price. Rising imports would have forced the Commission either to purchase more into intervention or to fund greater exports. Greater Community Preference, in contrast, both dampened import volumes and exacted higher levies from those imports that continued.

Mechanisms for surplus disposal

The relatively high and assured returns for wheat encouraged EC farmers to produce surpluses of common wheat throughout the 1970s. But, because EC production of the other cereal crops was less than adequate to meet domestic demand, the Community was not concerned about wheat surpluses. UK economist John Marsh concludes that 'symbolically the assurance of an adequate supply of cereals, guaranteed by policy, is the token of food security, which a generation who knew war and post-war shortages of food prized highly.'[4] In particular, the Community sought to dispose of the surpluses by using a combination of incentives for alternative uses, Community storage, food aid donations and exports.

Alternative uses

The Community primarily encouraged farmers to use low-quality wheats as animal feed in the place of imported cereal substitutes or the traditional barley and maize feed-grains that were in perpetual shortage in the EC. By 1972 almost 39 per cent of the wheat produced in the Community was consumed as feed, compared with only about 24 per cent in 1966. But the end of the denaturing programme and rising prices made common wheat less competitive with imported feed, so that by the late 1970s less than 30 per cent of the wheat produced in EC was fed to animals.

Common wheat was an expensive nutrient source compared with imported oilseed cakes and non-cereal substitutes. In the EC, cereals substitutes cost only about 1.2 times more than cereals (the ratio was 2.5 in the US), which encouraged farmers to use substitutes instead of maize, barley and feed wheat.[5] Although the high price regime in Europe was a major reason for the price difference, it was also believed that part of the differential was because cereal substitutes (i.e. corn gluten, citrus pulp and manioc) were priced by the exporters at or below cost of production. US corn gluten, for example, was readily available because it was a by-product of corn-sugar production, which resulted from the trade protection provided to US cane and beet sugar producers. Farmers also thought that manioc was available to the EC at artificially low prices because Thailand provided subsidies to tapioca producers. Competition from cereal substitutes became acute during the 1970s because the Community had surrendered during the Dillon Round of the GATT the prerogative to tax oilseed and non-grain feed imports (i.e. bound the duty at zero for soya and corn gluten).

The Community responded to surpluses in the late 1960s with a subsidy to denature surplus wheat (i.e. contaminate it with fish oil so that it could not be used for human consumption) which was then offered at lower prices to the EC livestock industry. This policy lasted until 1974, when the world price soared; thereafter it became the high-cost option for surplus disposal. At the same time, rising concern about world food scarcity radically changed taxpayers' and politicians' views of the morality of diverting food from its best use. Consequently the denaturing programme was terminated.

The French government and wheat producers association (AGPB), however, continued to advocate the use of domestic wheat as an animal feed.[6] After the denaturing programme ended, they pressed the Commission and Council to raise the target price faster than the intervention price and to renegotiate the GATT-bound duties. France also supplemented this with its own programmes. The Office National Interprofessionnel pour les Céréales (ONIC) collected a levy on all cereals marketed in France and used the funds to build feed lots to use French feed wheats. Generally the other producing countries were less concerned about feed markets because they did not have any surplus wheat.

The Community responded in 1975 to French demands with a series of measures to make low-quality wheats competitive as feed. In 1975–6, the Commission began to align barley and maize prices and moved the maize marketing year into line with the other cereals. Then in 1976 the Commission proposed and the Council accepted a single intervention price for common wheat, barley and maize and a new reference price for wheat of bread-making quality (a premium compensated farmers for lower yields). But, as discussed in Chapter 2, the cereal grading system was unable to differentiate properly between feed and bread-quality wheats, so that much of the low-quality wheat that did not command a premium on commercial markets ended in EC intervention. Thus, throughout the 1970s, the Community was unable to manage the domestic circulation of cereals to halt the growth in surpluses requiring disposal.

Storage

Surplus production was also stored in public or private facilities under the intervention programme. Even though the budget did not fully count the depreciation costs of intervention storage, public purchase and storage of surpluses was generally regarded as an expensive option. With a guaranteed buying system and little on-farm storage, stockpiles usually ended up in intervention stores in the surplus countries, where the Community incurred finance, technical storage and wastage costs.

The focus of the stock policy during the 1970s was undoubtedly security of supply rather than disposal. Wild gyrations in supply and prices on international markets, which began in 1972 and continued through 1976, spurred the Community to hold the average ratio of stocks to domestic use at about 21 per cent (i.e. close to the 20 per cent ratio that usually accompanies stable prices).[7] In contrast, the major exporting countries (especially the US and Canada) held greater stocks to reduce wasteful competition on generally slack world markets. The world-wide stock-to-use ratio dropped well below the lowest EC level during 1972–4, which caused world wheat prices almost to treble. As world-wide production rebounded, the world stock-to-use ratio soared to almost 32 per cent in 1976–7. As a result, US offer prices fell more than 25 per cent in 1976. The Community avoided these sharp swings in prices as it maintained steady stocks and used external markets as a swing destination for, or source of, residual quantities of wheat.

In the Stocktaking in 1974–5, the Commission proposed an 'active storage policy for cereals' to absorb cyclical fluctuations in production, ensure domestic supplies and fulfil international obligations,[8] but the Council never accepted this approach. An active storage policy is a necessary adjunct to the development of a commercial policy for wheat. To ensure customers are satisfied, the Community would have to hold precautionary supplies which would raise the stock-to-use ratio above the average 21 per cent recorded in the 1970s. As exports were generally one-time shipments, the Community was able to live without an active storage system.

Food aid

After decolonization in Africa and Asia in the 1960s, war and revolution became commonplace. Although EC member states were no longer responsible for these countries, instability in those regions endangered European trade and investments. France and the UK, through La Francophonie and the Commonwealth, and the EC, through the Yaoundé and Lomé Conventions, attempted to calm political conflicts in the former colonies in Africa, the Caribbean and the Pacific but endemic and episodic famine increased tension and conflict. Food aid was one solution.

Community aid formally began on 1 July 1968 with the Food Aid (Cereals) Convention, negotiated at the International Wheat Council meetings during the Kennedy Round of the GATT. Before that time, all food aid was disbursed by the member states. The EC initially agreed to contribute 1.035 Mt annually, to be supplied by either the Community or by individual member countries. In 1968–9, only 29 per cent of the cereals aid was given by the Community; that figure rose steadily until 1985–6 when the Community gave about 70 per cent of the 1.67 Mt committed.

Food aid allocations are set by the Council on advice of the Commission, subject to the commitments in the Food Aid (Cereals) Convention. Shipments are administered both by the member states and the Commission and the costs are allocated partly to Title 6 of the EAGGF budget (the refund portion of the aid) and partly to the development budget (the remainder of the cost of the aid).[9] Aid planning is managed by the Development and Cooperation Directorate of the Commission (DG–VIII). The Cereals Management Committee, consequently, had only indirect influence on shipments (e.g. determining when shipments could move) and consequently was unable to make direct use of the shipments to develop commercial markets. Some other food exporters have used aid shipments both to develop consumer tastes in LDCs and as a bonus to encourage commercial sales.

Evidence suggests that during the 1970s the EC generally regarded food aid as a means of disposing of surplus cereals rather than as a means to develop markets.[10] Although the Community between 1968 and 1978 supplied virtually all of the grain that it had committed under the 1968 Food Aid Convention, it shipped the grain at times and under conditions that best suited the Community. The aid was not tailored to the recipient's needs. During that decade the Community exceeded its annual commitment whenever it had supplies surplus to its domestic needs (i.e. in 1974–5 and 1977) and cut back on shipments during or following any year when the EC cereals crop was poor (i.e. 1971–2 and 1976)[11] World demand for food aid exceeded supply throughout the period, so the EC's volatile pattern of shipments did not enhance its image as a reliable source.

In 1974 the Commission proposed changes in the Community food aid policy. Supplies of wheat and other cereals had expanded faster than domestic demand and the Commission wanted to dispose of more as aid. The FAO World Food Conference in 1974 supported the Commission's position and asked developed countries to expand their annual cereals aid commitments to 10 Mt in order to meet larger food deficits throughout the Third World. The Commission accepted this approach and proposed it double the amount of aid disbursed by the Community (rather than by member states) and to distribute more to LDCs via the World Food Program and the International Red Cross.[12] Although the EP and the ESC supported the Commission's proposal, farmers and the ministries of agriculture were unenthusiastic because the additional costs (for restitutions and, until 1975, purchases) would be borne by the EAGGF and could squeeze other farm priorities. When drought hit in 1976, the Commission withdrew the plan because the member states rejected any increase in commitments when domestic supplies were short. Reform of the food aid system then waited until the 1980s.

Exports

When the Community found it had wheat that could not be disposed cheaply as feed, stored or given as aid, it opted to move its surpluses on to external markets. The export market was viewed as a cheap storage system because short-term exports could be cut off with impunity while physical stockpiling required finance, storage and depreciation costs. The export system, therefore, remained undeveloped at the Community level; the Commission failed to develop more than a custodial or bookkeeping role during the 1960s and 1970s.

Refunds (or restitutions) were the only EC-controlled instrument to support exports. 'Common law' or standing refunds, granted for cereals exported as grain (and, after 1981, for processed cereals and cereals by-products), were generally confined to sales to countries bordering the EC with known, verifiable requirements. In contrast, 'awarded' refunds were paid for unprocessed cereals exported to all destinations. The Commission, on the advice of the Management Committee for Cereals made weekly awards which fixed a maximum figure for export refunds, on the basis of offers submitted by Community operators. The fixed refund offers (which included the MCA refund) were limited to set periods, markets and volumes.[13] During the 1970s, DG–VI and the Management Committee for Cereals — comprised of members of national agricultural ministries — generally set tenders whenever domestic stocks looked set to exceed the desired stock-to-use ratio. The tenders were short term and more often than not open to all takers. Consequently, the export system did not develop long-term customers but simply disposed of surpluses at the lowest cost.

The export system was most strongly supported by France. Events during the 1960s and 1970s had amply demonstrated that food was useful both as a weapon and as a diplomatic tool; France insisted that the Community continue to have an export presence to counter the dominant power of the US.[14] France, which had been a significant wheat exporter since shortly after the Second World War, also believed it had an export 'vocation'; wheat exports helped offset part of its large balance of payments deficits. As wheat production rose in France and the world market expanded, France saw the commercial potential of wheat exports and pushed the Community to develop an active export policy.

Neither Germany nor the UK was particularly interested in export policy. Both governments during the 1970s were preoccupied with ensuring adequate quantities of food imports at reasonable prices, which often put them at odds with France.

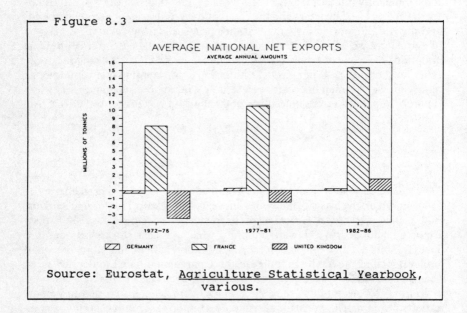

Figure 8.3

AVERAGE NATIONAL NET EXPORTS
AVERAGE ANNUAL AMOUNTS

Source: Eurostat, *Agriculture Statistical Yearbook*, various.

The Commission, prodded by the French government, proposed in 1975 that the EC enter fixed-term supply contracts to provide greater continuity for export shipments and perhaps cut the subsidy for exports.[15] It recommended that the Community enter a twelve-month contract with Egypt to supply in 1975–6 a minimum of 1 Mt of wheat and wheat flour. Israel and Algeria were targeted for similar contracts.[16] The EP supported the proposal but the ESC withheld support because it believed the Community should not implement any agreement before the IWA discussions were complete. While France pushed for the contracts, the MAFF, with NFU support, expressed concern that long-term agreements would institutionalize existing surpluses or create new ones. UK farmers and the MAFF instead preferred to renew the IWA to provide both security of supply and price stability. Germany and the Netherlands also rejected the proposal. The 1976 drought scuttled this proposal, much as it did the food aid proposals. 'Divisions of opinion in the Commission developed' during the year and the Council never acted.[17]

As a result, France developed and operated its own cereals export system outside the EC sphere. French cereals farmers, with state assistance, managed a comprehensive system to distribute, store and finance their export sales. The cereal co-operatives owned enough capacity to store and market about 70 per cent of the French wheat crop and thereby acted as agents for about 40–45% per cent of the French cereals exported.[18] As the market became more competitive in the 1970s, the French co-operatives also developed close links with the multi-national grain traders to ensure that they maximized their commercial prospects.[19] To support the system, French farmers paid a para-fiscal levy on all cereals marketed to ONIC, which then used some of the funds to provide credit guarantees on cereal exports.[20] The Compagnie Français d'Assurances pour le Commerce Extérieur (COFACE), a French government agency, also provides credit guarantees for cereals exports (generally six-month guarantees on 95 per cent of the credit at market rates of interest). Consequently, French cereals producers greatly expanded their exports through the 1970s, earning the admiration and support of President Giscard.

The Community, meanwhile, directed its attention to negotiations through the GATT. The assortment of domestic policies operating in the EC in 1976 when the substantive GATT discussions began, however, provided little scope for the Community to develop its commercial interests.

The EC in the GATT

The Community approach to GATT negotiations was determined by the domestic focus of the CAP. At first, the EC needed to complete the CAP, so the Commission and France used the Dillon and Kennedy Rounds in the 1960s to force recalcitrant member states to complete the system and then to protect it from outside influences. The Community also used the Tokyo Round to defend the policy. However, once that was assured the EC expanded its objectives to include its commercial interests.

Domestically, the Commission and the national governments dominated the GATT trade negotiations. Although domestic policy actors were consulted at the beginning of each round, the negotiating system deprived them of real impact on the decision. The Commission negotiated for the EC, guided by the Council's approved strategy (embodied in a directive) and directed by the 113 Committee of national officials (per the Treaty of Rome). The secrecy and remoteness of the talks and the negotiating process isolated farmers (who were not overly concerned with the trade discussions, provided the Community system of pricing and preferences prevailed). The EP and ESC were also isolated because the

Treaty of Rome does not require they be consulted on commercial agreements under Article 113.

GATT negotiations before 1973

Prior to 1973 the Commission and Council used the GATT strategically to build the Community policy system. The Dillon Round was used to get GATT approval for the European customs union and the general parameters of the common policies while the Commission and France worked together in the Kennedy Round to finesse introduction of the wheat price regime. Then, in 1966, with the CAP cereals regime largely decided, the Commission focused for the first time on ensuring a protected position for Europe in the world wheat market.

Although the CAP was first discussed at GATT committee meetings in 1958, the farm policy was not fully scrutinized until the closing stages of the Dillon Round because the market mechanisms had not been approved by the Council. After they were enacted in 1962, Article XXIV of the GATT forced the EC to negotiate with the countries that would be affected by the new customs union. Negotiations, especially with the US, concluded when the EC agreed to compensate affected agricultural exporters for lost markets by allowing an unlimited quantity of oilseeds, seedcake and cereal substitutes to enter the Community duty free. The EC believes it fully 'paid for' the variable levy system because that decision opened the EC to world market influences and raised the cost of the CAP price support schemes.[21] In exchange, the EC believed the CAP was accepted by all GATT signatory states. Although US farmers were not pleased, the US government accepted that the protectionist farm policy in the EC was necessary to help Europe recover from the war and to encourage the former combatants to unite against the new common enemy — the USSR.[22]

The Commission then used the agricultural talks in 1962–7 to force member states to complete the CAP. Warley concludes that DG–VI had a 'single-minded preoccupation with creating and protecting the CAP' and used the Kennedy Round 'not to alternate the CAP's external effects but to secure its completion.'[23] This defensive posture, which fitted well with the existing power structures, was championed at the negotiations by both the Commission and France and strongly supported within Europe by the farm lobby. The Commission 'declared its complete agreement with the USA on their [farm issues] inclusion in the negotiations, but, before committing itself on the international plane it needed to complete its own agricultural policy and in particular fix the level of common agricultural prices.'[24] France — worried that US imports would ruin French farmers' opportunity to become Germany's primary supplier — demanded that the CAP price and financial regimes be completed before talks began. M. Deleau, president of COPA, agreed that 'the existence of the CAP is an essential prerequisite for negotiations on agricultural products in GATT and such policy cannot be called into question.'[25]

The German government might have been willing to bargain access to EC food markets in exchange for freer world trade in manufactures, but France withheld support for the EC position on industrial tariffs until Germany agreed to complete the CAP price and financing arrangements.[26] To force quick agreement by Germany, France pushed the Council in February 1964 to propose at the GATT the *montant de soutien* system. Under the proposal, contracting countries would bind the maximum level of support for agriculture for three years. The *montant de soutien* was equal to the difference between the world and domestic prices, adjusted for any direct subsidies to the farm sector; consequently, agricultural trade discussions could not really begin until Germany agreed to set the prices.[27] The strategy succeeded and by 1966 the Community had established the price regime for cereals.

In 1966, after the 'empty chair crisis' was resolved and prices set, the Commission and Council presented detailed proposals to the GATT to protect the future development of the EC wheat market. In response to demands from the traditional world wheat exporters, the EC offered to bind the Community's self-sufficiency ratio for grains at 90 per cent and to store or export as non-commercial aid any EC surpluses. The offer would not have seriously hurt the domestic industry because the prevailing level of self-sufficiency in the EC was only about 85 per cent.

In 1967 the GATT negotiations concluded without any agricultural agreement because the EC was unwilling to cut its *montant de soutien* by 10 per cent or to convert its self-sufficiency ratio to a quantitative guarantee. Under the authority of Article XX(h) of the GATT, the farm traders reconvened the talks at the International Wheat Council and concluded an International Grains Agreement (IGA) to begin in 1967. The new Wheat Trade Convention established minimum and maximum prices, set commitments for importers to buy agreed percentages of their purchases from member countries and dictated that exporters would adopt special measures whenever the price bands were breached. A related Food Aid (Cereals) Convention provided for long-term cereals aid commitments. The Trade Convention failed in June 1968 when bumper crops pushed market prices below the minimum prices set in the agreement.

GATT relations (1973–9)

The 1973–9 period saw a dramatic turnaround in the Community approach to world food trade and the GATT. When the Community entered the trade negotiations in 1973 its defensive posture was dictated by its status as the largest importer in the world.[28] But, by 1979, the EC changed its external orientation, especially for cereals, to match its developing competitive status and export interests.

Even before negotiations began in the Tokyo Round of the GATT, the EC was forced to defend itself against claims resulting from the enlargement of the Community. The accession of the UK, Denmark and Ireland in 1973 affected other traders and Article XXIV forced the Community to negotiate with them and satisfy their claims. In August 1974 the talks ended without a conclusive result. Australia and the US 'agreed to disagree' with the EC on cereals because they considered their legal rights were jeopardized by accession of the UK and Denmark; they instead decided 'to continue discussions with a view to seeking, through international negotiations, agreed solutions to the problems arising in the field of international trade in cereals.'[29]

Meanwhile, the Community faced a number of attacks on its policy under the Article XXIII disputes procedure. Table 8.1 shows that between 1973 when the Tokyo Round negotiations opened and the conclusion of the talks in 1979, EC policies were challenged at least nine times by other agricultural exporters; previously all challenges had been directed at the member states. Although none of the challenges forced any appreciable change in EC policy for cereals or other sectors, they forced the Commission to review its export policies. In 1973 the EC initiated its first legal challenge at the GATT and henceforward lodged counter complaints with the GATT whenever its policies were threatened either by retaliation or countervailing duties. The Community, however, did not use the legal route to open other markets; it simply used it to defend its position.

Table 8.1 GATT Article XXIII dispute settlement proceedings against the EC

Date	Plaintiff	Issue
1974	Canada	EC concessions on grains (Art. XXIV:6)
1976	USA	EC measures on animal feed proteins; use of surplus dairy products in feed
1976	USA	EC fruit and vegetable rules; minimum import price regime
1976	Australia	Ditto
1977	Chile	EC malted barley export subsidies
1978	Australia	EC sugar export refunds/export subsidies
1978	Brazil	EC sugar export refunds/export subsidies
1979	Chile	Discriminatory import rules on apples

Sources: Petersmann (1986), pp. 67–70; Hudec (1988), pp. 46–51

The accession negotiations and the legal cases convinced the Community that its farm policy was not secure under international law. Lardinois noted in 1976 that the US could attack with impunity the CAP as 'protectionist' and 'anti-GATT' because the US did not have obligations for farm products under the GATT. He objected that the 'grandfather clause' (written into the Treaty via the 1951 Torquay Protocol) and the 1955 waiver (under Art. XXV:5) gave the US complete freedom from GATT discipline in the area of farm policy.[30] In the Tokyo Round the Community set out to rectify that imbalance.

Thus, at the beginning the Community saw the agricultural talks in defensive terms.[31] Although a Commission Communication in April 1973 affirmed that the 'principles of the CAP' could not be questioned, French Foreign Minister Michel Jobert was displeased because the Commission was not positive enough in defence of the CAP.[32] Because of his pressure, the final negotiating strategy adopted by the Council of Foreign Ministers in May 1973 declared that the 'CAP principles *and* their mechanisms' could not be matters for negotiation because of the 'fundamental and specific characteristics of agriculture'. The Community then demanded at the GATT that the agricultural talks be separated from the general tariff negotiations. Although the major food exporters were unhappy with that approach, the GATT ministers met in Tokyo in September 1973 and acquiesced: Article 3(e) of the declaration recognized that agricultural talks must 'take account of the special characteristics and problems of this sector' and subsequently separated them from the tariff talks.

The farm trade talks then proceeded in two distinct phases. The Commission argued that Europe must seek 'the expansion of trade in stable world markets', first through a negotiated 'code of good conduct covering export practices' and second via international commodity agreements (ICAs) for wheat, flour, feed grains, rice, sugar and some milk products.[33] Thus, the GATT continued to examine subsidies and export practices while, in 1975, the wheat and grain trade issues were moved to parallel talks at the IWC.

The Community laboured in the main agricultural forum to defend the basic features of the CAP. Wide ranging proposals to reform GATT Article XVI:3 (export subsidies) would have forced the Community to a complete overhaul of the CAP; if the Community could no longer provide export subsidies (i.e. restitutions or refunds), the CAP would quickly become unworkable. The Community entered the final stage of the discussions firmly convinced that it 'should make its agreement subject to retaining the full text of Art. XVI, particularly paragraph 3, which is sufficient as it stands and therefore needs no interpretive clauses.'[34] The US government, however, had assured its farmers that the GATT agreement would include some action on international trade in farm products. In early 1979, when the US negotiating mandate was about to expire and invalidate all the work in other areas, the two sides reached a compromise. The EC accepted a new interpretive code for subsidies when the US Trade Representative (USTR) assured Gundelach that the US did not plan to use the new code to attack EC policies.[35] The US had wanted the interpretive code to prohibit or at least severely curtail EC export refunds but had little choice but to accept the face-saving subsidies code.

Article 10 of the new Subsidies Code declared that signatories 'agree not to grant directly or indirectly any export subsidy on certain primary products in a manner which results in the signatory granting such subsidy having more than an equitable share of world export trade in such product, account being taken of the shares of the signatories in trade in the product concerned during a previous representative period and any special factors which may have affected or may be affecting trade in such a product.' The code suited the EC because it was vague: definitions for 'equitable share' and 'representative period' were couched with enough caveats so that they could not really bind while 'subsidy' was not defined.[36]

The Community gained significantly more than it surrendered in this part of the negotiations. First, Article 10 of the code categorically accepted the legality of export subsidies for primary agricultural products. Second, Article 11 of the code confirmed that subsidies other than for exports would be permitted to promote social and economic policy objectives. The code explicitly allowed subsidies to eliminate industrial, economic and social disadvantages of specific regions, to restructure industry, to sustain employment, to encourage R&D and to avoid environmental problems. These provisions effectively approved the complete panoply of price supports, structural programmes and social policies that underpinned the CAP.

The outcome of the GATT subsidies negotiations had a significant impact on wheat talks at the IWC. Initially, the Community sought to negotiate a new IGA to get stability in wheat and feed grain markets and to protect further the CAP market systems. The Community hoped to reach a market sharing arrangement that would protect both its needs as a major food importer and its export interests in Africa. In May 1977, the European Council called for the GATT to develop 'a mutually acceptable approach to agriculture that will achieve increased expansion and stabilization of trade and greater assurance of world food supplies.' But they argued that 'such progress should not remove the right of individual countries under existing international agreements to avoid significant market disruption.'[37] Ertl suggested 'that Australia and New Zealand find markets in their own region — Indonesia, Hong Kong and Japan' while 'Europe and the US can share Africa and South America.'[38]

In January 1978 a special meeting of the IWC asked the Secretary General of the FAO to convene a conference to negotiate a new IWA.[39] The EC entered those talks as spokesman for the group of importing countries (with 314 out of 1,000 importer votes at the IWC and 102 votes out of 1,000 exporter votes in 1973–4).[40] When the opening positions had been tabled, the EC and most of the LDCs agreed that the floor price should be kept at about US$115/t, that the ceiling price should only be a little higher and that stock actions should be triggered whenever prices breach firm price bands. The EC wanted to go further and to extend the agreement to all cereals; as a major importer of feed cereals, it believed that an agreement for wheat alone would not be very useful. The only major disagreement between Europe and the LDCs was over reserve stocks. The LDCs wanted large stocks to ensure adequate supplies in poor crop years while the EC wanted relatively small stocks, so that they could export or dispose of their surpluses rather than store them.

The US, the major exporter, wanted a wheat-only agreement to include a higher floor price (US$145/t), a higher ceiling price (US$215–225/t) and stock accumulation triggered by farmer-owned stocks rather than by market prices. The US also wanted higher world stocks (25–30 Mt) so that EC surpluses would be stored rather than sold on the international market; the EC at that time had surplus wheat production about equal to the American demands for reserve stocks.

At the beginning of 1977 the four traditional exporters — the US, Canada, Australia and Argentina — met frequently to develop an exporters' position. When negotiations began in earnest at an IWC/UNCTAD conference in Geneva in 1978, the traditional exporters included the EC and Japan in their discussions but excluded the LDCs from the substantive talks on trigger prices and stock holding.[41]

By the time the negotiations were suspended *sine die* in 1979, the US and EC had significantly narrowed the gap between their respective positions, but a wide gap had opened between the LDCs and Europe. The US had accepted that the agreement could include other cereals as in the 1967 IGA and that reserves could be triggered by prices rather than changes in farmer-owned stocks. Meanwhile, the Community had accepted a higher floor and ceiling price and had indicated that it would share in a larger world reserve stock (Table 8.2). As a result, the EC moved firmly into the exporters' camp in the talks.

Table 8.2 Bargaining positions in the IWC grain talks (1977–9)

	Stock levels Mt	Floor price US$/t	Ceiling price US$/t	Trigger mechanism	Products covered
EEC					
Opening	12–15	115	na	fixed prices	all grains
Final	20–22	125/140	195	fixed prices	all grains
LDCs					
Opening	25–30	115	na	fixed prices	na
Final	excluding LDCs	125–30	160	nc	na
US					
Opening	25–30	145	215–25	farm stocks	wheat
Final	25	125/140	200	prices	wheat +
Canada	30	140–55	225	–	wheat
Australia	<25	140–55	180	–	wheat
Argentina	<25	140–55	–	–	wheat
Japan	–	100	–	–	–

Sources: International Herald Tribune, Financial Times, The Times and *The Guardian*

The Commission, satisfied that the subsidies code would jeopardize neither EC market mechanisms nor EC trade expansion, was willing to strike a deal with the US. In November 1978 it asked the Council for approval to complete an agreement but France, fearing that the IWA agreement might limit export expansion, used its standing reserve on the GATT talks to force negotiations to continue.[42] As a result, the IWA talks failed. The main GATT agreements had to be completed early in 1979 to meet the conditions of the US Trade Act; the wheat discussions were severed from the larger package and ended without agreement.

In reality the talks were doomed when the EC moved from the import to export side of the negotiations because the LDCs were left without a spokesman. Although the US and EC positions had moved closer, the major importer group of LDCs completely rejected the potential outcome to which the exporters were converging.[43] This deadlock ultimately killed the international wheat agreement and ended the trade talks for the 1970s.[44]

Conclusion

Opinion in the EC built during the late 1970s for the Community to develop an active export policy. In 1977, the ESC looked beyond the GATT negotiations and called for the Community to create a 'genuine agricultural trade policy' to include commercially-motivated ICAs, long-term supply agreements, export contracts and new credit vehicles. Then in 1978 the EP recommended that the EC use the GATT disputes settlement system more actively to protect and support its commercial interests. These pronouncements heralded change.

Cereals traders in DG–VI, French and UK wheat producers and the government in France were beginning to see Europe as a world competitor.

The Commission also thought so. It believed the outcome of the GATT negotiations in the agriculture sector — without a new IWA but with official recognition that the general and specific instruments of the CAP wheat policy were legal — was 'satisfactory because it enables the Community to consolidate its agricultural policy.'[45] The EC had successfully ensured that 'the CAP was not called into question and the basic principle behind and operation of, its mechanisms, including those most open to attack by our partners, such as levies and refunds, remain intact.'[46] In particular, Article XVI:3 continued to allow export subsidies for agricultural products and Article 10 of the new Subsidies Code did not restrict Community action. Furthermore, Article 11 of the code explicitly authorized subsidies for many social objectives that had never previously been sanctioned. Thus, the Community found the international rules were pliable when changes in the 1980s forced the EC to adjust.

Notes

1. Tangermann (1983), p. 50
2. N. Butler (1983), p. 113.
3. IMF (1988), pp. 122–5.
4. J. Marsh, 'Summary', in Beard (1986), p. 10.
5. Duchêne, Szczepanik and Legg (1985), p. 140.
6. *Financial Times*, 24–6–77.
7. Phillips (1989) p. 308.
8. *Newsletter on the CAP #3*, March 1975, p. 45.
9. Before 1975, the entire cost of food aid was allocated to Title 6 of the EAGGF budget. The Commission estimates that prior to 1975 about 193 M UA was allocated to the EAGGF budget to purchase cereals to ship as aid.
10. Bard (1972), p. 43.
11. Phillips (1989), p. 310.
12. *Bulletin of the ECs, 3/74*, pp. 30–4.
13. OECD (1987c), p. 84.
14. *Financial Times*, 11–11–75.
15. Duchêne, Szczepanik and Legg (1985), p. 205.
16. *Financial Times*, 1–8–75.
17. House of Lords (1981a), p. 70.
18. Foxall (1982), p. 16.
19. Morgan (1979), p. 310.
20. OECD (1987b), p. 201.
21. Petersmann (1986), p. 41.
22. Warley (1976), p. 330.
23. *Ibid.*, p. 342.
24. Casadio (1973), p. 11.
25. *Ibid.*, p. 38.
26. *Ibid.*, p. 25.
27. *Ibid.*, p. 124.
28. *Green Europe 217*, pp. 44 and 46; Phillips (1989), p. 321.
29. *Bulletin of the ECs 7–8/74*, p. 19.
30. *Newsletter on the CAP #7*, September 1976, p. 2.

31. The genesis for the MTN was also defensive. In 1972 the US imposed a 10 per cent surcharge on imports in an effort to reduce its balance of payments deficit. France and Germany protested, but in the end agreed to revalue their exchange rates and to work within the EC to initiate a new round of multilateral trade negotiations; in exchange the US ended the surcharge.

32. Jackson, Louis and Matsushita (1984), pp. 24–6.

33. *Bulletin of the ECs Supplement 2/73*, p. 9–10.

34. *COM(78)275*, p. 12.

35. Hudec (1988), p. 40, reported that USTR Robert Strauss sent Gundelach a letter to confirm US intentions.

36. The 'equitable market share' was adjusted for 'developments on world markets' while the reference period includes the three most recent calendar years in which 'normal market conditions' existed.

37. Golt (1978), pp. 4–5.

38. *Financial Times*, 8–11–78.

39. Cohn (1979), p. 135, argues that the talks were shifted to the IWC and supervised by UNCTAD rather than the GATT to avoid the problems that arose in 1967. The USSR refused to join the 1967 IGA because it was not renegotiable when non-GATT members were invited to participate. Non-participation by the USSR and other CPEs (especially China) meant that the 1967 arrangement could not control world prices.

40. *Bulletin of the EC, 6/73*, p. 66.

41. Cohn (1979), p. 140.

42. *The Times*, 27–11–78; *Financial Times*, 14–12–79.

43. Cohn (1979), p. 137, writes that the LDCs wanted help to build domestic storage and handling systems for their share of the reserve stocks but the major exporters refused because they hoped to make profits storing the grain for the LDCs. The LDCs therefore refused to consider holding stocks to support the market.

44. G. Schuh, 'The changing context of food and agricultural development policy', in Gittinger, Leslie and Hoisington (1987), p. 80, argues that the IWA probably would not have worked in the 1980s because wide swings in the US dollar relative to other currencies would have triggered stock action. After the Bretton Woods system ended in 1971, the ECU–US dollar exchange rate varied by as much as 20 per cent in a single year and by about 40 per cent over the entire period. Between 1955 and 1969, the ECU–US dollar exchange rate moved less than 4 per cent in any single year and only about 11 per cent over the entire period.

45. *COM(79)514*, p. 68.

46. *Ibid.*, p. 9.

Chapter 9

Export competition in the 1980s

The Community developed a comprehensive commercial policy for wheat during the 1980s through a series of unilateral, bilateral and multilateral efforts. Although the obvious reason for the new policy was that the Community needed to find an outlet for surplus production, development of the trade policy only occurred when major changes in the power structures and bargains overcame strong resistance within the Community.

By 1979 changes in the structures and bargains in the Community had forced the Commission and Council to begin to re-examine the wheat policy. As a result, the Community shifted position and came close to striking a new IWA that would assist Europe to realize its potential gains from commercial exports. Although the wheat talks became stalemated and the only new GATT measures were embodied in a subsidies code, the Community welcomed the outcome.

Beginning in 1979, the Community realized that the security imperative had changed. As discussed in Chapter 2, the pre-1979 security concerns had begun to shift as East-West relations improved and the EC recognized the rising economic interdependence of food and industrial production. Germany's minister for defence in 1980 recognized this and warned that the CAP threatened the ability of Australia and New Zealand to play an effective military role in their region and could lead to a full-scale trade dispute which would endanger Community imports of energy and raw materials.[1] Meanwhile, new information technologies reduced the possibility of major market dislocations caused by 'grain robberies'. Furthermore, because of changes in the production structures by 1980, the Commission recognized that EC food security could probably be met by the 25 per cent of farmers who produce about 75 per cent of farm output and who need neither income nor price support.[2]

The Community also was pushed to change by the rapid growth in production and surpluses. By the early 1980s, the EC annually produced about 10 Mt more wheat than it could use. Operation of the CAP price and structures policies during the 1970s also had dramatically improved competitiveness of large wheat producers in Europe (Table 2.1). The Community had two options: it could tighten controls on domestic production and consumption through administrative edict (i.e. quotas) and opt out of the export market, or it could re-structure its price and trade policy towards market forces to capitalize on its new position as a competitive producer. As demonstrated in Chapters 3 to 7, the Community opted to redirect the domestic wheat policy to market conditions. As a result, the Community had to ensure that commercial farmers could find outlets for their product; the EC was compelled to look to exports. Rising volatility in the financial markets, however, had increased risks encountered in export competition so that European farmers needed help to export. Henceforward, the Community sought to use the GATT to support domestic reform and to promote its export interests, which represented a fundamental shift from the defensive posture in the 1970s.

The EC would have been unable to develop an active export policy without changes in the underlying bargains in the Community. New bargains between the Commission and large wheat farmers replaced the old agricultural policy compact that had developed the defensive, inward-looking wheat policy of the 1960s and 1970s. As the EC farm sector consolidated and specialized, the newly-dominant, world-competitive producers demanded greater access to world market opportunities. This split between commercial and peasant farmers enabled the Commission and Council to override powerful conservative forces in Europe. Within Germany, the Minister of Economics in 1979 had suggested that the EC forgo an export policy for agriculture in order to improve the prospects for trade negotiations to ensure raw materials imports.[3] Meanwhile, the UK government rejected the development of an EC export policy and instead suggested that each member state deal with its own surpluses.[4] The Commission prevailed because it got strong support from a number of important quarters. In particular, France decided in 1985 to support the Commission's proposals and thereafter became the strongest proponent of reform. These changes enabled the EC to reform the domestic price regime so that the Community could develop an export policy.

The Uruguay Round of GATT negotiations faces new opportunities because of these changes. For the Community, the exercise presents two main opportunities. First, if international agreement recognizes the EC's role as a natural competitor and establishes new rules for international food trade, the crippling export subsidy war could end. That would relieve the budgetary burden of the CAP and release funds to implement other programmes to support Community development. Second, the GATT could contribute to domestic reform. The new market approach outlined in Chapter 3 could still be overturned if conditions in the farm sector deteriorate. 'For the Commission it would certainly be helpful to be imbedded in an international agreement which would support its position vis-à-vis those member countries which still are against price cuts.'[5] On the other hand, the risks and consequences of failure are greater. If the GATT fails to recognize the EC as a 'natural' competitor in the wheat area, the Uruguay Round, and possibly the entire GATT system, could collapse.

The revised price system

The domestic price system and international trade policy for wheat are inseparably linked. The operation of the price system determines where and how much wheat is produced, how it is marketed and the levels of subsidies required for exports. During the 1970s, the price system was devoted to supporting farm incomes irrespective of market conditions, which left little room for the Community to develop a sustained export presence on the world market. The two goals were incompatible because of the expense and logistics.

Beginning in 1977, rapidly increasing supplies of common wheat and negotiations in the Tokyo Round of the GATT caused the Commission to re-examine the price system. Henceforward, the Commission attempted to frame prices to adapt domestic production to market conditions (both domestic and international), rather than to ameliorate domestic problems. Then, after 1980, Community opinion began to shift. By the mid-1980s the farm policy community which had successfully managed the development of the CAP was gone. In its place, a new farm policy community had united behind reform of the CAP.

In 1980 the Commission for the first time suggested that Community prices should be aligned with world prices. It pursued that line of argument in the Mandate of 30 May 1980, concluding that the support (i.e. target) price for cereals in the US was a 'valid point of reference' for the world price.[6] The Commissioners had explicitly rejected aligning EC prices with world prices for a number of reasons:

It is unlikely that European consumers could be supplied for long at low and stable world prices if Community supply, because of reduction in production, would depend to a greater extent on imports. World market prices are notoriously volatile because the quantities involved in international trade are often marginal in relation to total production (e.g. sugar, cereals, dairy products) and may reflect short-term fluctuations in production . . . Therefore, the Commission is convinced that a generalized and systematic alignment to world market prices would not be a practical policy guideline.[7]

They also did not envisage cutting nominal prices; rather, they hoped inflation would close the approximately 20 per cent gap between the two regions.

The Commission generally followed this pricing strategy until 1985. By 1982 the guarantee threshold system was in place and the EC–US price gap had begun to narrow. But, in 1985, the weakening US dollar increased the price gap and the Commission decided that nominal EC prices would need to be cut if the Community was to close the gap. When the 1985 price cut was vetoed by Germany in the Agricultural Council, the Commission initiated a review of the options, which were eventually published in the *Green Paper*. A major rift developed within the Agricultural Directorate-General over the options. Parts of DG–VI pushed strongly during the review for the Commission to continue to set prices to support incomes and to use a variety of soft options (including land set-asides and quotas) to dampen growth in surpluses and budget outlays. As shown in Chapter 4, the cereals traders prevailed and a market focus was adopted by DG–VI.[8] Even then, the market-pricing approach met resistance in the full Commission: the German Commissioner voted against the *Green Paper* in 1985 because he rejected the central premise that EC prices should be aligned with world (i.e. US) prices.[9] Nevertheless, the majority prevailed and thereafter the Commission worked to make the price and intervention systems support the export policy, rather than the reverse.

The Commission's *Green Paper* in 1985 set the tone for reforms over the next several years: 'As for exports, arrangements whereby the producers themselves can take over export risks, if they were to be systematically introduced, could be incorporated into the market organizations ... by restricting to specified quantities the price and disposal guarantees granted by the Community at levels above world prices. Beyond these quantities, disposal would be the responsibility of the producers themselves, at world market prices.'[10]

Meanwhile, in preliminary discussions in 1985 leading to the Punta del Este conference, agricultural trade representatives from many of the GATT signatory states concluded that 'export subsidies could be permitted in the GATT system as long as they are financed by producers themselves rather than being paid for by the taxpayer.'[11] The Commission shortly afterward proposed producer co-responsibility levies to fund export refunds. In practice, the new levy differed little from the levies already paid by French cereals producers to ONIC to finance export marketing (which had never been challenged as subsidies in multilateral forums). Beard says that as a result, 'it can be argued by the EC authorities in international negotiations that EC exports are not being subsidized and that they are therefore legitimate competitive sales, because of the co-responsibility levies contributing to the cost of surplus disposal and export subsidies.'[12]

In the following few years the Commission manipulated the price and inter-vention systems to achieve the changes proposed in the 1985 *Green Paper*. In par-ticular, the Commission forced through the Council new rules that realigned prices closer to US prices (Figure 9.1)[13] and effectively moved much of the financial responsibility for exports to farmers.

In 1986 the Commission proposed a 3 per cent co-responsibility levy on common wheat to finance approximately half of the cost of exporting surpluses.[14] Although the Council adopted the levy only on the basis that the funds would be used to develop domestic uses, it agreed that the funds should be given to DG–VI rather than put into general revenue. In practice, there was nothing to ensure against the levy being used to finance exports. The 1988 budget stabilizers levy worked in the same way. Furthermore, the Council set the production threshold for cereals (beyond which prices would automatically fall) at 160 Mt because that

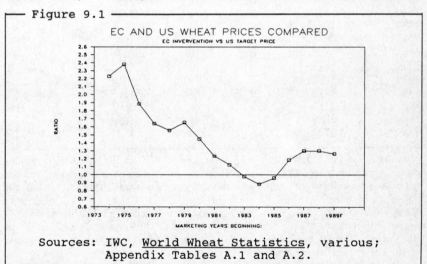

— Figure 9.1 —

EC AND US WHEAT PRICES COMPARED
EC INVERVENTION VS US TARGET PRICE

Sources: IWC, <u>World Wheat Statistics</u>, various; Appendix Tables A.1 and A.2.

represented the net average annual consumption of domestic and imported cereals in the Community. Amounts over that level would need to be exported. Taking all the changes together, in just two years the Commission both set in motion an automatic system to close the gap between support prices in the EC and the US and got producers accepting a greater share of the cost of exports.

Table 9.1 shows the impact of these changes on export finances. Revenues from co-responsibility in 1989 were forecast to pay for more than one-third of the cost of exporting cereals. When the refunds for food aid (which are included in the export cost in the EC but are generally excluded in other exporters' budgets) and the revenues earned from the variable levy on cereal imports are removed, the net cost of exporting cereals was substantially lower.[15] Imports of cereal substitutes, which forced domestic production on to world markets, also contributed significantly to the cost of export restitutions (as much as 800 M ECU in 1982). If, as some groups in the EC argue, the costs of those exports were not assessed to the export policy, then the net cost of cereals exports approached zero in 1989, which put the EC in a strong position to sustain its export effort.

The Commission also reduced the role for official prices. Until 1983 the

Table 9.1 EAGGF expenditures on cereal exports

	Export refunds[1]	Co-resp. levies	Refunds on aid	Net refunds[2]	Import levies[3]	Net cost[4]
1973	567	0	0	567	−25	592
1974	92	0	0	92	54	146
1975	416	0	1	414	192	222
1976	494	0	45	450	331	119
1977	360	0	31	329	298	31
1978	832	0	52	780	317	463
1979	1182	0	30	1152	266	886
1980	1175	0	26	1149	198	951
1981	1206	0	21	1185	219	966
1982	1065	0	24	1041	226	815
1983	1525	0	16	1059	167	892
1984	918	0	15	903	141	762
1985	1077	0	14	1063	203	860
1986	1711	56	60	1595	319	1276
1987	3157	379	86	2692	500	2192
1988F	2805	814	141	1850	350	1500
1989F	2773	1119	133	1521	300	1221

Notes: M UA in 1973–7, M EUA in 1978–80, and M ECU in 1981–;[1] includes refunds on aid shipments; before 1975 it also included the purchase cost of cereals aid;[2] refunds net of co-responsibility and refunds on aid;[3] for common wheat, estimated to equal the difference between the threshold price and the US #2 HWO FOB Gulf offer price multiplied by the total tonnage of wheat imported;[4] equals net refunds less the import levy
Sources: EC Budgets, *OJ* No. L Series, *Nimexe* for EC wheat imports, Canadian Wheat Board *Annual Reports* for US wheat prices, *ASC* for the EC threshold prices, *EC Economy* for the US–EC exchange rates

intervention price represented a solid floor under the market price and, as such, was used as the relevant price for comparison with other competitors. Then the Commission used its powers under Reg.(EEC) 2727/75 to 'restore' intervention to its original role as 'a safety net to cushion farmers against short-term production fluctuations which are not structural in nature.'[16] Chapter 3 illustrates that, as a result, market prices have been consistently below intervention prices since 1983 and farmers have had to respond more to market signals than according to government direction.

The combination of realigned prices, producer co-responsibility for exports and restricted intervention activity has strengthened the European wheat sector's potential to take advantage of commercial opportunities in the world markets. The Commission believes the domestic price system is now a 'sound basis for export growth.'[17]

Developing marketing tools

The Community sought throughout the 1980s to build upon its domestic reforms in order to assure growing opportunities for commercial wheat producers. As before 1979, the Community still had four key alternative outlets for surplus wheat: food aid, feed or industrial usage, storage or export. Whereas the Community generally preferred during the 1970s to store or donate as aid its surplus cereals, in the 1980s the EC sought to develop long-term, commercial outlets for the excess wheat. Food aid shipments continued, but aid policy was reshaped to focus on assisting economic development in the Third World rather than simply on disposal of EC surpluses. Domestic storage remained significant but was reshaped to operate as an adjunct to export policy rather than as an alternative. In place of those outlets, the Community encouraged alternative, commercially-viable domestic uses for wheat (i.e. animal feed or industrial feedstock) and created mechanisms to develop continuous exports. In short, the Community shifted its focus from 'surplus disposal' toward development of commercial markets.[18]

Food aid

The European food aid programme during the 1980s moved from being merely a mechanism for surplus disposal towards a true development-based policy. The EC during the 1980s grew 'increasingly to accept that its food aid commitment should be a continuing one no matter what the state of its internal supply situation.'[19]

The change in EC food aid policy was precipitated by the rapid expansion in exportable surpluses. During the 1970s the Community was frequently threatened with domestic shortfalls. As food aid was viewed largely as a means of surplus disposal (accounting for an average 43 per cent of total surpluses in 1969–78), the Community was quite willing to cut aid shipments to supply the domestic market. During the 1980s, however, the Community found its surpluses were large enough so that even when the Community faced a major crop failure, it had sufficient produce to supply both domestic and foreign aid commitments (Figure 9.2).[20]. Consequently, annual aid shipments during the 1980s reflected needs of receiving countries rather than short-term market problems in the Community.

In 1979, the Commission proposed a new Food Aid Regulation 'to transform food aid into an independent policy aimed at development objectives.'[21] The newly elected EP also began to push for the Community to develop a more responsible aid policy. In 1982 the Council finally approved revised regulations that focused European food aid on development goals — raising the standard of nutrition, helping with emergencies and contributing to balanced economic and social development in the recipient countries — and thereby divorced food aid from disposal of European surpluses. Since then the Community has diversified its methods of giving aid so that in some cases the food aid provided by the EC does not even originate in the Community (i.e. triangular arrangements). Much of the EC's cereals aid is also shipped multilaterally, a turnaround from 1968–78 when the Community shipped less than 15 per cent of its aid via multilateral arrangements or agencies. In the 1980s on average about 30 per cent of the aid was shipped multilaterally and in 1985 about 539,000 tonnes, almost half of the Community aid that year, was shipped through multilateral arrangements.

Alternative uses

After the Community ended the wheat denaturing programme in 1973, it decided to seek alternative uses for the rising surpluses of low-grade wheats. First, the Community sought to increase the use of low-quality wheat as animal

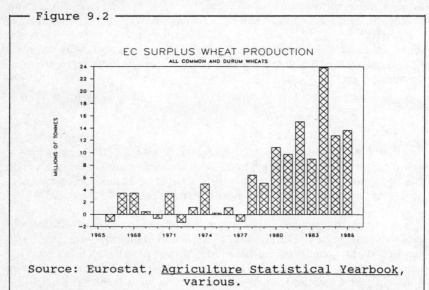

Figure 9.2

EC SURPLUS WHEAT PRODUCTION
ALL COMMON AND DURUM WHEATS

Source: Eurostat, Agriculture Statistical Yearbook, various.

feed, initially by 'completing the CAP' (i.e. limit imports of cereal substitutes) and then by reform of the price system. Then, in the late 1980s, it encouraged processors to use more wheat as a feed stock for industrial products.

As discussed in Chapter 8, the price 'silo' (with bread wheat paid a premium over the common cereal feed price) was not particularly successful in encouraging greater animal feed consumption of low-quality wheat. When that approach failed to solve the problem, the Community sought to reduce imports of non-cereal feeds. By 1979 the derogations of the CAP cereals markets (i.e. zero-bound duties under the GATT) caused the Community serious headaches. During the 1980s, the Community annually imported about 30 Mt of soya and cereal substitutes, which was more than double the exportable production for common wheat. Without its GATT obligation, the Community would likely have reduced imports of these substitutes and fed a significantly higher proportion of its common wheat to animals. By 1982, the cost of importing 9 Mt of manioc and corn gluten feeds had risen to 650 M ECU, or about two-thirds of the net costs of wheat exports.[22]

Pressure to negotiate changes to these bindings built over the late 1970s and into the 1980s. French farmers in particular were convinced that imports of low-cost cereal substitutes were the primary cause of weak domestic demand for their wheat and a major factor behind the fall in EC domestic market prices toward the intervention levels. Especially following the introduction of the cereals co-responsibility levy in 1986, FNSEA pressed the French government to have the Council tighten Community Preference.[23] But the feed industry, consumer associations and the UK government generally opposed the French proposals. At the European level the French farm lobby had convinced the EP in the late 1970s to support GATT negotiations to limit imports of these competing products but after 1979 MEPs on the committees on external economic relations and consumer affairs developed contrary positions. Meanwhile, the ESC generally supported farmer demands to limit cereal substitutes but not if that caused a trade war with the US.

The Commission decided as early as 1982 to try to limit imports of soya and cereal substitutes. It first opened negotiations for a voluntary export restraint (VER) agreement with the exporters of manioc, the major cereal substitute not produced in the US. GATT Article XXVIII allows contracting countries to modify bindings of specific products provided they provide compensation.[24] In April 1982 the Commission reached a tentative agreement with Thailand and Indonesia, paving the way for the EC to suspend the bound duties on manioc. In July 1982 the Council approved a nine-year deal with Thailand, which was not a GATT member, that initially limited it to 5.5 Mt imports and gradually reduced that to 4.5 Mt by 1986, at a maximum *ad valorem* levy of 6 per cent. In exchange Thailand got grants to aid rural development and agricultural diversification in manioc dependent regions. Indonesia and Brazil, both GATT members, were to share (85 per cent and 15 per cent respectively) a 0.588 Mt quota in 1982, which would rise to 0.97 Mt in 1986, subject to a 6 per cent *ad valorem* duty.[25] In 1986, the quotas for Thailand (by then a GATT member), Indonesia and Brazil were extended to 1990 and new quotas were developed for China and other non-GATT members for the 1987–9 period.[26]

US shipments of soya and corn gluten feeds were more difficult to control.

The Commission first proposed in 1982 that the Community should negotiate under Article XXVIII to limit imports of US soya and corn gluten feeds. But that appeared to have been simply part of an effort to finesse the 1982 price package past the French government in the Council rather than a serious attempt to act.[27] As pressure grew, the Commission was forced to respond. In 1984 Council finally authorized the Commission to open negotiations with exporters of maize starch residues (i.e. corn gluten feeds), spent grains (from brewing and distilling) and maize cake. The Commission began discussions with the US in July 1984 but failed to reach any agreement.[28] The Commission was careful to avoid a full-scale battle over this issue because of the increasing importance of world markets for the Community. When it became obvious that the US would not budge, the Commission decided that it would have to use price cuts to improve the competitiveness of EC wheats as animal feed.

The set of measures aimed at realigning wheat and feed cereals prices, combined with the limitations on imports of manioc, had some success by the mid-1980s. The feed use of common wheat rose to an average 21.1 Mt in 1983–6 from an average 13.5 Mt in the previous four years. But exportable surpluses of wheat continued to rise.

The Community decided in the late 1980s to reintroduce subsidies for domestic feed merchants to incorporate common wheat into feeds. At the end of 1988 the Council agreed to pay subsidies to livestock producers who use compounds that include at least 20 per cent EC cereals. Subsidies rise progressively with the proportion of EC cereals used.[29] In total, the Commission planned to make 2–3 Mt of surplus cereals available for feed under this plan.

Meanwhile, the Commission worked after 1980 to develop industrial uses for wheat and other surplus cereals. Once the Commission had shifted its scrutiny from farmers to the larger agro-industrial complex, it saw potential to direct some of the rising surpluses into industrial processes. After 1983 the Commission pushed biomass and ethanol production as a potentially large outlet for low quality wheats. Although the Community had some success with this approach — industrial usage of common wheat rose to 1.3 Mt in 1986–7 from only 0.135 Mt in 1972–3[30] — the expanded usage represented only about 2 per cent of total domestic usage.

Storage

After 1980, the Commission and the Cereals Management Committee directed its stocks policy much more in response to export imperatives. During the 1970s, the Committee maintained a steady domestic stock-to-use ratio by adjusting exports and aid shipments in line with disposable surpluses. Long-term commitments were assiduously avoided. After 1980, however, the Commission was faced with significantly larger surpluses (an average 13 Mt per year compared with only 4 Mt during the 1970s) and a more competitive international market. The Community could no longer hope to store all the exportable grain, nor did it expect to ship it as aid or use it in the livestock industry or for industrial processes. The Community needed an active, long-term export policy, with appropriate storage practices. Consequently, the stock-to-use ratio was allowed to swing more widely than in the 1970s. In both 1981 and 1983, for example, the

Community increased exports by more than the increase in production, which caused the stock-to-use ratio to drop below the level that was historically viewed as consistent with domestic price stability. At the same time, a higher stock-to-use ratio was maintained throughout the period (24 per cent versus 21 per cent in the 1973–80 period) at least partly to guarantee the EC could meet market commitments.[31]

The Commission also held some stocks for strategic purposes. In 1981 the US challenged the EC export subsidies under the 1979 GATT Subsidies Code: it argued that EC subsidies for wheat flour exports allowed Community wheat producers to gain market share at the expense of other exporters. Before the case was adjudicated, the EC announced at the 1982 GATT Ministerial that it would limit its exports to 14 per cent of the world wheat market, which was about the share it had captured during 1980–2.[32] Even though the disputes panel failed to conclude whether EC wheat flour exports exceeded the 'equitable share' standard of the subsidies code, the Community after 1983 was willing to hold larger stocks than strictly needed for domestic purposes partly in order to placate the EC's major competitors.

Export mechanisms

The consultative agencies led the development of new export mechanisms. As early as 1977 the ESC called for a 'genuine agricultural trade policy'. Then after the 1979 election, the new EP supported France's call for the Community to develop medium- and long-term agreements and to provide a greater variety of incentives to exports (e.g. credit).[33] The Commission generally accepted that approach in the 1980s.

Before the Commission asked for greater powers or new mechanisms, it used its management powers to improve the existing export machinery to enable it to move maximum volumes through the export system at the best price. In particular, the Commission created advance settings for refund payments (thereby ensuring that sales were made when buyers were ready, even if the volumes were not yet available), introduced differentiated and special refunds (which allowed the Commission to target exports to specific markets and to practise market price differentiation) and developed product balance sheets (which enabled DG–VI to plan its export campaigns).[34] These innovations were critical factors in a number of Community sales during the 1980s. In 1983, for example, the Commission used a 'special export refund' to regain the Egypt wheat flour market after the US made a subsidized flour sale.[35] Then, in 1986, when the US made an Export Enhancement Program (EEP) offer to the USSR, the Commission was able to offer a special refund (more than 8 ECU/t) in advance of the new marketing year because the product balance sheets showed that the Community would have available supply in the new year. In this way, the EC was able to beat the US offer and complete a 1 Mt sale.[36] Again, in 1988, the Commission countered US EEP offers to China and the USSR with special wheat export subsidies of 4.5 ECU/t (in addition to the existing standing refund offer).[37] The Commission also got Council approval in 1981 to provide restitutions on exports of processed cereal products.[38] Thus, after 1981, the Commission was able to offer export packages of multiple products from numerous food groups, which gave it greater marketing power.

But the Commission was not content with those tools. It felt that the export system lacked continuity; it was unable to maximize export revenues or volumes because it was constrained to single-year sales and was only allowed to use export refunds to regulate volume, price and destination. The Commission argued that, without further mechanisms, it could not optimize the timing, volume or price of export sales; as a result, exports were unnecessarily expensive. Furthermore, the Community's customers wanted the greater security of supply that would flow from long-term agreements. The Commission therefore pressed the Council in 1980 for permission to develop long-term framework agreements (LTFAs or multi-annual supply agreements) to protect important EC food export markets.[39] These three- to five-year agreements, covering only part of expected total export volumes, would 'regularize sales' by establishing the price conditions, safeguard rules and minimum and maximum annual volumes of a variety of products that the Community would agree to export. If integrated into development programmes of LDCs or tied to multi-annual food aid agreements, these contracts would also help stabilize world markets by assuring EC customers secure supplies. In March 1982, the Commission asked Council to allow it to open negotiations on LTFAs with Algeria, Egypt, Morocco and Tunisia, but the Council did not approve.[40]

France, in particular, was unhappy with the Community's limited number of export mechanisms for wheat. As rising EC production after 1979 restricted the commercial opportunities within the Community, France wanted the EC to develop an active export policy so that French farmers could replace their lost EC sales with new world markets.[41] As early as 1975 France pressed the Community to make long-term framework agreements with Europe's major trading partners but, as mentioned in Chapter 8, that attempt failed. When the Community did not pursue long-term exports, France negotiated with China and eventually signed in September 1980 an agreement to sell 0.5 Mt to 0.7 Mt of wheat annually between August 1980 and July 1983. Then, in October 1982 France concluded a three-year agreement in principle to boost French food exports to the Soviet Union; the deal included commitments for between 1 Mt and 3 Mt of wheat each year over the period.[42] Nevertheless, France continued to press for Community action. In October 1983 the French minister of agriculture proposed that the Community create an EC Cereals Export Board to act as a central selling agency, similar to the Canadian or Australian Wheat Boards, but the proposal died because the Commission declined to forward it to the Council.[43]

Meanwhile, the Commission attempted to develop credit mechanisms to support EC wheat exports. In 1981 the Commission offered to co-ordinate the existing national credit agencies (to reduce competition between member states) and to develop an EC credit system for food exports.[44] As with LTFAs, however, Council refused to act and the member states were left to develop their own programmes.

Again, France led in the development of credit instruments. After October 1982 the US used a blend of zero-interest export credits and credit guarantees to 'regain lost market share' in the Mediterranean market. By February 1984, after the first full year of the three-year EEP programme, it had disbursed

US$601 M of blended credit for wheat sales to Algeria, Egypt, Morocco and Tunisia, areas France regarded as traditional markets.[45] Consequently, when the Commission failed to get authority to extend either credit or credit guarantees for EC wheat exports, France decided to expand its own credit offerings. The French government granted, both to export companies and importing countries, two- and three-year credit packages at market rates of interest, with a COFACE guarantee for 95 per cent of the total amount. Previously COFACE extended credit guarantees to exporters only for political and commercial risks and for no longer than six months.

Although of lesser importance, UK and German exports of wheat were on the rise, which encouraged those two countries to develop their own export mechanisms. In the UK, the Home-Grown Cereals Authority provides market intelligence, promotes R&D and acts as the EC agent for intervention buying, storage and disposal of surplus cereals and rapeseed, but does not provide any export assistance. The Export Credit Guarantee Department (ECGD) of the Department of Trade and Industry, traditionally only involved with grain exports in a minor way, was permitted at the end of 1984 to extend credit and credit guarantees for all bulk grain sales to government and public agencies for a maximum of two years and, in cases where other countries were offering credit, for up to three years.[46] The IWC, however, does not think the ECGD used this facility often between then and 1989. Even without further support, however, UK producers were clearly set to capitalize on their new export capacity. The UK invested heavily in port and grain handling facilities during the late 1970s and early 1980s, so that by the mid-1980s the UK could move about 9 Mt annually.[47]

In Germany, support for cereals exports comes mainly from producer financed agencies. The Marktabsatzfond, a marketing fund set up in 1969, was reformed in the 1980s so that its export efforts were financed entirely by levies on agricultural products sold in Germany (before 1979–80 it received government funding). It spends a significant portion of its budget to promote exports, particularly to traditional markets in Eastern Europe.

In 1985, the Commission's *Green Paper* signalled a new phase in the search for more EC export mechanisms. Once the new co-responsibility system was in place, the Commission proposed to develop related trade policy instruments. Commercial farmers, largely in France, demanded that they have greater opportunities to sell abroad if their domestic support was to be cut. In the *Green Paper*, the Commission recommended that export refunds should be further varied by quality, intended use and destination and that the Community should become more active in the credit area. In particular, the Commission proposed to harmonize existing national credit and insurance practices, to encourage the use of ECU-denominated loans (to reduce exchange risks), to regulate national loan subsidies to ensure they accord with the OECD code for credit for industrial products,[48] to develop an EC-level export credit programme and to negotiate multi-annual supply contracts.[49] The Council did not respond and national measures continued to proliferate.

In 1988, after the outstanding domestic concerns were resolved at the special Brussels Summit, the Commission returned to the Council for approval for a Community-based export system. The Commission again offered to co-ordinate national credit agencies (COFACE, ECGD and Marktabsatzfond) in order to harmonize national loans on hard commercial food exports (using OECD guidelines). It also proposed to develop an EC scheme of reduced-rate loans to support exports to the poorest debtor nations in Africa. The credit programme would provide subsidies of 35–100 per cent of the loan interest rate for up to three years, while loan principals would be guaranteed for the EC exporters.[50] The Canadian Wheat Board estimated that the proposed budget of 76 M ECU in 1989 would have been adequate to finance about 2 Mt of wheat sales (equal to about 10 per cent of the 1989 EC export campaign).[51] The Council had not decided on that set of proposals by Spring 1990.

Although the trade policy was not in full operation in 1989, it was possible to see its scope. The Commission would co-ordinate national LTFAs and credit arrangements (which are largely financed through para-fiscal levies on producers) until the Council approves a set of EC supply agreements and credit measures (also financed by producers through co-responsibility levies). When fully operational, the system would rival any now functioning in the major competing countries.

The EC in the GATT

Faced with the changed orientation of the CAP and strong domestic pressure for export expansion, the Community adopted an aggressive strategy for the Uruguay Round of GATT negotiations which began in 1986. Whereas in the Tokyo Round the EC sought to protect and defend its domestic farm policy, in the Uruguay Round until early 1990 it sought to consolidate its domestic reforms and expand its position in world wheat markets. In particular, the EC wants the GATT to confirm it is a 'natural' competitor and to grant it the privileges that flow from such a position, such as the right to defend its market share and the opportunity to enter new markets.

The Community entered the negotiations in the run up to the Punta del Este conference in a strong position, having begun the process to recast its domestic price system to support its international goals. The domestic reforms between 1983 and 1988 were closely linked with the international negotiations. The co-responsibility and stabilizer systems (which incorporate levies, a maximum guaranteed quantity and automatic price cuts) provided the Community with a solid base for export growth because, as indicated above, the levies contribute a large and growing share of the export subsidy costs of the CAP. As well, the mechanisms modulate prices in line with market conditions.

With its domestic programmes largely in order, the Commission sought to develop a matching strong external position. As in the 1970s, the Community faced a variety of legal and political challenges to its export policies (Table 9.2) but, in contrast to the earlier period, the Commission responded aggressively to those attacks. The Community's new response to trade irritations was 'a quick, sharp and rather belligerent threat of retaliation, often listing the actual products.'[52] For example, the EC retaliated to the barrage of US litigation in 1981 and 1982 with cases against the US subsidized sale of wheat flour to Egypt in 1983 and against tobacco and wine import restrictions in 1985. In the 1980s the EC also frequently blocked panel decisions and then negotiated bilaterally with the other litigants to resolve the disputes.[53] After 1979 the Commission also began to use GATT Article XXIII to pry open foreign markets for European exports. Furthermore, in 1984 the EC Foreign Ministers Council adopted a 'New Commercial Policy Instrument', similar to the Section 301 provisions of the US Trade Act of 1974, which permits private EC citizens to complain about GATT violations of other countries and establishes a series of steps by which EC officials could be forced to respond with GATT lawsuits against offenders.[54]

Then the Community brought before the GATT Council meeting on 22 September 1988 a complaint against the 1955 waiver granted for US agricultural

Table 9.2 Key farm trade disputes at the GATT (1980–9)

GATT Article XXIII dispute settlement proceedings:

Date	Plaintiff	Issue
1980	Canada	EC restrictions on imports of beef
1980	USA	UK restraints on poultry imports
1981	Australia	EC canned fruit production subsidies
1982	EC	Switzerland measures on table grapes
1982	Australia+	EC sugar export subsidies
1982	USA	EC production aids on canned fruit
1982	USA	EC tariff on Med. citrus imports
1983	EC	USA tobacco policies
1984	EC	Chile dairy products policies
1984	Australia	EC beef and veal regime
1985	EC	Canadian provincial liquor boards
1986	EC	Canadian limits on beef imports
1987	EC	Japan label rules & distribution systems for bulk wine and beer
1988	USA	EC meat hormone ban
1988	Chile	EC import licenses for dessert apples
1988	US	EC subsidies to feed processors
1988	US	EC restrictions on imports of apples
1988	EC	US 1955 waiver
1988	EC	US duties on EEC products in response to Hormone Directive

Formal dispute settlement proceedings under the framework of the 1979 Tokyo Round trade agreements:

Date	Plaintiff	Issue
1981	USA	EC export subsidies on wheat flour
1982	USA	EC export subsidies on pasta
1982	USA	EC export subsidies on poultry
1983	USA	EC export subsidies on sugar
1983	EC	US wheat flour sale to Egypt
1985	EC	US countervailing duty action on wine

+ also Austria, Brazil, Columbia, Cuba, Dominican Rep., India, Nicaragua, Peru and Philippines
Sources: Petersmann (1986), pp. 67–71, 370–76; Hudec (1988), pp. 46–51; OECD (1988, 1989).

laws. The Community argued that the waiver was both the major infringement of the GATT in the agricultural area and the main source of 'disequilibria, tensions and weakening of the trading system'.[55] The EC and US had held consultations under Article XXIII:2 during 1987 and 1988, but failed to resolve their differences. The US offered to address the waiver in the Uruguay Round negotiations but the EC wanted to remove that bargaining chip before the talks got to the substantive stage. The EC pressed the GATT Council to establish a panel to review US sugar policies (exempted under the waiver) and, if no agreement could be reached, to vote by a two-thirds majority to remove the waiver. The GATT in July 1989 established a panel to review the case and in January 1990 decided against the EC. Insiders reported, however, that because the decision was based on a technicality there is room for the EC to pursue the claim further.[56]

Meanwhile, momentum behind the Uruguay Round of the GATT increased. Compared with past multilateral trade negotiations, this round developed a different focus. In the Tokyo Round discussion centred on tariff levels and the profusion of export subsidies and non-tariff trade barriers. The Uruguay Round, in contrast, quickly evolved into an exercise to establish ground rules to limit both domestic and international policies that distort trade.

In March 1985 the Council set out its objectives for the new GATT Round. Both the Commission and Council agreed that the Community should seek 'more satisfactory arrangements for trade in agricultural products which would not call into question the fundamental principles of the CAP.'[57] The Community would not countenance prohibition of export subsidies or the variable import levy because both instruments were fundamental to the domestic organization of the markets and necessary for any expansion of the EC's market share. About that time, Bruno Julian, the EC agricultural representative at the GATT, warned that 'the EC believes it is entitled to a fair share of the world market and will be aggressive in trying to obtain this share.'[58] In support of that goal, the Community quietly let lapse its 1982 commitment to hold its share of the world wheat market to 14 per cent; during 1984–6 the EC market share averaged more than 17 per cent and rose to 20 per cent in 1988 and 1989.

The Community stonewalled at the GATT opening meeting until the other countries accepted a significantly less dogmatic ministerial declaration than either the US or the Cairns Group desired. The final declaration simply stated that the contracting parties 'agreed that there is an urgent need to bring more discipline and predictability to world agricultural trade.' The talks were not committed, as the US argued, to total liberalization of farm trade, but simply to 'increase discipline'.[59] Furthermore, export subsidies were not singled out as a key issue.

Although the opening salvos in the trade talks appeared similar to past negotiations, there was a significant difference. In earlier GATT rounds the EC sought to defend domestic interests from outside forces; in the Uruguay Round the Commission seeks to use the GATT talks to protect its own reform initiatives from domestic pressures. Although the Commission and European Council want lower domestic support prices and a commercially directed export policy for wheat, there are still large numbers of farmers and many politicians who would like to reverse the changes. The Commission, therefore, seeks through the

GATT to embed the new CAP orientation in an international agreement.[60] Whereas the EC chose to protect the CAP mechanisms in the Tokyo Round by removing agriculture from the agenda (i.e. to the IWC and into discussions leading to interpretive codes),[61] this time it wants agriculture fully on the GATT agenda. The domestic reforms over 1984–8 brought the CAP largely into line with the terms of the GATT and the subsidies code negotiated at the end of the Tokyo Round, so the Community has little to fear from GATT discipline. The Commission judges that it could actually gain if agriculture were brought fully under the rules and obligations of the GATT because it could use the disputes settlement system to resolve differences about state trading rules and the subsidies code (without resort to export subsidy wars).

The Commission decided early in the negotiations that it could best serve both its domestic interests and international market goals by pushing for adoption of a revised form of *montant de soutien*, similar to that proposed in the Kennedy Round negotiations. The Commission believes such a system would help entrench its domestic reforms, permit it to 'balance' Community Preference so that cereal substitutes and oilseed imports are treated as any other imported foodstuff, allow it to extend export subsidies to processed food products and, most importantly, help to reduce the predatory price competition in international markets. The Commission subsequently accepted that a modified producer subsidy equivalent (PSE) system could be used if it takes account only of measures with a significant incidence on trade, if it includes a method to quantify production constraints and if it accommodates problems related to world price and currency fluctuations.[62] The OECD, the US, Canada and the Cairns group also appeared willing to consider a similar sort of system to measure and bind farm support.

The EC in 1987–8 expanded its proposal. It suggested to the GATT Negotiating Group on Agriculture that each country bind for a period of five years its total support for cereals, rice, sugar, oilseeds, dairy products and beef and veal at the level prevailing in 1984 (chosen so that the EC would get total credit in the negotiations for the significant reforms that it had implemented afterwards). The subsidy level would be measured by comparing domestic support prices (ECUs in the EC) with a fixed external reference price (expressed in national currency terms in order to remove distortions caused by changes in exchange rates). Each country could then adjust support for specific commodities without limitation, provided the aggregate level of support remained at or below the bound amount. At the end of five years the system would be reviewed and the Community suggested that it would then accept a long-term phased reduction in agricultural support that affects international markets.[63] The Community additionally sought to force state trading agencies to operate more openly (i.e. transparently);[64] the EC has difficulty setting the proper refund and import levies because the Canadian and Australian Wheat Boards do not disclose their sale prices.[65]

As outlined, the policy was sharply at odds with the US goal of complete liberalization by the year 2000.[66] When the trade ministers met in Montreal in December 1988, the differences became obvious. The US and the EC failed to agree on the wording for either the mid-term review or the negotiating mandate for the remainder of the talks. The entire GATT Round was then jeopardized because the trade ministers refused to proceed with the other areas until there was progress on agriculture.

In April 1989 the US and EC finally resolved their differences. After four months of wrangling over the words related to the ultimate goal of the talks, the trade ministers agreed to seek 'a fair and market-oriented agricultural trading system' and 'provide for substantial progressive reductions in agricultural support and protection sustained over an agreed period of time, resulting in correcting and preventing restrictions and distortions in world agriculture markets.'[67] The ministers also agreed that the EC would get credit for the positive measures it had adopted since the Punta Del Este meeting in September 1986, thereby embedding past reforms in international agreement. Furthermore, the deal specified that support prices for producers (in ECUs for the EC) should not be raised in the short term above the level which prevailed in April 1989. Consequently, when the Agricultural Council met later in April, it had little alternative but to accept the Commission proposals for the 1989–90 marketing year.

Conclusion

During the 1980–9 period, the Community successfully replaced its old, inward-looking trade policy (which was designed to protect small family farms) with a fledgling commercial export policy to assist competitive farmers to realize their commercial potential. Although the new intervention rules and co-responsibility levies had not brought EC prices in line with US prices by 1990, nor had the Council approved the full selection of export mechanisms offered by the Commission, the shape of the Community's trade policy for the 1990s was clearly visible. As a result, the Uruguay Round of the GATT is extremely important for both the Commission and Community, because it represents 'a unique opportunity to encourage and consolidate the reforms — indispensable as they are — in agricultural policies in the various countries, and to improve, on a lasting basis, conditions on world markets.'[68]

Notes

1. Pearce (1981), p. 61.
2. *Ibid.*, p. 99
3. *Financial Times*, 9–7–79.
4. *The Times*, 21–11–80.
5. Tangermann (1988), p. 35.
6. *COM (81) 608*, p. 24.
7. *Ibid.*, p. 8.
8. *Agra Europe*, 1140, 5–7–85.
9. *Financial Times*, 16–6–85.
10. *COM (85) 333*, p. 41.
11. Zietz and Valdés (1988), p. 52.
12. Beard (1986), p. 54.
13. The data in Figure 9.1. is not adjusted for US land set-asides or EC changes to related measures. If they could be quantified, the narrowing in the gap might be

more pronounced because between 1986 and 1989 the US reduced its set-aside requirements (which effectively raised the value of the US deficiency programme) and the EC undercut the operation of intervention (which reduced the value of EC support prices).

14. *COM (86) 20, p. B3.
15. Food aid is financed under the EAGGF Guarantee Section of the budget (Reg. (EEC) 2681/74.) The export refund portion of the cost is assigned to titles 1 and 2 while the world market value of the gift is assigned to title 9.
16. ASC 1988, p. 16.
17. Bull. EC 3–84, p. 14.
18. The Commission's rhetoric changed about that time. It no longer referred to 'surpluses' for disposal but to 'exportable surpluses'.
19. Fennell (1987b), p. 105.
20. See Phillips (1989), p. 343. Between 1979 and 1985, cereals aid shipped accounted for less than 10 per cent of the EC exportable surpluses of wheat.
21. Green Europe, 216, p. 3.
22. COM(81)608, Annex 9.
23. Financial Times, 11–2–86.
24. If satisfactory compensation cannot be negotiated, then the affected country can retaliate with equivalent measures.
25. Bull. EC 7/8–1982, p. 37.
26. Bull. EC 11–1986, p. 69.
27. Financial Times, 8–4–82.
28. ASC 1984, pp. 27 and 79.
29. Agra Europe, 1312, 11–11–88.
30. Eurostat, Supply Balance Sheets.
31. Phillips (1989), p. 352.
32. Petit (1985), p. 59.
33. EP Doc 1–37/80, 24–3–80, p. 22.
34. Bull. EC 7/8–1981, p. 21.
35. Bull. EC 10–1983, p. 58.
36. International Herald Tribune, 15–8–86.
37. Canadian Wheat Board, Weekly News Summary, Week 13, Oct. 24–8, 1988.
38. General Secretariat of the Council, 29th Review of the Council's Work 1981, p. 184.
39. COM(81)429, 10–8–81, pp. 1–2.
40. COM(82)73, 4–3–82.
41. Pearce (1981), p. 97.
42. Agra Europe (1983), p. 46.
43. Petit et al. (1987), p. 31.
44. Bull. EC 7/8–1981, p. 21.
45. F. Clerc, 'French Attitudes', in Tracy and Hodac (1979), p. 363, noted that there is an 'advantage for the Community in having available agricultural product which can be exported to countries of the Mediterranean, the Near East and above all Africa, where the Community is seeking to develop its political relationship.' J. Lynn and A. Jay, Yes, Prime Minister (London, 1986), p. 31, present a wonderful satire of European geopolitical concerns of the CAP which is uncomfortably close to this statement.
46. IWC (1988), p. 3:10.
47. F. Rees, 'The EEC and the UK's cereals processing industry', in Swinbank and Burns (1984), p. 106.
48. OECD (1987a), pp. 231–8, sets guidelines, which include the maximum proportion of credit allowable per trade (85 per cent), the maximum term (10 years) and the minimum interest rate (SDR rate less 10 basis points).

49. *COM(85)333*, p. 46.
50. *Agra Europe*, 1296, 22–7–88, p. 2.
51. Canadian Wheat Board, *Weekly News Summary*, Week 4, Aug. 22–6, 1988.
52. Hudec (1988), pp. 30–1.
53. See Phillips (1989), p. 362n.
54. Hudec (1988), p. 35.
55. GATT, *Focus*, #57, Sept./Oct. 1988, p. 1.
56. *The Globe and Mail*, 10–1–90.
57. General Secretariat of the Council, *33rd Review of the Council's Work 1985*, p. 105.
58. D. Hayes and A. Schmitz, 'Price and welfare implications of current conflicts between the agricultural policies of the US and the EC', in Baldwin *et al.* (1988), p. 69.
59. GATT, *Press Communiqué*, 1396, 25–9–86, p. 7.
60. Tangermann (1988), p. 35.
61. ICAs (e.g. IWA) are not governed by GATT disputes settlement procedure. The subsidies code is also not part of the formal GATT treaty, so it is more difficult to police than other trade rules.
62. National Consumer Council (1988), p. 80.
63. GATT, *Focus*, #50, p. 5, #56; p. 4; and #58, p. 7. Also see Negotiating Group on Agriculture (GATT), *The EC Approach on Aggregate Measurement of Support* (Paris, MTN/GNG/NG5, 10–7–89).
64. Tangermann (1988), p. 36. A good example of EC concerns was reported in *The Western Producer*, 18–5–89. The Canadian Wheat Board announced that it would no longer comment publicly on sales.
65. Morgan (1979), p. 295.
66. *Financial Times*, 15–10–88.
67. GATT, *Focus: Uruguay Round Special Issue*, #61, May 1989, pp. 4–5.
68. *ASC 1988*, p. 26.

Chapter 10

Lessons for policy-makers

Changes in the CAP wheat policy during the 1980s were the result of significant shifts in the power structures and concomitant changes in some of the critical bargains in the system. It follows that further change can only come as quickly as those features shift, which creates both constraints and opportunities in the Uruguay Round of the GATT. In short, the GATT negotiators must accept that 'politics is the art of the possible'. They may continue to strive for the ideal, but in the end they must accept the 'possible' or fail. The foregoing analysis, using the international political economy approach, illuminates the vital linkages between the political and economic spheres to determine the 'possible'.

Trade policy poses a particular problem for analysis and policy development because it depends critically on the domestic economic and policy systems in the trading nations. This study provides some hope for the GATT Round because it shows that the EC has already made some of the significant reforms that are prerequisites for a successful trade negotiation. The foregoing analysis, in particular, shows that the domestic reforms in the EC entail more than mere tinkering with mechanisms; they represent fundamental changes in attitudes and outlook. Avery notes that during the 1970s CAP reform caused apprehension in political circles and for many 'the very term "reform of agricultural policy" was taboo.'[1] During the 1980s, virtually all actors in the policy community came to accept that reform was necessary and most believed that it was desirable.

The challenge for the Uruguay Round GATT negotiators is to recognize the changes within the Community (i.e. that Europe is a natural wheat trader) and to develop a new trading environment that will secure and build upon the domestic reforms in the European Community.

The new power structures

Since 1970, the shifting structures, more than anything else, caused greater diversity in both the economic and political systems. The changes in structures, however, are not complete; they are only part of long-term movements occurring world-wide. Consequently, neither the policy community nor the resulting economic systems are stable; they will continue to be pressed to change.

The security structure is perhaps the least certain. The thaw in East–West relations in the 1980s and the major economic and political reform efforts in the USSR and Eastern Europe are far from secure. There are many road-blocks and pitfalls that could stall or reverse the reforms. Nevertheless, international conflicts are highly unlikely to follow the conventional patterns (i.e. lengthy battles and blockades) while the failure of the US embargo of the USSR in the early 1980s demonstrated that countries have little to fear from disruption of supply during peacetime. As discussed in Chapter 2, food self-sufficiency is no longer physically possible. World-wide integration of production has virtually eliminated the potential for any country to be truly self-sufficient in any product. Now an open and fair trading system is more critical than any policy of national self-sufficiency. The CAP as it operated in the 1970s represented a major irritant in the trade system and threatened the basis of the transformed western security system.

Changes in the production structures are more predictable. The gap between commercial and peasant farms continues to widen: small farmers have neither motivation nor opportunities to become more competitive while large efficient farmers (now producing about 80 per cent of EC cereals) continuously apply new technologies and capital to increase productivity. Furthermore, in spite of the reforms of the price system, Community wheat and cereals output could rise sharply during the next decade. Spain, which in 1988 had more land seeded to wheat than any other member state except France, had wheat yields of only 40 per cent of the average in France, Germany and the UK. If yields increase in response to the higher prices now offered to Spanish producers, Spain conceivably could produce another 5 Mt of wheat and perhaps an additional 10 Mt of other cereals.

Although significant increases in productivity have made large European farmers competitive with other major exporters, they will face stiff competition in the coming years. The IWC estimates that the USSR, currently the largest single cereals importer, could become self-sufficient by 1993 if the new farm programme introduced during 1985–9 improves the efficiency of grain use, reduces post-harvest losses and raises yields.[2] As world wheat stocks are rebuilt in the 1990s and production rebounds in North America, lower Soviet imports should intensify competition among Europe, Canada, Australia and the US for the slowly growing markets in the developing world.[3]

Rapidly changing financial systems will also continue to press on farmers. The expansion of financial capital into the European farm sector in the post-war period allowed farmers to expand, consolidate and specialize but also exposed them to outside influences. In 1990 there was little prospect that financial conditions would return to the stability that characterized the 1960s. Nevertheless, the financial system rapidly innovates and may yet fill one of the missing elements in the developing EC market-based price system. Strange has noted that European farmers do not have ready access to and consequently do not use futures markets to insure themselves against poor prices.[4] As the security afforded farmers under the CAP price system is steadily eroded by reforms, the financial system will be pressed to develop a futures market for wheat and other cereals. The financial industry, spurred by deregulation and competition flowing from the Single Market, might rapidly fill this gap in the system, further reducing the need for regulated prices.

Finally, the knowledge base for farming and food production is booming, with scientific knowledge doubling about every ten years. So far, recombinant DNA techniques have not been directed fully to cereals; when they are, the potential for growth will be large. The US Office of Technical Assessment forecast in 1982 that wheat yields world-wide could rise 1.3 per cent per annum until the turn of the century because of new technologies and seeds.[5]

Overall, the power structures examined in Chapter 2 represent only a stage in the continually changing environment for the European and world wheat industry. There certainly will be more changes, many of which will push the system along the way it has been going since 1980; others may force re-evaluation and redirection of policy.

The evolving policy community

The biggest change since 1970 is the striking reversal in the influence of farmers on the system. The shifting power structures forced the policy community to adapt. In the 1970s, the CAP wheat policy represented an archetypical case of 'sacred cows herded by special interests'.[6] Since then the policy community has become both more diverse and more balanced, with the cows (the CAP mechanisms) less sacred and the special interests (farmers) less able to herd. Farmers still have influence, but more in line with their economic significance, while consumers, environmentalists and other non-farm groups now have a greater say in future directions. Overall, however, markets are the strongest force driving the system.

The farm lobbies in the three major cereals producing countries have all lost power and influence and appear to have little chance of regaining their lost position. The farm lobby in Germany is increasingly losing the unique position it maintained in the political and economic systems. The security imperative to have farmers in the regions bordering on East Germany will end with German re-unification while the massive shift from full- to part-time farming has sharply reduced the number of small and inefficient farmers who depend solely on their farm labours. French farmers also appear to have passed a key political threshold, highlighted by their inability to elect their favoured presidential candidate in either 1981 or 1989. Farmers are highly unlikely, even if a Gaullist president is elected, to rebuild the privileged corporatist relationship which sustained them during the 1960s and 1970s. UK farmers have already decided that their government is not receptive to their needs and now look for support from Brussels. A 1988 survey showed that 75 per cent of UK producers believe that the EC is a better farm policy-maker than the UK government and, as such, they are fully committed to the CAP.[7] Meanwhile, non-farm groups in most of the member states want to ensure that the new Single Market is completed and that the world trading system allows European firms to compete abroad. Consequently, support for farmers now comes less assuredly from the national capitals.

The Brussels farm policy community is also only a shadow of its former self. COPA and the strong farm lobbies in the European Parliament and the ESC have little chance of regaining their earlier power. DG–VI has also lost influence since 1980 because the administrative and political reforms and shift to market pricing allows non-farm interests to become more involved in agricultural policy formulation. Consequently, the agricultural policy community is increasingly unable to keep budget, foreign and trade ministers out of the farm policy debates.

The new price policy

The CAP no longer represents a 'licence to farmers to over-produce';[8] instead, the domestic market now largely determines the prices and marketing conditions. The reform of the CAP has come so slowly and in such fits and starts that many observers refuse to accept that it has really occurred. But a comparison of the system in the early 1970s with the system operating in 1989 clearly demonstrates the extent of the reforms (Chapter 3).

The main complaint of the EC's competitors is that Europe has not adopted complete free market pricing. That expectation plainly fits in the category of the ideal rather than the 'possible'. To give due credit, the Commission attempted to make the price system the sole market regulator in the mid-1980s but the cuts needed to restore market balance were too great for national governments to accept. Koester estimated in 1981 that real EC wheat prices would have to be cut by 4–6 per cent annually merely to halt the growth in surpluses. In West Germany, that would have led to annual nominal cuts of as much as 2 per cent.[9] The Australian Bureau of Agricultural Economics in 1985 concluded that the investment stimulus to yields was so great that total EC agricultural production would have risen by more than 10 per cent during 1973–82 even if real prices had fallen at 4 per cent per annum.[10] More recently, a Canadian study of the international wheat markets forecast that even if EC prices are cut to only US$80/t, the EC would still produce about 70 Mt of wheat.[11] The Council in the mid 1980s rejected such large price cuts and the Commission was forced to seek other methods to stabilize production and costs.

The financial interdependence of farming clearly limits the opportunities for overall policy reform. Cereals farmers in France, Germany and the UK have high debt levels and, in most cases, land represents a large proportion of their investment. Because land prices generally reflect the expected returns from production (and there are few alternative uses for cropped land), even small changes in the level of domestic support for cereals translate into significant changes in land prices. Consequently, heavily indebted cereals farmers (who are usually the most efficient producers)[12] are particularly vulnerable to land price fluctuations. Major changes in the pricing structure, therefore, could eliminate a significant portion of cereal farmers' net worth. The Kiel Institute of World Economics estimates that complete liberalization of the CAP would cause farm land prices in Germany to drop by 17 per cent[13] while other studies suggest the relative shadow prices for farm land would decline by two-thirds to three-quarters,[14] which could translate into price cuts of up to 50 per cent.[15] In addition to endangering a large number of farms, such declines in land prices would threaten many farm-based financial institutions and agricultural suppliers.[16] In spite of these constraints, the Community did achieve significant reform between 1985 and 1989.

Reforms of the cereals policy are and likely will remain less than total liberalization. Cereals are different from many commodities. Compared with mineral products and even livestock production, the cereals production cycle is quite long, with little opportunity to adjust production decisions once the process has started (i.e. the price elasticity of supply is very low in the short term). Adjusting prices after the crop is sown has little or no effect on final production levels. Hence, the Community and most farmers are unenthusiastic about freely floating prices during the marketing year.

The opportunity cost for much of the agricultural land, labour and capital is also low in the short to medium term, so governments will always provide some assistance to farm families. Farm land, the specialized buildings and farm machinery and the skills acquired in the operation of small holdings have little value outside the farm sector.

Perhaps most important of all, governments have a significant investment to protect in rural areas and limited resources to replicate those services in urban areas if the population were to move. Governments have generally made large per capita public investment in rural roads, schools, hospitals and public utilities and, therefore, have a strong economic reason to support the rural economy, which has been overwhelmingly farm-based. In the 1970s and early 1980s, the Community supported farmers largely through higher prices. But, with the reform of the price system in the 1980s, the Commission decided to use a wider variety of programmes to put rural development 'in the forefront of the European Community's objectives.'[17]

Although prices have been cut and intervention systems have been increasingly tightened since 1985, EC market prices have not fully responded. The tight world wheat situation has offset much of the impact of the lower support in Europe and masks the changes in the policy. First the depreciating dollar and then drought in North America in 1988 and 1989 supported the world wheat price in ECU terms, so that the Community has been able to sell abroad with lower net subsidies. Domestic growing conditions in 1985–8 were also not as favourable as in 1984, so that the volumes of grain were not onerous. Consequently, the Commission until 1989 was able to sustain domestic prices above the reduced support levels without exceeding the budgetary limits. The farm lobbies recognize that the domestic wheat price in the EC should drop in line with the reduced price and intervention support whenever yields stabilize in both North America and Europe.

Constraints and opportunities for GATT negotiators

The reform of the EC wheat price policy and the emergence of the Community as a 'natural' competitor in world markets constrain the scope of possible outcomes and present opportunities for progress. The direction chosen will depend on how the international community responds to the EC.

The farm talks in the Uruguay Round negotiations are vitally important because failure could jeopardize the entire GATT process. The opening of the new round of negotiations was delayed in 1986 because of disagreements over farm trade issues and at the start of 1989 progress in the non-farm areas was stalled for four months because negotiators were unable to agree on a mid-term report for the agricultural negotiations. Ultimately, failure to resolve the outstanding farm trade issues could also endanger existing GATT agreements. Governments in the US and the Cairns Group countries, in particular, have over-sold the prospects for farm policy reform; if the promised reforms do not materialize, farmers in those countries might force new retaliatory trade actions. The negotiators in the Uruguay Round must ensure that they do not destroy the benefits of past agreements in the quest for a new, more comprehensive package.

Traditionally, the GATT is based on the view that 'the world is not rich enough to despise efficiency.'[18] Although that motivation possibly dominates other countries or other commodities, it is not the key concern of Community negotiators in the area of agricultural trade. Instead, the Community seeks acceptance of its developing export orientation and support for its domestic approach. Graham Avery, a Commission official, believes that the GATT should 'harness the external pressures to help, rather than hinder, the process of reform' in the EC.[19] Therefore, the GATT must develop a workable way to reduce support and bolster the rules governing farm trade.

The EC and the traditional exporters have already agreed in principle that they would be willing to bind and gradually reduce agricultural support, using some type of aggregate measurement: the producer subsidy equivalent (PSE) measure proposed by the FAO and OECD or the 'trade distorting' equivalent measure proposed by Canada.[20] They have also all expressed willingness to examine how variable levies and other non-tariff barriers can be 'tariffied'. Provided these options do not jeopardise the EC policy of supporting farmers via regulated prices, the EC might accept this approach because it would allow it to reduce support for some sectors (e.g. cereals) while sustaining or increasing the support for other sectors (e.g. milk). Although total support would be bound (and gradually reduced), this approach would enable the EC to realign its external protection (i.e. higher duties on cereal substitutes) and to provide for some ameliorating measures to offset price movements caused by largely monetary-induced exchange rate fluctuations.

Furthermore, the GATT can no longer ignore the Community's export interests; at the very least, any agreement must recognize the EC as a legitimate competitor. Even in 1989, the prevailing opinion among the traditional wheat traders (i.e. the US, Canada, Australia and Argentina) was that the EC should not export. But the Community cannot easily be denied a position in world markets. EC cereals farmers are now among the most competitive in the world (Table 2.1) and their export aspirations are widely supported within the Community. An opinion survey in 1987 showed an overwhelming majority of respondents believed the EC should maintain its role as the second largest food exporter (Figure 10.1).[21] Traditional exporters should press instead for the Community to realign its domestic support closer to world levels and to develop a system of producer-financed export subsidies to replace its current budget-based system of export restitutions. As shown in Chapter 9, the Community is already moving in that direction. Now, most of all, it needs support through the GATT to sustain the reforms.

The GATT will also need to accommodate Community and developing world concerns over the impact of macroeconomic policy on trade. For both LDCs and the EC, the link between protection and exchange rate misalignments has become a major issue.[22] Resolution of the US current account and budgetary

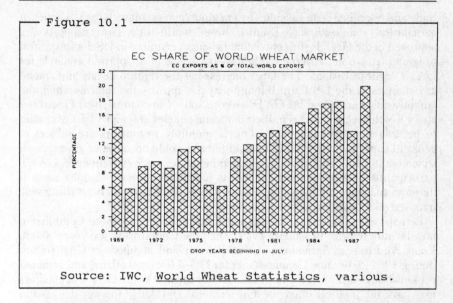

Figure 10.1

EC SHARE OF WORLD WHEAT MARKET
EC EXPORTS AS % OF TOTAL WORLD EXPORTS

CROP YEARS BEGINNING IN JULY

Source: IWC, World Wheat Statistics, various.

deficits, in particular, poses the most difficulty. US economist William Cline estimates that exchange rates will have to change significantly for the US current account deficit to be reduced to a sustainable level. In the EC, that would require a major realignment in the EMS, including a 17 per cent revaluation of the DM against the French franc,[23] which would wreak havoc with the agri-monetary system and the whole CAP wheat price regime. Although at first glance this threatens to make the negotiations more complex, exchange rate adjustments may provide a critical opening for reform in the EC. The Commission has announced that it wants to end the agri-monetary system by the beginning of 1992 so that intra-EC trade in food products will compete on the same basis as non-agricultural products in the newly completed Single Market. By then revaluations of the DM may have opened the gap between the green and real ECU (already about 13.7 per cent) to such a degree that all producers would suffer a price cut if the green ECU were set equal to the real ECU. If by that time the GATT has negotiated firm commitments to hold the line on domestic price support for farmers, the Community might be persuaded to allow effective ECU prices to drop by the amount of the correcting factor, provided both income support and direct cash payments could be made. The GATT should seek an agreement that will establish a framework to guide these Community reforms.

The GATT negotiators must quickly resolve the confusion and disagreement emanating from the different national negotiating mandates and strategies. One critical difference between the EC and US is that the US Trade Representative's (USTR) mandate is set once and for all by the Congress in the Trade Act, while the Commission's mandate is continuously revised. The USTR can offer to negotiate almost anything (such as complete liberalization of farm trade) without causing major protests from the national constituencies because anything outside the negotiating mandate must be ratified by Congress. In this round, the 1988 US Trade Act only authorizes the President to negotiate rules for agricultural trade and to reduce farm subsidies in a manner 'consistent with the US policy of agricultural stabilization.'[24] Even if lower world-wide farm supports are approved in the GATT, the concomitant changes required in US domestic farm programmes are not covered by the fast-track system of approval available for GATT tariff provisions. The US Congress has the right to debate and amend any changes of the US Farm Bill and may not approve the reforms which the administration accepts at the GATT negotiations.[25] In contrast, the EC member states which accept changes in their domestic policies at the GATT are certain to be able to implement them. The Community negotiators are subject to constant supervision by the 113 Committee and would not advance any proposal which could incite opposition in the member states. As a consequence, GATT participants must not assume the EC is unnecessarily obstructionist when it hesitates to make ambitious proposals; it simply has a different negotiating style imposed on it by its mandate.

Perhaps most important, the balance of power in the European Commission now favours reform. In January 1989, when the Commission was reappointed, Frans Andriessen, Agricultural Commissioner and architect of CAP reform during 1984–8, became Commissioner for DG–I (external affairs) and assumed responsibility for the GATT negotiations. For the first time EC trade negotiators may have the political influence and technical knowledge to sway debate and offset the influence of defensive elements in DG–VI. Support also extends into the national governments and to farmers themselves. France, Germany and the UK all support the GATT negotiations and each is willing to make further changes in the CAP in exchange for concessions in other areas. Meanwhile, commercial farmers in Europe generally support farm reform, provided it comes gradually. Daniel Green argues that farmers are 'not rejecting change; for in no other industry have men kept abreast of a rapidly changing technology quite so successfully.' Rather they want change to come at an 'evolutionary rather than a revolutionary pace.'[26] Better than most, farmers know that they must survive the short term to take advantage of the long-run benefits of reform.

Finally, the GATT negotiators must look closely at the calendar. The scheduled final year for the Uruguay Round negotiations roughly coincides with two major domestic events. First, the 1985 US Farm Security Act must be renewed in or shortly after 1990. Second, the EC budgetary, production and price rules set in 1988 are only established until the end of the 1991–2 marketing year; afterwards, the Community must either extend or replace the system. Although farmers are unlikely to be able to force the EC to return to using prices to support farm incomes, the Community could reverse its support for a market-based price and marketing system and introduce stronger administrative controls over the market (e.g. through quotas and market guarantees), which would virtually eliminate any chance for fair competition in the international market. The GATT negotiators and their political masters must decide whether to accept the possible or, in pursuit of the ideal, risk failure.

Conclusion

This study provides a different perspective on the EC and the current GATT round of negotiations for a wide range of participants: those at the table, others who help them prepare and the many actors in the trade policy community. First, traditional analytical approaches for trade issues may no longer be appropriate. The multidisciplinary international political economy approach adopted here provides significantly greater depth of understanding than single-discipline approaches. Second, there have been fundamental shifts in the structures and bargains that nurture and support the wheat policy system in the European Community. The development of commercial competitiveness, diffusion of interests and increased pace of change within the EC has radically altered the farm policy community. The policy 'cartel' of the 1960s and 1970s has been replaced by a constantly shifting set of looser bargains. Third, the policy orientation inside the Community has been transformed. The EC now wants to capitalize on its new commercial opportunities for wheat production and export; earlier, the Community sought to defend and preserve the distinct social aspects of farming. Consequently, the EC now seeks a commercial arrangement within the GATT, which at least means that they are talking the same language as the traditional exporters. The main difference between the two is a question of speed and degree of adjustment, not of direction. These changes present new challenges and opportunities to participants in the GATT.

Notes

1. Avery (1987), p. 162.
2. *The Western Producer*, 22–12–88.
3. *Ibid.*, 4–5–89.
4. Strange (1986), p. 113.
5. M. Phillips, 'Enhancing competitiveness', in Federal Reserve Bank of Kansas City (1985), p. 31.
6. BBC broadcast, 30–10–87.
7. Centre for Agri Food marketing study results reported in *Financial Times*, 25–11–88.
8. Philip (1989), p. 6.
9. Koester (1981), p. 10.
10. Bureau of Agricultural Economics (1985), p. 318.
11. Furtan *et al.* (1988), p. 129.
12. *ASC 1988*, p. 61, shows that in 1985–6, the largest 14 per cent of farms had 40 per cent of the capital in agriculture and the lowest net worth as a percentage of liabilities.
13. Centre for International Economics (1988), p. 28.
14. *Ibid.*, p. 28.
15. P. Pierani and K. Frohberg, 'Impact of CAP trade liberalization on agricultural supply', in Tarditi *et al.* (1989), p. 136.
16. K. Thomson, 'Budgetary and economic effects of CAP trade liberalization', in Tarditi *et al.* (1989), p. 117, estimates that the farm supply industry would suffer losses of nearly 60 BECU if the CAP were liberalized.
17. Avery (1989).
18. Warley (1976), p. 364.
19. Avery (1987), p. 163.

20. GATT, *News of the Uruguay Round*: #007, 14–7–87, p. 4; #011, 12–11–87, pp. 2–3; and #017, 30–6–88.

21. National Consumer Council (1988), pp. 190, 196 and 198. About 67.1 per cent of Germans, 83.8 per cent of the French and 72.3 per cent in the UK agreed that 'the EC should maintain its role as the second largest exporter of agricultural products by improving competitiveness'. For the Community as a whole, 70.7 per cent responded yes and only 8 per cent disagreed.

22. Valdés (1987), p. 575.

23. *The Economist*, 6–5–89, p. 95.

24. US Government, *Omnibus Trade and Competitiveness Act of 1988*, P.L.100, 23–8–88, S.1101(7.B).

25. *Ibid.*, S.1102(b).

26. Green (1975), p. 126.

Appendix A

Wheat prices and agri-monetary rates

Table A.1 EC wheat price proposals and decisions (ECU/tonne; marketing years)

		Target price	% Ch	Intervention price	% Ch	Reference price	% Ch
1972–3	Year-end	137.58	—	126.64	—	—	—
1973–4	Proposal	141.37	2.8%	130.13	2.8%	—	—
	Decision	138.96	1.0%	127.91	1.0%	—	—
	Year-end	138.96	1.0%	127.91	1.0%	—	—
1974–5	Proposal A	141.73	2.0%	127.91	0.0%	—	—
	Decision A	147.30	6.0%	133.02	4.0%	—	—
	Proposal B	153.19	10.2%	138.34	8.2%	—	—
	Decision B	154.66	11.3%	139.67	9.2%	—	—
	Year-end	154.66	11.3%	139.67	9.2%	—	—
1975–6	Proposal	170.12	10.0%	152.24	9.0%	—	—
	Decision	168.58	9.0%	152.24	9.0%	—	—
	Year-end	168.58	9.0%	152.24	9.0%	—	—
1976–7	Proposal	184.38	9.4%	143.45	–5.8%	162.73	6.9%
	Decision	183.76	9.0%	140.24	–7.9%	158.37	4.0%
	Year-end	183.76	9.0%	140.24	–7.9%	158.37	4.0%
1977–8	Proposal	189.20	3.0%	144.47	3.0%	163.21	3.1%
	Decision	191.11	4.0%	145.15	3.5%	163.92	3.5%
	Year-end	191.11	4.0%	145.15	3.5%	163.92	3.5%
1978–9	Proposal	196.32	2.7%	146.97	1.3%	169.01	3.1%
	Decision	196.32	2.7%	146.97	1.3%	165.58	1.0%
	Year-end	196.32	2.7%	146.97	1.3%	165.58	1.0%
1979–80	Proposal	196.32	0.0%	146.97	0.0%	165.58	0.0%
	Decision	201.42	2.6%	149.47	1.7%	168.06	1.5%
	Year-end	201.42	2.6%	149.47	1.7%	168.06	1.5%
1980–1	Proposal	208.97	3.7%	152.15	1.8%	171.00	1.7%
	Decision	214.01	6.3%	155.88	4.3%	175.20	4.2%
	Year-end	214.01	6.3%	155.88	4.3%	175.20	4.2%

Table A.1 EC wheat price proposals and decisions (ECU/tonne; marketing years) (con't)

		Target price	% Ch	Intervention price	% Ch	Reference price	%Ch
1981–2	Proposal	213.13	8.0%	165.23	6.0%	182.21	4.0%
	Decision	230.55	7.7%	165.23	6.0%	192.72	10.0%
	Year-end	230.55	7.7%	165.23	6.0%	192.72	10.0%
1982–3	Proposal	246.81	7.1%	176.10	6.6%	205.40	6.6%
	Decision	250.61	8.7%	179.27	8.5%	209.10	8.5%
	Year-end	250.61	8.7%	179.27	8.5%	209.10	8.5%
1983–4	Proposal	261.41	4.3%	186.44	4.0%	217.46	4.0%
	– Co-resp.	261.41	4.3%	184.58	3.0%	215.29	3.0%
	Decision	261.41	4.3%	184.58	3.0%	215.29	3.0%
	Year-end	261.41	4.3%	184.58	3.0%	215.29	3.0%
1984–5	Proposal	261.41	0.0%	184.58	0.0%	215.29	0.0%
	Decision	259.08	–0.9%	182.73	–1.0%	213.14	–1.0%
	Year-end	259.08	–0.9%	182.73	–1.0%	213.14	–1.0%
1985–6	Proposal	262.97	1.5%	185.47	1.5%	216.34	1.5%
	– Co-resp.	249.82	–3.6%	176.20	–3.6%	205.52	–3.6%
	Interim	254.98	–1.6%	179.44	–1.8%	209.30	–1.8%
	Year-end	254.98	–1.6%	179.44	–1.8%	209.30	–1.8%
1986–7	Proposal	256.16	0.5%	179.44	0.0%	—	—
	Decision	256.16	0.5%	179.44	0.0%	—	—
	Year-end	256.16	0.5%	179.44	0.0%	—	—
1987–8	Proposal A	251.63	–1.8%	175.85	–2.0%	—	—
	Proposal B	256.10	0.0%	179.44	0.0%	—	—
	Decision	256.10	0.0%	179.44	0.0%	—	—
	Year-end	256.10	0.0%	179.44	0.0%	—	—
1988–9	Proposal	250.30	–2.3%	179.44	0.0%	—	—
	Decision	250.30	–2.3%	179.44	0.0%	—	—
	Year-end	250.30	–2.3%	179.44	0.0%	—	—
1989–90	Proposal	247.78	–1.0%	174.06	–3.0%	—	—
	Decision	247.78	–1.0%	174.06	–3.0%	—	—

Notes: Prices before 1979 converted at 1 ECU = 1.208953 × UA; the percentage difference in the reference price in 1976–7 is the change from the intervention price for 1975–6.
Sources: Commission Proposals, *ASC* (various)

Table A.2 Agri-monetary rates for the green ECU, franc, pound and DM (marketing years)

		Conversion factor for green ECU	Franc green rate	Pound green rate	DM green rate
1972–3	Year-end	—	4.59422	0.382168	3.02741
1973–4	Proposal	—	na	na	2.94385
	Decision	—	4.59422	0.382168	3.02741
	Year-end	—	4.59422	0.382168	3.02741
1974–5	Proposal A	—	4.59422	0.382168	3.02741
	Decision B	—	4.59422	0.382168	3.02741
	Proposal A	—	4.59422	0.382168	3.02741
	Decision B	—	4.59422	0.412489	3.02741
	Year-end	—	4.59422	0.412489	3.02741
1975–6	Proposal	—	4.74658	na	2.86467
	Decision	—	4.65955	0.421638	2.96018
	Year-end	—	4.65955	0.471156	2.96018
1976–7	Proposal	—	4.65955	0.471156	2.84843
	Decision	—	4.65955	0.471156	2.87922
	Year-end	—	4.65955	0.471156	2.87922
1977–8	Proposal	—	4.78294	0.500910	2.79407
	Decision	—	4.78142	0.485244	2.82276
	Year-end	—	4.96381	0.485244	2.82276
1978–9	Proposal	—	4.96381	0.500995	2.79049
	Decision	—	5.14920	0.524589	2.81432
	Year-end	—	5.42697	0.524589	2.81432
1979–80	Proposal	—	5.42021	0.552200	2.81432
	Decision	—	5.50961	0.581264	2.78341
	Year-end	—	5.56725	0.618655	2.78341
1980–1	Proposal	—	5.76891	0.618655	2.75175
	Decision	—	5.84700	0.618655	2.75175
	Year-end	—	5.99526	0.618655	2.75175
1981–2	Proposal	—	5.84700	0.582603	2.60723
	Decision	—	5.99526	0.618655	2.65660
	Year-end	—	6.19564	0.618655	2.65660
1982–3	Proposal	—	6.08656	0.592604	2.53140
	Decision	—	6.19564	0.618655	2.57524
	Year-end	—	6.19564	0.618655	2.57524
1983–4	Proposal	—	6.37174	0.604167	2.49870
	Decision	—	6.49211	0.618655	2.52875
	Year-end	—	6.49211	0.618655	2.52875

Table A.2 Agri-monetary rates for the green ECU, franc, pound and DM (marketing years) (con't)

		Conversion factor for green ECU	Franc green rate	Pound green rate	DM green rate
1984–5	Proposal	—	6.67790	0.593946	2.37039
	Decision	1.033651	6.86866	0.618655	2.52875
	Year-end	1.033651	6.86866	0.618655	2.39792
1985–6	Proposal	1.033651	7.01590	0.618655	2.38516
	Interim	1.033651	7.00089	0.618655	2.39792
	Year-end	1.083682	7.00089	0.618655	2.39792
1986–7	Proposal	1.083682	7.10590	0.618655	2.39792
	Decision	1.083682	7.09967	0.626994	2.39792
	Year-end	1.125696	7.09967	0.626994	2.39792
1987–8	Proposal A	1.125696	7.43388	0.646618	2.39792
	Proposal B	1.125696	7.43388	0.646618	2.34069
	Decision	1.137282	7.47587	0.656148	2.39792
	Year-end	1.137282	7.47587	0.656148	2.39792
1988–9	Proposal	1.137282	7.47587	0.656148	2.37360
	Decision	1.137282	7.58418	0.675071	2.37360
	Year-end	1.137282	7.58418	0.675071	2.37360
1989–90	Proposal	1.137282	7.47587	0.675071	2.37360
	Decision	1.137282	7.69787	0.701383	2.37360

Notes: Rates before 1979 were converted at 1 ECU = 1.208953 UA; in 1978 the franc green rate was changed after the Commission proposal, so the existing rate has been entered rather than the proposed rate; national currency prices = ECU price × green rate × conversion factor (after 1984).
Sources: Commission proposals; *ASC* (various); and Commission (1988c), *Taux de Conversion*

Appendix B

Table B.1 Sources for EC wheat price proposals, opinions and decisions (1973–88)

Market year	Commission proposal (COM and date)	ESC plenary opinion (reference and date)	EP agriculture draft (reference and date)	EP plenary opinion (decision and date)	Council decision (date)***
1973–4	COM(73)445/453	OJ No. C 69, 28–8–73	Doc 24/73	OJ No. C 26, 30–4–73	1–5–73
1974–5A	COM(74)30, 16–1–74	OJ No. C 88, 26–7–74	Doc 366/73	OJ No. C 23, 8–3–74	23–3–74
1974–5B	COM(74)1446, 29–9–74	No opinion	Doc 248/74, 14–9–74	OJ No. C 118, 3–10–75	2–10–74
1975–6	COM(74)2001, 27–11–74	OJ No. C 47, 27–2–75	Doc 473/74, 13–1–5	OJ No. C 32, 11–2–75	12–2–75
1976–7	COM(75)600, 10–12–75	OJ No. C 50, 4–3–76	Doc 522/75, 5–2–76	OJ No. C 53, 8–3–76	6–3–76
1977–8	COM(77)100, 28–2–77	OJ No. C 77, 30–3–77	Doc 9/77, 21–3–77	OJ No. C 93, 18–4–77	25–4–77
1978–9	COM(77)525, 8–12–77	OJ No. C 101, 26–4–78	Doc 579/77, 13–3–78	OJ No. C 85, 10–4–78	12–5–78
1979–8	COM(79)10, 5–2–79	OJ No. C 171, 9–7–79	Doc 675/78, 12–3–79	OJ No. C 93, 9–4–79	21–6–79
1980–1	COM(80)10, 7–2–80	OJ No. C 182, 21–7–80	Doc 1–37/80, 24–3–80	OJ No. C 97, 21–4–80	30–5–80
1981–2	COM(81)50, 20–2–81	OJ No. C 159, 29–6–81	Doc 1–50/81, 19–3–81	OJ No. C 90, 21–4–81	2–4–81
1982–3	COM(82)10, 27–1–82	OJ No. C 114, 6–5–82	Doc 1–30/82/A, 19–3–82	OJ No. C 104, 11–4–82	18–5–82
1983–4	COM(82)650, 21–12–82	OJ No. C 124, 9–5–83	Doc 1–1325/82/A, 28–2–83	OJ No. C 96, 11–4–83	17–5–83
1984–5	COM(84)20, 21–1–84	OJ No. C 103, 16–4–84	Doc 1–1508/83, 2–3–84	OJ No. C 104, 16–4–84	31–3–84
1985–6	COM(85)50, 30–1–85	No opinion	Doc 2–1770/84, 4–3–85	OJ No. C 94, 15–4–85	**
1986–7	COM(86)20, 13–2–86	OJ No. C 181, 20–5–86	Doc A2–8/86/A/B/C	OJ No. C 120, 20–5–86	25–4–86
1987–8	COM(87)1, 24–2–87*	OJ No. C 150, 9–6–87	Doc A2–40/87, 29–4–87	OJ No. C 156, 15–6–87	30–6–87
1988–9	COM(88)120, 25–4–88	OJ No. C 175, 4–7–88	Doc A2–108/88	OJ No. C 187, 18–7–88	14–7–88

Notes: 1974–5A and 1974–5B were both acted upon; * Revised 16–3–87; ** Council never approved the cereals price decisions; the Commission implemented an interim set; *** The best sources for information are the *Bulletin of the ECs, OJ* L Series, *Green Europe Newsflash*, and the Home-Grown Cereals Authority *Marketing Reports*.

Bibliography

All European Community documents are listed chronologically under the relevant agency (i.e. Commission, ESC, EP) except the periodicals *Green Europe* and *Eurobarometre* (listed separately) and the Commission's annual price proposals and related EP and ESC opinions (included in Table B.1). The key sources for European farm affairs are: Commission Communications (COMs); EP committee opinions (Doc EP/PE); ESC committee opinions (CES series); the *Official Journal (OJ);* the monthly *Bulletin of the ECs (Bull. EC);* and the annual *Agricultural Situation in the Community (ASC).*

Agra Europe (various). London, England.

Agra Europe (1983). *The Common Agricultural Policy's Role in International Trade.* London: Agra Europe.

Andrlik, E. (1981). 'Farmers and the state: agricultural interests in West German politics.' *West European Politics,* 4:1, pp. 104–19.

Ardagh, J. (1987). *Germany and the Germans.* London: Hamish Hamilton.

Avery, G. (1984). 'The Common Agricultural Policy: a turning point.' *Common Market Law Review,* 21:3, pp. 481–504.

—— (1987). 'Farm policy: chances for reform.' *The World Today (RIIA),* 43:8–9, pp. 160–5.

—— (1989). *From Farm Policy to Rural Policy: The Challenge for Europe.* London: Speech at the Central Association of Agriculture Valuers, 3 April.

Averyt, W. (1977). *Agro Politics in the EC: Interest Groups and the CAP.* London: Praeger.

Baldwin, R. (1979). *The MTN: Toward Greater Liberalization.* Washington: American Enterprise Institute.

Baldwin, R. *et al.* (eds) (1988). *Issues in US-EC Trade Relations.* London: University of Chicago Press.

Bale, M. and Koester, U. (1983). 'Maginot line of European farm policies.' *The World Economy,* 6:4, pp. 373–92.

Bard, R. (1972). *Food Aid and International Agricultural Trade.* London: Lexington Books.

Barkema, A. and Drabenstott, M. (1988). 'Can U.S. and Great Plains agriculture compete in the world market?' *Economic Review,* 73:2, pp. 3–17.

Beard, N. (1986). *Against the Grain? The EC Cereals Policy*. London: Knight Frank & Rutley.

Bieber, R. and Palmer, M. (1975). 'Power at the top — The EC Council in theory and practice.' *The World Today (RIIA)*, 31:8, pp. 310–18.

Body, R. (1984). *Farming in the Clouds*. London: Temple Smith.

Bowler, I. (1985). *Agriculture under the Common Agricultural Policy: A Geography*. Manchester: Manchester University Press.

Braudel, F. (1981). *Civilization and Capitalism: 15th–18th Centuries, Vol. 1*. New York: Harper and Row.

Buckwell, A. *et al.* (1982). *The Costs of the Common Agricultural Policy*. London: Croom Helm.

Bulmer, S. and Paterson, W. (1987). *The Federal Republic of Germany and the European Community*. London: Allen & Unwin.

Bureau Européen des Unions de Consommateurs (1985). *Bureau Européen des Unions de Consommateurs*. Brussels: BEUC.

—— (1987). *EEC Food Surpluses: A Symbol of Failure: BEUC's views on the CAP and what should be done to reform it*. Brussels: BEUC/104/87.

—— (1989). *Comments on the Agricultural Conclusions of the Mid-Term Review of the Uruguay Round*. Brussels: BEUC.

Bureau of Agricultural Economics (1985). *Agricultural Policies in the European Community: Their Origins, Nature and Effects on Production and Trade*, Policy monograph no. 2. Canberra: Australian Government.

Burrell, A. *et al.* (1984). *Statistical Handbook of UK Agriculture*, 2nd ed. Ashford, Kent: CEAS, Wye College.

Burtin, J. (1987). *The Common Agricultural Policy and its Reform*, 4th ed. Luxembourg: EC Commission.

Butler, M. (1986). *Europe: More Than a Continent*. London: Heinemann.

Butler, N. (1983). 'The ploughshares war between Europe and America.' *Foreign Affairs*, 62:1, pp. 105–22.

—— (1986). *The International Grain Trade: Problems and Prospects*. London: Croom Helm.

Canadian Wheat Board (various). *Grain Matters: A Letter from the Canadian Wheat Board*. Winnipeg: CWB.

—— (various). *Weekly News Summary*. Winnipeg: CWB.

Casadio, G. (1973). *Transatlantic Trade: US-EEC Confrontation in the GATT Process*. Farnborough: Saxon.

Caspari, C. (1983). *The Common Agricultural Policy: The Direction of Change*, Special Report #159. London: The Economist Intelligence Unit.

Centre for International Economics (1988). *Macroeconomic Consequences of Farm Support Policies: Global Study Overview*. Canberra: CIE.

Club de Bruxelles (1988). *New Options for European Agriculture in 1988–89*. Brussels: European News Agency.

Cohn, T. (1979). 'The 1978–79 negotiations for an international wheat agreement: an opportunity lost?' *International Journal (Can)*, 35:1, pp. 132–49.

Commission of the ECs (annual). *Agricultural Situation in the Community: Annual Report (ASC)*. Brussels: Commission of the EC.

—— (annual). *Commission Proposal to the Council on the Fixing of Prices for Certain Agricultural Products and Connected Measures*. Brussels: Commission of the ECs (see Table B.1).

—— (annual). *General Report on Activities of the European Communities*. Luxembourg: Commission of the EC.

—— (monthly). *Bulletin of the Economic Community*. Brussels: Commission of the ECs.

—— (various). *European Economy*. Luxembourg: Commission of the ECs.

——. *COM(73)1850: Memorandum: Agriculture 1973–88*. 5–11–73.

——. *COM(75)100: Stocktaking of the CAP*. 4–3–75.

——. *COM(78)20: Economic Effects of the Agri-Monetary System*. 10–2–78.

——. *COM(78)275: GATT Multilateral Talks*. 16–6–78.

——. *COM(78)700: Future Development of the CAP*. 29–11–78.

——. *COM(79)514: GATT Multilateral Talks — Final Report and Proposals*. 10–10–79.

——. *COM(79)710: Changes in the CAP to Help Balance the Markets and Streamline Expenditures*. 30–11–79.

——. *COM(80)800: Reflections on the CAP*. 5–12–80.

——. *COM(81)300: Commission Report on the Mandate of 30 May 1980*. 24–6–81.

——. *COM(81)429: Negotiation of Framework Agreements related to Multi-Annual Supply of Agricultural Products*. 10–8–81.

——. *COM(81)608: Mandate of 30 May 1980: Guidelines for European Agriculture*. 23–10–81.

——. *COM(82)73: Recommendations for a Council Decision on the Directives to be Followed in Negotiations for Multi-Annual Supply Agreements*. 4–3–82.

——. *COM(82)175: Changes to the Conditions under which Certain Products for Use as Animal Feed are Imported into the Community*. 19–4–82.

——. *COM(83)380: Further Guidelines for the Development of the CAP*. 20–6–83.

——. *COM(83)500: CAP: Proposals of the Commission*. 28–7–83.

——. (1984). *Public Expenditure on Agriculture*, Study P.229. Brussels: DG–VI, Commission of the ECs.

——. *COM(85)333: Perspectives for the Common Agricultural Policy*. 15–7–85 (also known as the *Green Paper*).

——. *COM(85)700: Memorandum on adjustment of the market organization for cereals*. 14–11–85.

——. *COM(85)750: A Future for Community Agriculture: Commission Guidelines Following Consultations in Connection with the 'Green Paper'*. 18–12–85.

——. *COM(86)30: Council Regulations for Cereals*. 11–2–86.

——. (1987). *CAP Working Notes: Cereals and Rice and Animal Feed*. Brussels: DG–VI.

——. *COM(87)64: Report on the Agri-Monetary System*. 27–2–87.

——. *COM(87)168: Economic Effects of the Agri-Monetary System, Updated 1987*. 14–8–87.

——. *COM(87)410: Review of Action Taken to Control the Agricultural Markets & Outlook for the CAP*. 3–8–87.

——. *COM(87)452: Implementation of Agricultural Stabilizers, Vol I*. 1–10–87.

——. *COM(88)1: Set Asides of Agricultural Land and Extensification*. 18–1–88, revised 27–4–88.

——. *COM(88)84: Proposals for Set Asides*. 31–3–88.

—— (1988a). *Produits Agricoles: Prix et Montants Fixes (Marché Unique)*. Bruxelles: 2591/VI/74, 25eme revision, 26 April 1988.

—— (1988b). *Taux de Conversion a utiliser dans le Cadre de la PAC.* Brussels: DG VI/A4, 4916/VI/81, Rev. 87, 9 September 1988.

Cottrell, R. (1987). *The Sacred Cow: The Folly of Europe's Food Mountains.* London: Grafton.

Cox, G., Lowe, P. and Winter, M. (1986). *Agriculture: People and Policies.* London: Allen and Unwin.

Daily Telegraph, The (various). London.

Davey, B., Josling, T. and McFarquhar, A. (1976). *Agriculture and the State: British Policy in a World Context.* London: Macmillan.

Debatisse, M. (1981). *EEC Organization of the Cereals Markets: Principles and Consequences,* CEAS report #10. Ashford, Kent: Wye College.

Duchêne, F., Szczepanik, E. and Legg, W. (1985). *New Limits on European Agriculture: Politics & the CAP.* London: Croom Helm.

Economic & Social Committee (annual). *Annual Reports of the Economic and Social Committee.* Brussels: ESC.

—— (annual). *Opinion on Commission Proposal to the Council on the Fixing of Prices for Certain Agricultural Products and Connected Measures.* Brussels: CES & *OJ* Series (see Table B.1).

——. *Opinion on Community's Approach to the coming MTN in GATT. OJ* No. C 62, 31–7–73, p. 22.

——. *Opinion on the Development of an Overall Approach to Trade in View of the Coming MTN in GATT. OJ* No. C 115, 28–9–74, p. 1.

——. *Opinion on Improvement of the CAP. OJ* No. C 115, 28–9–74, p. 22.

——. *Opinion on the Agricultural Aspects of the MTN in GATT. OJ* No. C 115, 28–9–74, p. 32.

——. *Opinion on the Developing Countries in the GATT Negotiations. OJ* No. C 62, 15–3–75, p.12.

——. *'Opinion on the Stocktaking.' Newsletter on the CAP,* 1 (January 1976).

——. *Opinion on CAP in the International Context. OJ* No. C 61, 10–3–77, p. 1.

——. *Opinion on the GATT Multilateral Trade Negotiations. OJ* No. C 126, 28–5–77, p. 7.

——. (1980). *European Interest Groups and their Relationship with the Economic and Social Committee.* Westmead, England: Saxon House.

——. *Opinion on the Reform of the CAP. OJ* No. C 348, 31–12–81, p. 27.

——. *Opinion on the Perspectives for the CAP. OJ* No. C 330, 20–12–85, p. 12.

——. *Opinion on the Forthcoming Round of GATT Negotiations.* CES(86)512, 22–5–86.

——. *Own-Opinion on Current US Economic & Political Developments & GATT.* CES(87)634, July 1987.

——. *Opinion on Commission Proposals on Aids to Agriculture, Framework for Aids and Proposals for Cessation of Farming.* CES(87)798, Sept 1987.

——. *Opinion on the Implementation of Agricultural Stabilizers. OJ* No. C 356, 31–12–87, p.34l; *OJ* No. C 80, 28–3–88, p.28.

——. *Own-Opinion on the Agriculture Proposals in the Single Act. OJ* No. C 356, 31–12–87, p.35.

——. *Opinion on the Prospects of the GATT Negotiations for Agriculture.* CES(88)1099, 27–10–88.

Economist, The (various). London.

Edinger, L. (1986). *West German Politics*. New York: Columbia University Press.
Eurobarometre, 27. Luxembourg: Commission of the EC, June 1987.
—— (special issue). *Europeans and their Agriculture*. Luxembourg: Commission of the EC, February, 1988.
European Parliament (annual). *Opinion on Commission Proposal to the Council on the Fixing of Prices for Certain Agricultural Products and Connected Measures*. Brussels: EP Doc & *OJ* Series (see Table B.1).
——. *Opinion on COM(73)1850 concerning Improvement of the CAP*. *OJ* No. C 23, 8–3–74, p. 41.
——. *Resolution on the Community's Approach to the coming MTN in GATT*. *OJ* No. C 62, 31–7–73, p. 22.
——. *Resolution on the Community's Position in the GATT Negotiations*. *OJ* No. C 157, 14–7–75, p. 26.
——. 'Resolution on the Stocktaking.' *Newsletter on the CAP*, 1 (January 1976).
——. *Report on COM(76)616 (MCA System review)*. EP Doc 522/76, 7–2–77.
——. *Resolution on the MTN in GATT*. *OJ* No. C 163, 10–7–78, p. 26.
——. *Resolution on the Conclusion by the EC of the GATT MTN (Tokyo Round)*. *OJ* No. C 4, 7–1–80, p. 55.
——. *Report on the Commission's Proposals to Change the CAP to Help Balance the Markets, COM(79)710*. EP Doc. 1–37/80; *OJ* No. C 97, 21–4–80, p. 34.
——. *EP's position on the framing of the price proposals for 1983/84*. EP Doc. 1–837/82, 10–11–82.
——. *Report on New Guidelines for Community Structural Policy*. EP Doc. 1–923/83, 14–11–83.
——. *Report on COM(83)500*. EP Doc 1–987/83.
——. *Report on Impact of the EMS on the CAP (COM(83)586)*. EP Doc. 1–1139/83, 5&8–12–83.
——. *Report on COM(83)604 Amending Cereals Organization (threshold)*. EP Doc. 1–1373/83, 13–2–84.
——. *Report on Future of the CAP, COM(85)333*. PE Doc. A 2–185/85, 16–12–85.
——. *Report on Application of Agricultural Stabilizers*. PE Doc. A 2–194/87, 5–11–87.
——. *Opinion on Aids to Agricultural Income*. PE Doc. A2–162/87; *OJ* No. C 318, 30–11–87, p.45.
——. *Opinion on Agricultural Stabilizers*. PE Doc. A2–194/87; *OJ* No. C 345, 21–12–87, p.158.
Eurostat (various). *Agricultural Prices and Selected Series from the Cronos Data Bank*. Luxembourg: EC Commission.
——. (various). *Agriculture Statistical Yearbook*. Luxembourg: EC Commission.
——. (various). *Crop Production*. Luxembourg: EC Commission.
——. (various). *Supply Balance Sheets*. Luxembourg: EC Commission.
——. (various). *Agriculture Statistical Yearbook*. Luxembourg: EC Commission.
Federal Reserve Bank of Kansas City (1985). *Competing in the World Marketplace: The Challenge for American Agriculture*, Symposium. Kansas City: FRBKC.
Fennell, R. (1979). *The Common Agricultural Policy of the European Community*. London: Granada.
——. (1987a). 'Reform of the CAP: shadow or substance.' *Journal of Common Market Studies*, 26:1, pp. 61–77.

——. (1987b). *The Common Agricultural Policy of the European Community*, 2nd ed. Oxford: BSP Professional Books.

Financial Times (various). London.

Finger, J. and Nogués, L. (1987). 'International control of subsidies and countervailing duties.' *World Bank Economic Review*, 1:4, pp. 707–25.

Finger, J. and Olechowski, A. (eds) (1987). *The Uruguay Round: A Handbook on the MTN*. Washington: IBRD.

Fitzmaurice, J. (1985). 'Session 3: the EP in Brussels', in A. Robinson, and A. Webb, *The European Parliament in the EC Policy Process*, Studies in Euro Politics #9. London: Policy Studies Institute.

Foxall, G. (1982). *Co-operative Marketing in European Agriculture*. Aldershot, England: Gower.

Frankel, J. (1970). *National Interest*. London: Pall Mall.

Franklin, M. (1988). *Rich Man's Farming: The Crisis in Agriculture*. London: Routledge.

Furtan, W. *et al.* (1988). *International Wheat Markets: The Options Available to Saskatchewan*. Saskatoon, Canada: Department of Agricultural Economics, University of Saskatchewan.

GATT (1988). *Basic Instruments and Selected Documents*, 26th Supplement. Geneva.

——. (various). *FOCUS: GATT Newsletter. Geneva.*

——. (various). *News of the Uruguay Round of the MTN*. Geneva.

—— (various). *Press Communiqué*. Geneva.

General Secretariat of the Council. *Review of the Council's Work*. Brussels: Council of the ECs, Annual.

George, S. (1985). *Politics and Policy in the European Community*. Oxford: Clarendon.

Gilpin, R. (1987). *The Political Economy of International Relations*. Princeton, NJ: Princeton University Press.

Gittinger, J., Leslie, J. and Hoisington, C. (eds) (1987). *Food Policy: Integrating Supply, Distribution and Consumption*. London: Johns Hopkins University Press.

Globe and Mail, The (various). Toronto.

Golt, S. (1978). *The GATT Negotiations 1973–79: The Closing Stage*. London: British-North American Committee.

Green, D. (1975). *The Politics of Food*. London: Gordon Cremonesi.

Green Europe (various). Brussels: EC Commission.

Guardian, The (various). London.

Haen, H. de, Johnson, G.L. and Tangermann, S. (eds) (1985). *Agriculture & International Trade*. London: Macmillan.

Harris, S. and Swinbank, A. (1978). 'Price fixing under the CAP: proposition & decision – the example of the 1978/79 price review.' *Food Policy*, 3:4, pp. 256–71.

Harris, S., Swinbank, A. and Wilkinson, G. (eds) (1983). *The Food and Farm Policies of the European Community*. Chichester: John Wiley and Sons.

Harvey, D. (1982). 'National interests and the CAP.' *Food Policy*, 7:3, pp. 174–90.

Harvey, D. and Thomson, K. (1985). 'Costs, benefits & the future of the Common Agricultural Policy.' *Journal of Common Market Studies*, 24:1, pp. 1–20.

Hathaway, D. (1987). *Agriculture and the GATT: Rewriting the Rules*, Policy Analyses in International Economics #20. Washington: Institute for International Economics.

Hayward, J. (1982). 'Mobilizing private interests in the service of public ambitions', in J. Richardson (ed.), *Policy Styles in Western Europe*. London: Allen & Unwin.

Hedges, I. (1967). 'Kennedy Round agricultural negotiations and the world grains agreement.' *Journal of Farm Economics*, 49:5, pp. 1332-41.

Hendriks, G. (1987). 'The politics of food: the case of the Federal Republic of Germany.' *Food Policy*, 12:1, pp. 35-45.

Henig, S. (1980). *Power and Decision in Europe: The Political Institutions of the European Community*. London: Europotentials Press.

Hiemstra, S. and Shane, M. (1988). *Monetary Factors Influencing GATT Negotiations on Agriculture*, Foreign Agricultural Economic Report 236. Washington: USDA.

Hill, B. (1984). *The Common Agricultural Policy: Past, Present and Future*. London: Methuen.

Home-Grown Cereals Authority (1988). *Cereals Statistics 1988*. London: HGCA.

——. (various). *Marketing Notes (Supplement to the Weekly Bulletin)*. London: HGCA.

House of Lords, 1981-82 Session (1981a). *2nd Report of the Select Committee on the EC: Agricultural Trade Policy*. London: HMSO.

——, 1981-82 Session (1981b). *7th Report of the Select Committee on the EC: State Aids to Agriculture*. London: HMSO.

——, 1985-86 Session (1986). *6th Report of the Select Committee on the EC: Cereals*. London: HMSO.

Howarth, R. (1985). *Farming for Farmers? A Critique of Agricultural Support Policy*. London: The Institute for Economic Affairs.

Hudec, R. (1988). 'Legal issues in US-EC trade policy: GATT litigation 1960-85', in Baldwin *et al.* (1988).

Insel, B. (1985). 'A world awash in grain.' *Foreign Affairs*, 63:4, pp. 892-911.

International Herald Tribune (various). Paris.

International Monetary Fund (1988). *The CAP of the EC: Principles and Consequences*. Washington: IMF DM/88/1.

International Wheat Council (1988). *Wheat Support Policies and Export Practices in Five Major Exporting Countries*, Secretariat Paper #16. London: IWC.

—— (various). *World Wheat Statistics*. London: IWC.

Jackson, J., Louis, J.-V. and Matsushita, M. (1984). *Implementing the Tokyo Round: National Constitutions and International Economic Rules*. Ann Arbor: University of Michigan Press.

Johnson, D.G. (1973). *World Agriculture in Disarray*. London: Macmillan.

—— (1977). *The Soviet Impact on World Grain Trade*. London: British-North American Committee.

Josling, T. and Harris, S. (1976). 'Europe's green money.' *The Three Banks Review*, 109, pp. 57-72.

Keeler, J. (1987). *The Politics of Neocorporatism in France: Farmers, the State and Agricultural Policy Making in the Fifth Republic*. Oxford: OUP.

Kennedy, S. (1983). 'Reflections on the geopolitics of food', *Paper for the Annual Meeting of the International Studies Association.* Mexico City: mimeo.

Keohane, R. and Nye, J. (eds) (1977). *Power and Independence: World Politics in Transition.* Boston: Little, Brown & Co.

Kirchner, E. (1980). 'Interest group behaviour at the community level', in L. Hurwitz (ed), *Contemporary Perspectives on European Integration: Attitudes, Non Government Behaviour, and Collective Decision Making,* European Studies #4. London: Aldwych Press.

—— (1984). *The European Parliament: Performance and Prospects.* Aldershot, Hampshire: Gower.

Kirchner, E. and Schwaiger, K. (1981). *The Role of Interest Groups in the European Community.* Aldershot, Hampshire: Gower.

Koester, U. (1981). 'The chances for a thorough reform of the CAP.' *Intereconomics,* Jan/Feb, pp. 7–12.

Krasner, S. (ed.) (1983). *International Regimes.* London: Cornell University Press.

Lodge, J. and Herman, V. (1980). 'The ESC in EEC Decision Making.' *International Organization,* 34:2, pp. 265–84.

Malenbaum, W. (1953). *The World Wheat Economy, 1885–1939.* Cambridge, Mass.

Marsh, J. and Swanney, P. (1980). *Agriculture and the European Community.* London: Allen and Unwin.

—— (1983). 'The Common Agricultural Policy', in J. Lodge (ed.), *Institutions & Policies of the European Community.* London: Frances Pinter.

McCalla A. and Josling, T. (1985). *Agricultural Policies and World Markets.* London: Collier Macmillan.

McMahon, J. (1988). *European Trade Policy in Agricultural Products.* London: Martinus Nijhoff.

Morgan, D. (1979). *Merchants of Grain.* Middlesex: Penguin.

Murphy, M. (1985). *Report on Farming in the Eastern Counties of England: Changes in the Economic Aspects of Farming with Data for Farm Business Analysis.* Cambridge: Department of Land Economy.

National Consumer Council (1988). *Consumers and the Common Agricultural Policy.* London: HMSO.

Neville-Rolfe, E. (1984). *The Politics of Agriculture in the European Community.* London: Policy Studies Institute.

Observer, The (various). London.

OECD (various). *Review of Agricultural Policies in OECD Member Countries, Annual.* Paris: OECD.

—— (various). *The OECD Observer.* Paris, France.

—— (1982). *Problems of Agricultural Trade.* Paris: OECD.

—— (1983). *Prospects for Soviet Agriculture Production and Trade.* Paris: OECD.

—— (1987a). *The Export Credit Financing Systems in OECD Countries.* Paris: OECD.

—— (1987b). *National Policies and Agricultural Trade.* Paris: OECD.

—— (1987c). *National Policies & Agricultural Trade: Study on the EEC.* Paris: OECD.

—— (1988, 1989). *Agricultural Policies, Markets and Trade: Monitoring and*

Outlook, 1988 & 1989. Paris: OECD.

Olson, M. (1965). *The Logic of Collective Action: Public Goods and the Theory of Groups.* London: Harvard University Press.

Paarlberg, R. (1988). *Fixing Farm Trade: Policy Options for the United States.* Cambridge: Ballinger.

Pearce, J. (1981). *The Common Agricultural Policy: Prospects for Change,* Chatham House Papers 13. London: Routledge & Kegan Paul.

—— (1983). 'The Common Agricultural Policy: the accumulation of special interests', in Wallace, Wallace & Webb (1983).

Petersmann, E.-U. (1986). 'The EEC as a GATT member', in M. Hilf, F. Jacobs and E.-U. Petersmann (eds) (1986), *The European Community and GATT.* London: Kluwer Law & Tax Publishers.

Petit, M. (1985). *Determinants of Agricultural Policies in the US and the EC,* Report 51. NY: IFPRI.

Petit, M. *et al.* (1987). *Agricultural Policy Formation in the EC: The Birth of Milk Quotas and CAP Reform,* Developments in Agricultural Economics #4. Oxford: Elsevier.

Philip, A. (1985). *Pressure Groups in the EC,* Occasional Paper #2. London: UACES.

—— (1989). *Domestic Political Processes Influencing Agricultural Trade Policy: Balancing International Pressures & Domestic Demands.* Toronto: Institute for Research into Public Policy.

Phillips, P. (1989). 'The making of the European Community's wheat policy 1973–88: an international political economy analysis.' PhD dissertation (London).

Poullet, E. and Deprez, G. (1977). 'The place of the Commission within the institutional system', in C. Sasse *et al., Decision Making in the European Community.* London: Praeger.

Priebe, H., Bergmann, D. and Horring, J. (1972). *Fields of Conflict in European Farm Policy.* London: Trade Policy Research Centre.

Puchala, D. and Hopkins, R. (1983). 'International regimes: lessons from inductive analysis', in Krasner (1983).

Ritson, C. and Tangermann, S. (1979). 'The economics and politics of MCAs.' *European Review of Agricultural Economics,* 6:2, pp. 119–64.

Rosenfeld, C., Girling, B. and Reid, I. (eds) (1980). *Farm Financing and Farm Indebtedness in the Community.* Ashford, Kent: CEAS, Wye College.

Rosenthal, G. (1975). *The Men Behind the Decisions: Cases in European Policy-Making.* London: Lexington Books.

Rubin, S. and Graham, T. (eds) (1984). *Managing Trade Relations in the 1980s: Issues Involved in the GATT Ministerial Meeting of 1982.* Totowa, NJ: Rowman & Allen.

Runge, C. (1988). 'The Assault on Agricultural Protectionism.' *Foreign Affairs,* 67:1, pp. 133–50.

Runge, C. and Witzke, H. von (1987). 'Institutional change in the Common Agricultural Policy of the EC'. *American Journal of Agricultural Economics,* 69:2, pp. 213–22.

Schmitz, A. and Bawden, D. (1973). *The World Wheat Economy: An Empirical Analysis,* Giannini Foundation Monograph #32. Berkeley, Ca.

Schmitz, A. *et al.* (1981). *Grain Export Cartels.* Cambridge, Mass: Ballinger.

Snyder, F. (1985). *Law of the Common Agricultural Policy.* London: Sweet & Maxwell.

Spero, J. (1985). *The Politics of International Economic Relations,* 3rd ed. London: Allen & Unwin.

Stoeckel, A. (1985). *Intersectoral Effects of the CAP: Growth, Trade and Unemployment,* Occasional Paper No. 95. Canberra: Australian Government.

Strange, S. (1983). 'Cave! Hic dragones: a critique of regime analysis', in Krasner (1983).

—— (1984), ed. *Paths to International Political Economy.* London: Allen & Unwin.

—— (1985). 'International political economy: the story so far & the way ahead.' *International Political Economy Yearbook,* 1, pp. 13–25.

—— (1986). *Casino Capitalism.* Oxford: Basil Blackwell.

—— (1988). *States and Markets: An Introduction to International Political Economy.* London: Pinter.

Strange, S. and Tooze, R. (eds) (1981). *The International Politics of Surplus Capacity.* London: Allen & Unwin.

Swinbank, A. (1979). 'The "objective method": a critique'. *European Review of Agricultural Economics,* 6:3, pp. 303–17.

Swinbank, A. and Burns, J. (eds) (1984). *The EEC and the Food Industries.* Reading: Department of Agricultural Economics & Management.

Tangermann, S. (1979). 'Germany's role within the CAP: domestic problems in international perspective'. *Journal of Agricultural Economics,* 30, pp. 241–56.

—— (1983). 'What is different about European agricultural protectionism'. *The World Economy,* 6:1, pp. 39–57.

—— (1988). 'The EC perspective on agriculture in the Uruguay Round', in C. Roberts (ed.), *Trade, Aid and Policy Reform,* Proceedings of the 8th Agriculture Sector Symposium. Washington: IBRD.

Tangermann, S. *et al.* (1987). 'Multilateral negotiations on farm-support levels'. *The World Economy,* 10:3, pp. 265–81.

Tarditi, S. *et al.* (eds) (1989). *Agricultural Trade Liberalization and the European Community.* Oxford: Clarendon.

Taylor, P. (1983). *The Limits of European Integration.* London: Croom Helm.

Thomson, K. and Harvey, D. (1981). 'The efficiency of the CAP'. *European Review of Agricultural Economics,* 8:1, pp. 57–83.

Times, The (various). London.

Tracy, M. (1982). *Agriculture in Western Europe: Challenge and Response 1880–1980,* 2nd ed. London: Granada.

Tracy, M. and Hodac, I. (eds) (1979). *Prospects for Agriculture in the European Economic Community.* Bruges: De Tempel.

Tugendhat, C. (1986). *Making Sense of Europe.* Middlesex: Penguin.

Valdés, A. (1987). 'Agriculture in the Uruguay Round: interests of developing countries.' *World Bank Economic Review,* 1:4, pp. 571–93.

Vasey, M. (1985). 'The 1985 farm price negotiations and the reform of the CAP.' *Common Market Law Review,* 22:4, pp. 649–72.

Veer, J. de (1979). 'The objective method: an element in the process of fixing guide prices within the Common Agricultural Policy.' *European Review of Agricultural*

Economics, 6:3, pp. 279-301.

Wallace, H., Wallace, W. and Webb, C. (eds) (1983). *Policy-Making in the European Community*, 2nd ed. London: John Wiley and Sons.

Wall Street Journal (Europe) (various). Paris.

Walters, A. (1987). 'The economic consequences of agricultural support: a survey.' *OECD Economic Studies*, 9, pp. 7-54.

Warley, T. (1976). 'Part III: Western trade in agricultural products.' *International Economic Relations of the Western World 1959-71, Vol. 1, Politics and Trade*, ed. A. Shonfield. London: OUP.

—— (1987). 'Issues facing agriculture in the GATT negotiations.' *Canadian Journal of Agricultural Economics*, 35:3, pp. 425-49.

Western Producer, The (various). Saskatoon, Canada.

Winham, G. (1986). *International Trade & the Tokyo Round Negotiations*. Princeton, NJ: Princeton University Press.

World Bank (1986). *World Development Report 1986*. Oxford: OUP.

Zietz, J. and Valdés, A. (1988). *Agriculture in the GATT: An Analysis of Alternative Approaches to Reform*, Research Report 70. Washington: IFPRI.

Index